THE POSSIBILITY
OF BELIEF

The Way Back to Hope

Duncan Bayliss

Pikeawassa Press

The Possibility of Belief, The way back to hope

First edition published 2022

Published by Pikeawassa Press

Paperback ISBN 978-1-7397435-1-2
E-book ISBN 978-1-7391435-0-5

Authors are cited in the text in the format:

(Author's name *Title of their work,* page number)

I have referenced this way because I believe the two main and commonly used alternative referencing conventions do not work well for the reader in this sort of book. Numbered referencing requires searching in a numbered list for publication details which can be tedious. Harvard referencing gives the author's name and date of publication but not the title. Whereas listing the author and title helps the reader quickly see which sources are used most often and will assist in remembering which book or source might be worth reading next for more details.

Bible quotations are from the New International Version - NIV (1984) unless otherwise stated. The name of a book is followed by the chapter number, then the verse abbreviated to vs, generally in the form:

(John 3 vs 16)

ESV refers to the English Standard Version

CONTENTS

ACKNOWLEDGE-MENTS

I have covered a lot of issues and arguments for a short book and I am indebted to many other authors. I have read across a wide range of subject areas over many years in preparing this material and I have attempted to attribute sources fully. However, if I have inadvertently failed to acknowledge any sources, I would welcome the correction and gladly acknowledge them in updates.

The arguments and evidence presented here are not novel and are covered well in many, in-depth publications. However, I have not found them all drawn together in one introductory volume such as this.

Please see this book as a steppingstone to a fuller understanding and do explore the sources suggested in the Further Reading section.

I must give especial thanks to:

John Walton for detailed comments on the text and to Conrad Vine of AFM for comments and encouragement to keep writing. Crispen de Lange read drafts and encouraged too. My father Peter Bayliss undertook proof reading. Christopher Bayliss encouraged me to simplify and then to publish.

Many others read and commented on drafts or parts of the final book including Daniel Vine, Cedric Vine, Jeremy Johnson.

The books of Francis Schaeffer including *Escape From Reason* and *The God Who Is There*, were foundational to a long journey of reading and discovery in understanding secularism and rebutting it.

The cover was designed by Christopher Bayliss incorporating the advice of Rob Waller.

PREFACE

This book considers whether Christian belief is possible on a reasonable basis.

A book like this can in a sense never be finished, it can only be a starting point. I hope that it will stimulate many discussions between Christians and non-believers, because contrary to the message put out by secular culture, I believe there is a reasonable and credible basis for Christian belief.

The Possibility of Belief sets out an overview of what should be considered to help people settle the question of whether Christian belief is reasonable, and so it explores the landscape of faith and how that differs from a secular worldview.

If you have come to this book without an introduction by anyone, then I hope you will find it allows you to explore Christian belief in a satisfactory way and to open up conversations with believers.

If you are already a Christian, I hope this book will challenge you to take the time to build a rigorous basis for your belief and to make sure it is anchored in reliable evidence. Christians are not asked to ignore the evidence and "just believe anyway". Christian belief is not a so-called "leap of faith" away from the evidence. Some of what is discussed will be challenging for many people who call themselves Christians, because sadly too many have only a vaguely worked out basis for their beliefs, when in fact there can be a very solid basis.

If you have been given this book by a believer, then after exploring what it discusses, a good way to find out if belief makes sense is by having conversations with someone you respect who does believe; someone who is prepared to go against the flow in western culture and who not only believes but also has a solid basis for their belief. Be prepared to challenge them and any answers they give. The truth always stands up to scrutiny.

We will consider belief
in an age of unbelief

Christian belief has more in common with getting to know the most helpful person you can imagine meeting, than with passing an exam or achieving a qualification. It is based on relationship not just statements of truth. It takes account of the world and ourselves, as they are really are, but it is more like opening a door to something new than just setting out arguments and evidence, although they do matter.

Belief is perhaps best explored through stories. In fact, we all live within a narrative, a story, about who we are, why we are here and what life is all about. However, the stories that many people have been telling each other in western countries turn out to be sadly lacking.

So, I have sought to tell simple stories and short reflections that explore different aspects of life, that credible belief must take account of. They each relate to some part of a greater reality that I hope might resonate with your life.

No-one has all the answers. However, whilst our knowledge may be partial, it can be based upon something reliable. That is not the story secular culture puts out about belief, but it is what we will explore.

We will consider belief in an age of unbelief. We will look at a range of basic questions that anyone can engage with and see whether there is a reasonable basis for belief in God and for knowing what is right in this life, and when we have considered the evidence, whether there is a reasonable basis for hope?

Hope should be based on a solid foundation not wishful thinking

Some chapters are quite easy reading, some are more technical. I don't claim to be an expert in all these areas. Neither will I accept that being labelled an "expert" is necessary to look at them critically and see if the answers we are offered by secular culture make sense, or whether there is a better way to account for all the evidence available to us.

Where more technical discussions are covered, I point to further reading that will help you consider those issues in more detail if you wish. My discussions of some issues will have their inadequacies, but they are a starting point which you can build out from. Very often it has only been possible to summarise some of the key lines of argument, but I have tried to make sure that what is included is as readable as possible.

I believe it is helpful to set out the overall framework of Christian belief and use that to consider a range of challenging questions. As we will see throughout this book, everything we think we know about questions such, as 'Where have we come from?' and 'Why are we here?' is interpreted within a framework. That is true of all science, all philosophy, all common sense, all religion; it is inescapable that what we "know" is known within a framework of understanding. So, it is important to look at the evidence and see what ideas, beliefs and framework, or worldview it can best support.

This book can help you consider the evidence, but it is only a starting point. It could easily have been ten times longer; the challenge has been to keep it to a manageable length. It can only be an introduction and further reading will be essential if you have unanswered questions on anything we look at.

The illustrations used are intended to give a readable way into what can seem some very difficult issues. The good news, however, is that by asking the right questions, we can find compelling and satisfying answers. We should rightly be suspicious when "experts" tell us what to think and believe, it is right to check out the evidence for ourselves. It is also the case that when claims are wrapped up in such complicated language that ordinary, but educated readers can't understand it, it is likely to be the case that the person making those claims doesn't understand them either.

Many apparently difficult questions boil down to something very simple in the end: for example, either there is a God or there is not; either there is a purpose to existence or there is not; either life is better explained by Random Chance or by Design. And the answers to such questions have immense implications.

I am convinced that when the evidence is laid out carefully it points to clear answers. The problem, it seems, lies not so much with the evidence as whether people are willing to follow where it leads.

Finally, it is important to be clear from the start, that belief is not an abstract concept or an academic exercise.

Belief is a lived experience, that should be built on a solid evidential basis.

There are compelling reasons not to dismiss Christian belief out of hand, let's look at some of them.

Duncan H. Bayliss, 2022

PART 1 WHAT MUST WE EXPLAIN?

1 INTRODUCTION

Will you follow the evidence?

In the late summer, before the clouds and rain come to dominate, the cold nights clear the air and the light in the alps has a special quality. A distant pinnacle seemed magnified, highlighted with a clarity beyond what ought to be possible and just beneath it was a refuge, small, made of the stone with a black metal roof, my next destination across a glacier. Mountains flowed without a cloud to interrupt the view in all directions away from Switzerland to Italy and France and it felt as though I could almost see to Austria to the east. The air tasted different. On the way up it was heavy with pollen from late summer haymaking, but here it seemed filtered, purified; the very essence of air itself.

To reach this point on a rocky ridge had taken patience, waiting for the right window in the weather forecast, but the views were worth the effort. Here on the edge of another dimension, the peaks and glaciers burned themselves into my memory. Taking photos seemed unnecessary, since they could never capture such a vast panorama and I knew I would never forget the scene. I climb up into mountains to be among them, rather than always to reach the top. I do it not for some abstract sense of achievement at conquering summits or from a romantic notion that I might climb a mountain and come down a different person, but because beauty is somehow essential. I feel the need to stock up on vistas to see me through the winter ahead, to recharge the mind's inner eye and to let my thoughts roam freely unencumbered by the constraints of the daily setting.

Mountains are challenging to travel in. We may be drawn by their beauty, but their unpredictability serves as a reminder of our own fragility, our presence there tolerated but not entirely natural. Steep slopes, deep gorges, rockslides, avalanches, high altitudes and thin air, glaciers, and the roaring torrents of mountain streams all make travel in mountains difficult. In the great mountain ranges of the world, the valleys can be miniature worlds in their own right.

Later in that trip in the alps, while finishing off a generous serving of Raclette in a pleasant restaurant, I asked what I might find in the next valley. I was astonished to find that neither the owner of this small restaurant, nor his family, had ever been there despite living in this place all their lives. Just a day's walk away, or three hours by car or bus, lay another valley full of possibilities, for me, redolent with the promise of new vistas and discoveries; only 10 kilometres in a direct line over the mountain and yet they had never been there! The next valley spoke German and they French, but that need not be an obstacle to curiosity. I climb mountains to clear my mind and my heart seeks out the next view and the next after that, always delighted to discover more natural beauty. Their apparent lack of curiosity about a valley so close by threw me, it was a completely different mindset.

Alain de Botton was onto something when he wrote,

> "Journeys are the midwives of thoughts. Few places are more conducive to internal conversations than a moving plane, ship or train. There is almost a quaint correlation between what is in front of our eyes

and the thoughts we are able to have in our heads: large thoughts at times requiring large views, new thoughts new places. Introspective reflections which are liable to stall are helped along by the flow of the landscape. The mind may be reluctant to think properly when thinking is all it is supposed to do." (Alain de Botton, *The Art of Travel*, page 57)

If you travel in the less developed regions of the world the isolation mindset in mountain communities becomes much more marked as the practical difficulties of travel between valleys increases. The people, language, culture, religion, clothing, diet and customs can vary dramatically from one valley to the next.

Now, picture yourself growing up in an isolated mountain village in one of the remotest parts of the world. Everyone seems to share the same values and beliefs. Everyone does things the same way, lives in the same kind of house, eats the same food, wears the same clothes, because that is just how things are done. All the houses are simple stone structures with stone slab roofs and walls around them, forming courtyards. Just about everyone is involved in subsistence farming and life is regulated and ruled by traditional practice and the elders of the community.

Then one day, rumours begin to circulate of a totally different world outside the deep valley where you live. In a community without television, or much in the way of books, or even radio reception it is exceptionally hard to imagine life in any other form than how it presents itself to you. The world around you is all you know. Occasionally people would come through selling metal pans and knives and ceramic bowls otherwise unavailable within the valley and they would tell stories and bring news from the outside world. A good story, told slowly and dramatically for effect, would be worth a meal and some hours beside the fire, as the community gathered round to take in the news and discuss what it meant. Many things might come up in the discussion, a new president, or a war in some far-off country, or worries about landslides further down the valley and rumours that maybe a wide track would be built up through the gorge to your village, with all the hopes and fears for what that would mean for your community. The tales they told seemed other worldly.

No-one in your family had been more that a days' travel in either direction except for grandad who was called out to go and fight and rarely talked about his time on the dusty plain trying to stay alive so he could come home and carry on providing for his family. A mixture of intense curiosity and an underlying fear of the unknown framed all you heard. Sometimes the talk would turn to a land of wide-open landscapes where you can see vast distances, of endless greenery and trees and grass; an almost mythical land of plenty. The talk would be of customs, clothes, medicines, foods and entertainments unheard of in your valley and from an early age you were determined that somehow, one day, you would find out if it was all just myth and legend? Was it too good to be true, or was it a real place that you could visit? The question would roll around your mind and you could be forgiven for thinking that people and life in the "outside world" would surely be just like those in yours. How different can one deep rocky valley be from another?

At the same time, it was not as though everything was perfect in your home village. If someone becomes sick, they either get better or die. The food is really bland and unvaried. A whole lifetime of bread, some sheep meat, milk and a bit of fruit in season gets pretty tedious. When arguments break out the village elders try to resolve them, but if they get really out of hand people can get killed and then there are honour killings in return. The vendettas can last generations. It's not heaven on earth.

One day, talking with one of the passing traders, you hear that the way out of the valley is supposed to be up a perilous ladder at the head of a gorge a few days walk away. No-one you have talked to in the village has ever climbed the ladder, some even deny its existence. Others said it was broken and didn't go anywhere, still others said it was made during the great war to enable you to cross a rocky ridge to another valley just like this one, but this man claims to have climbed it and that it leads to a land of abundance. You know what the elders and your family and friends all say: they say these men are full of tall stories and legends. People used to believe that kind of stuff in old times but now we know it is nonsense. As for the ladder, its broken and it doesn't go anywhere, so don't waste your time going to look at it. *Everyone knows nothing is up there.*

Yet it niggles you and niggles you. What if he is right? Maybe there is more to life than this valley, this rocky prison. So, you slip round to the hut where he is staying and quietly ask him to take you with him when he leaves. You ask to be shown the ladder. The next day, just before dawn, the air cold and dry, the valley eerily silent, you slip out of the village with your guide, leaving behind the flocks of sheep, sparse grass, endless rocks and little stone homes of the village, the long trek to the head of the gorge is tough. When you finally see the ladder, your heart sinks. It doesn't look climbable. It doesn't even look safe. It consists of metal rungs or staples embedded in a huge sheer cliff face. In fact, it looks obvious that everyone else in the village must be right, there can't be anything better up a ladder like that and the doubts creep in. As for finding a better life, what would be the point of risking everything to climb such a ladder to just end up in another valley full of rocks and sheep? Even so, a little voice keeps prompting you to check out the ladder. You think the options through. Stay where you are and insist that this valley is all there is, just like the village elders, or try to climb out. Why risk climbing? All there is to go on at this point is the word of someone you hardly know who claims to have been this way before. Plus, the tallest ladder you have climbed was no more than ten rungs onto the roof of the house and even that gave you a queasy stomach from the height. This one appears to go up out of sight forever on a sheer cliff face with only blue sky above.

Lost in your own thoughts and weighing up your fears and choices you fail to notice that your guide has already set out climbing and he starts calling down from much higher up,

"The view is amazing, I'm out of the shadow, it's so warm, you really should come and see for yourself. I can't describe how far I can see, and how green and beautiful it is."

"What have I got to lose?" you say to yourself and so, with encouragement from him you start climbing. The first rungs of the ladder do look to be solid enough to try testing, so stepping up, cautiously at first, they hold your weight. Then you climb some more. So far, so good, just remember his advice and don't look down!

A curious thing about the whole experience of starting on the ladder is that as you climb your perspective changes rapidly. Maybe there is something up there after all. As you emerge from the deep shadow of the valley, the sickening feeling in the pit of your stomach and the thumping of your heart pounding in your ears, take second place to new sensations. The ladder turns out to be much stronger once you are experiencing it, rather than just looking at it from below. It is solid and dependable, and your grip tightens, your legs stop trembling; you are going to be alright. Ascending steadily, it is possible to see much more than you ever have before. Excitement wells up as you wonder what more will be revealed. Some problem with perspective must have been distorting the view from the ground, because the ladder, rather than appearing to be almost endlessly long, now looks and feels solid and safe and very climbable and you think you can see the top. Your assumptions about the ladder had been wrong.

Still testing each rung carefully before you put your weight on it, you move higher with increasing confidence. The rungs seem to get stronger not weaker. Looking back one final time, the gorge below the ladder is now an insignificant part of a greater landscape that is larger more varied and beautiful than you ever imagined. The greatest surprise of all is that up here in this incredible place you are not alone. There are stone walls, paths, meadows, forest and houses all visible.

Stepping off confidently onto solid ground, everything about your former world seems so small and so insignificant, that you now can't imagine not climbing out of the valley of shadows. As you begin to walk around and explore, the world out of the gorge is everything you were told and more. It all now makes sense. The views are immense, the landscape sparkling in crystal clear air is bursting with beauty and life. It truly has to be seen to be believed. Rich forests and rushing streams, lush deep green meadows highlighted by an array of flowers of every hue. Sheep and cattle are grazing the fields. The scattered farmhouses with flowers on their balconies show that other people are not just surviving here as your community does in your own valley, eking out an existence. Here they are thriving. All of this stands in embarrassing contrast to the tiny stone hut that was home such a short time ago. The air is full of pine scent and bird song, the babbling brook is accompanied by the rustling of bushes in the breeze, it caresses your face as the sun warms your back. The experience is overwhelming, something akin to being released from lifelong imprisonment. It is as though you are experiencing freedom and the wonders of nature for the first time ever and you're brought to tears of joy. How could you have called it *living* without experiencing such beauty? How could it be called *life* to exist in deep shadows, while all the time such wonders were so nearby?

Quite simply, having the courage to climb one ladder has changed your perspective on everything, forever.

I have taken time to describe this metaphor in detail, because the image needs to be in mind throughout all that we will look at in this book. At this point you might be thinking that I can't be serious with the contrast I have painted between the world of belief and unbelief, between the valley of shadows of secularism and the beautiful landscape of belief and hope? Well truly I am, and I aim to show that it is not wishful thinking or some delusional escapism. Christian belief is real, based on solid evidence and available for anyone to explore. So, let's begin to examine why this is so.

Over the last century it has become the norm to talk about faith or belief as some sort of leap in the dark, away from solid ground and testable evidence and that picture is deeply embedded in many people's minds. No analogy is perfect, but the aim of this book is to challenge that view and to present the steps of a ladder that can be climbed towards belief and hope, a dependable robust ladder, rather than a leap in the dark. It aims to show you that contrary to the prevailing view, belief in Jesus is credible, reasonable and fits well with all the evidence you can find of the world around you and even of what you can know of yourself.

Exploring this evidence may well help you to come to belief, but that is a journey that should be undertaken based on an understanding of the evidence and then a willingness to act on it. Don't rush, test the evidence. At this point however, I am trusting that you are prepared to "follow the argument wherever it leads" (Anthony Flew: we will return to him in a later chapter). So, we will look at the evidence that makes the rungs on this ladder.

I am convinced that one of the main reasons that many people do not consider even trying to climb a ladder to faith or belief, is because they have been persuaded that it is not possible. They have been told that many rungs of the ladder are missing and that others are broken or simply too weak to stand on. So, they won't even consider trying, they are sure it would be pointless. The short chapters that follow will start looking at the evidence to make the case that belief is a reasonable step to take, that the evidence is there to rely on, and then point out where you can find out more.

Many objections are raised to the very possibility of belief, so much so, that the prevailing view in most western countries today is that belief is only possible when you ignore the evidence and take a leap in the dark. Nothing could be further from the truth. It is only when you *ignore* the evidence that it is easy to believe nothing much.

What are the supposedly missing and broken rungs? Most people in western countries are aware, at some level, that there have been several main lines of attack on Christian belief in the last 150 years.

The first line of sustained attack has been on the historical reliability of the book Christians base their beliefs on, the Bible. The popular conception of the result of a century and a half of those attacks by critics, is that there is little evidence for the existence of Jesus and that the other stories in the Bible are basically legend and not anything a reasonable person would base their life on. And if they are "made up" then why believe anything the Bible says?

The second line of attack has been through the ideas promulgated by Charles Darwin and others on evolution, which is now popularly perceived to explain the existence of all life without the need for any kind of God.

> "Those rejecting religious belief cite scientific theories of unguided chemical and biological evolution more frequently than any other reason for their loss of faith." (Stephen Meyer, *The Return of the God Hypothesis, Three Scientific Discoveries That Reveal the Mind Behind the Universe*, page 434)

A third line of attack has come from physics and astronomy with ideas around the origin of the universe as arising from a Big Bang. Again, as it is popularized, there is no need for a God, the universe just made itself.

Running hand in hand with these ideas have been many others that have been deadly to the faith of millions. For example, a fourth line of attack has been the claim that there is no such thing as truth. In fact, these attacks are closely interlinked, since if there is no God, or at least not one who is knowable, then we have no-one to answer to but ourselves. If everything evolved by Random Chance from 'molecules to man', then there is no ultimate basis for right and wrong, only what we agree amongst ourselves. Everything becomes relative and we are left with no real truth, just subjectivity. That is the place where western culture has ended up.

In a short book like this we can't deal with every objection, but we must look at some of these foundational views that affect everything else. We must engage with them since they underpin the world view of most secular or non-religious people in Europe, North America and many other countries, whether they realize it or not. Everyone has a world view, but not everyone's world view is based on careful consideration of the evidence. In fact, for many people all they have done is give it a quick look and move on.

We will consider each of those attacks on Christian belief just outlined and see if they stand up to scrutiny. To summarize in plain language, those secular views go something like this:

> The Universe came from a big bang a very long time ago. Somehow by Random Chance life started and evolved, ending up with us. There's no real meaning to life other than the meaning we make for ourselves. The Bible is made up stories. Jesus was no more than a good teacher with some interesting insights on ethics. There is no absolute right or wrong. Anyone who has faith in God is basically involved in wishful thinking, which most of the time is fairly harmless, but not based on anything reliable, or on any kind of solid evidence.

We will consider whether this is in fact a credible set of claims, as millions assume. Is all the evidence really stacked in favour of secular unbelief? Is it really the case that Christian belief isn't possible on any reasonable basis? Which fits better with the evidence?

We will look at some of the most basic evidence available and see whether, on balance, it supports either Christian belief, or an agnostic or atheistic and secular view of life. However, what most people do, most of the time, is to measure claims they encounter against the basic assumptions they already hold as "true" and then dismiss what doesn't agree with those assumptions or pre-suppositions. That approach makes some sense on a day-to-day basis, but there is a time for stepping back and checking whether the assumptions you hold to are actually based on anything like reliable evidence. They may be held by many other people, but they may also not be true.

So, to continue with the analogy that we started with, let's see if we can identify the basic steps on the ladder to belief and see how strong they are. Truth always stands up to scrutiny. I hope that in following the evidence you will find that belief is not only possible and reasonable but that it also makes surprisingly good sense of who you are, what your life is all about, and is true to the evidence in the world around you.

Every person's journey through life is different, but we all owe it to ourselves to face up to reality as it presents itself

> "Jacob, ... taking one of the stones there, he put it under his head and lay down to sleep. He had a dream in which he saw a ladder resting on the earth, with its top reaching to heaven."
>
> Moses, in the book of Genesis 28 vs 1

Let's climb a ladder

2 DO DOGS DREAM OF HEAVEN?

People are different

When I was a teenager, we had an Old English Sheep dog called Shingle. Shingle was a fantastic dog. She was very bouncy, full of fun and had quite a sense of humour. When I had to get up for school in the morning, she loved to run off with socks and hide them. She invented the game and she was addicted. Dad would open the bedroom door saying, "Go and get him up", and the dog would explode in. She knew she wasn't allowed on the bed to sleep so would jump onto the forbidden territory and bounce around a bit, then look for something to grab and run off with. If Mum took clean socks out and put them on my bed saying, "Come on, get up, time for school", Shingle would grab them and charge down the bungalow at full speed, bounce off an armchair, that she also wasn't supposed to go on, then hide the socks somewhere. The dog was only interested in today's clean socks because that would provoke a game.

So, I would get up and the search for the socks would begin. I was fascinated by this behaviour. Shingle would walk about watching out the corner of her eye pretending she knew nothing, looking so innocent, but as soon as my hand went behind the sofa, or under a chair, or behind a wastepaper bin to retrieve the socks she would pounce trying to get them back again. It was sophisticated behaviour for a dog, because she was not simply intent on taking the socks but on making me look for them and then join in a chase.

Of course, I could take another pair out the drawer and often did, but it was fun to join in with her game. If hiding socks didn't work for getting my sister and I up, then she would take to charging up and down the length of the bungalow at full speed with a pair of socks in her mouth, doing banked turns by bouncing off a chair in my parent's bedroom at one end and a chair in the lounge at the other. This was quite challenging behaviour to deal with, because at that point Shingle weighed about 50 pounds (23 Kg) and could cover the ground from one end of the house to the other in just a few massive strides.

Some mornings the only way to deal with this explosion of energy was to open the backdoor and she would charge round and round the garden as fast as possible for 5 minutes or so. In fact, every single day, at least once, she had to run around flat out often knocking things over, going as fast as possible for her "Mad 5" as we called it. It didn't necessarily happen first thing in the morning, it could be any time of day when the pent-up urge to simply charge about at high speed would come out and the best that we could do was to try to direct it in a safe direction. Lots of people had neat theories about how to deal with this. 'Don't reward her with attention, just ignore it' we were told. Well really, can you safely ignore a very large, very powerful, dog charging about like that? Others said, 'She needs more exercise'. They were missing the point. Shingle was an impressively fit dog who ran about 20-25 miles a week with my Dad. But anyway, we mostly just loved having a very fun dog, why would we want to drill the sheer joy of life out of her?

Where is this leading? Well, any dog lover will tell you about their dog's funny habits that make it so individual. Each dog really has its own personality and we can build quite complex relationships with them, yet much of what a dog is actually thinking is a mystery to us. We can guess at it, but we don't know. For example, Shingle loved chasing rabbits, or family members or friends, or other dogs or anything that was willing to run around and play chase. You could offer any number of theories as to what she thought about it or why she did it, but clearly, she loved doing it.

When she was sleeping, she would sometimes dream too. Her muscles would twitch, she would make whining noises and as far as anyone could tell she was dreaming about chasing something. We can only guess what the dreams included. Was she successful at catching rabbits in her dreams, when she never succeeded in reality?

The advances in our understanding of animal behaviour have brought fascinating insights. For example, Prairie dogs turn out to have quite a wide vocabulary and are able to communicate information about different types of threats approaching their 'town' (see for example, The New York Times Magazine in 2017, *Can Prairie Dogs Talk?*[1]). Young Prairie dogs have to learn the language and be trained in how to respond to the range of calls or whistles others make.

Bonobos, like Chimpanzees, and Gorillas have been able to use touch icons on a screen to indicate different types of food they want or learn basic sign language to express their wishes (see for example, IEEE, *Apes with Apps*[2]). Yet, whatever we have found out about animal behaviour there remains a noticeable gap between people and animals. For all the communication they can manage, I am not aware of any of them asking about the meaning of life.

When I think of our dog apparently dreaming, I have no reason to assume that she ever dreamt of heaven. It is not clear what thinking actually means in animals, but there is no evidence to believe that she thought of anything beyond this life and the immediate here and now. But people do. I haven't met anyone who doesn't at some time think about these things. In this very crucial respect, we are different from animals, we do think about what there is beyond our day-to-day existence. We do think about the purpose of life. This is something special about us that does require explanation.

No matter how meaningless someone might claim life to be, they are still engaging in that level of abstract and conceptual thought that sets them apart from the rest of nature around them, even when they are pondering how meaningless they think everything is!

It seems to me, that any explanation about who we are, must take account of all the dimensions of what it means to be human, and one central part of that is that we do reflect on these sorts of questions. Why should this be so? People are different from the rest of nature. Personality and sentience are not an illusion. You are reading this and considering the extent to which you agree with what I have said so far. You are living proof to yourself of the essential specialness of being human.

Despite all the advances in what we know about animals in terms of sentience there is a huge gulf between people and the rest of nature. We do dream about heaven and what comes after this life. It seems so integral to what we are, that it simply cannot be glossed over and ignored. We need a credible answer as to why should this be so? As you read on, we can think about whether this significant difference between us and the animal kingdom is in fact something that has an intentional cause. Indeed, the capacity to think about questions such as, 'What is the meaning of life?', is surely one of the most basic aspects of reality as we find and experience it.

Were we *intended* to be what we are, or are we better explained as being the result of blind, unthinking, random accidents of chance? Is there a greater mind and personality behind our having a mind and true personality?

You are special and your personality is not an illusion

"He has also set eternity in the hearts of men."
Solomon, Bronze Age King of Israel, in
Ecclesiastes 3 verse 11

3 THE SKY AT NIGHT

Where did everything come from?

I have been privileged to visit many wild places. The wild is an antidote to the busy, crowded life most people live in western countries. Once you are away from the background glow of light pollution that makes it hard to see the stars clearly, the sky comes alive. I recall lying back watching the stars at various times and being awe struck. Way out in the Rockies in Canada, backpacking with two friends, we pitched our tents and as the sun set, shooting stars appeared. The Perseids meteor shower filled the sky with trails of light as material from immense distances away burned up in our atmosphere. You would have to be deeply unreflective not to be struck by how small we are in such a vast universe.

Perhaps the defining photograph of the 20th century was the image of Earth taken from space by the Apollo mission. Suddenly all that we think of as solid and that sustains our life, is shown to be a blue-green ball in the unimaginable vastness of space. That image has spurred conservationists and campaigners, evangelists and a myriad of others.

The more you try to get your mind around the vast scale, and complexity of space, the more it can become too much to handle. It stretches so far beyond anything we directly experience that comparison becomes almost futile. Yet, some basic questions come to mind. Are we alone in the Universe? And where did it all come from?

When we turn to the question of the origin of 'life, the Universe and everything' (as Douglas Adams author of The Hitchhiker's guide to the galaxy put it), there are a few basic possibilities to consider. The present "consensus" in science, is that everything came from a big bang, from a single point expanding outwards that eventually settled down into everything that is now in existence in a universe that is still expanding. To be fair the apparent consensus is less certain than we are often led to believe. It may surprise you to know that a substantial number of physicists are unsure about this model, pointing to evidence they believe doesn't fit it or even undermines it, (such as the Horizon problem, which we will return to later). Therein lies a significant problem for science when looking at such questions. It develops models and theories about reality. However, no-one can literally go back in time, so we seek evidence from what is observable now and then model it backwards. The models may seem plausible, they may seem to fit much of the evidence we have at this point, but the history of science shows us again and again that these models will change. They are revised with new evidence, or new theories. Whatever form such models may take, they still can't go back beyond the modelled beginning of the universe. Before that science can know nothing.

Complex mathematical models have been built of the "Big bang" theory. Evidence has been gathered that supports it. Yet the real problem that this or any models really misses is this; what is the ultimate <u>cause</u> of reality in the first place? Did everything that exists spontaneously spring into existence without a cause at a so called 'singularity', then spontaneously expand and form into an ordered Universe? Or was there a cause that led to it?

It seems remarkable to me, that whilst we live within a Universe and on a planet where cause and effect are so immutable that all science has had to do is figure out the details of how that cause and effect works, most scientists still, as a matter of faith, insist that there was no cause to the existence of the Universe in the first place. This is often it seems because they do not want to *"allow a Divine foot in the door."* (Richard Lewontin quoted in *The New York Review*, p. 31, 9 January 1997).

Let's be blunt about this. Let's suppose that everything did come from a Big Bang. There is then by definition no way we can ever go back before that point to prove or disprove, on the basis of scientific observation, as to what the cause was. There is no logical or scientific reason to claim that the explanation that, "It just happened by itself spontaneously", is any better than the explanation, "God caused it". As David Berlinski puts it,

> "There is a very natural connection between the fact that the universe had a beginning and the hypothesis that it had a creator. It is a connection so plain, that glowing with its own energy, it may be seen in the dark." (David Berlinski *The Devil's Delusion, Atheism and its Scientific Pretensions*, page 71)

We will look elsewhere for further evidence to see which explanation is the more credible.

So, why is the Universe ordered and not a massive pile of chaos? It turns out that the maths behind the fine tuning of the Universe is quite incredible. If one of a range of forces or constants were just minutely different there would be no life here. This has been elaborated by many authors. If for example the gravitational constant were slightly different, stars would either burn out too quick or not be hot enough to produce heavy elements. If the electromagnetic force were slightly stronger or weaker molecules could not form. And the differences need only be extremely small. Multiple such "coincidences" need to be in place at the same time or there would be no life. (See for example, Stephen Meyer *Signature in the Cell* and *Darwin's Doubt*). This is not an incidental argument. We face two very simple alternatives: unexplained Random Chance or Design and intent.

Berlinski quotes Fred Hoyle the astronomer who observed that,

> "The universe looks like a put-up job."

In considering why this should be so, Berlinski observes that,

> "One answer is the answer that theologians have always offered: the universe looks like a put-up job because it is a put-up job. That this answer is obvious is no reason to think it false." (David Berlinski, *The Devil's Delusion, Atheism and its Scientific Pretensions*, page 112)

Since the Universe turns out to be not only unimaginably vast but also incredibly finely tuned, why should it be so? An obvious explanation is that a super-intelligence intended it to be that way. If we start at the level of the whole Universe and find that there are the hallmarks of incredible Design, then it is surely reasonable to consider that there might be a designer? The only reason to completely exclude this possibility is because of a decision already made separate from any evidence, that there could not be any God. That is a prior assumption rather than a willingness to be fair to the evidence as we find it.

That's what many people would call blind faith.

> "For the scientist who has lived by his faith in the power of reason, the story ends like a bad dream. He has scaled the mountains of ignorance; he is about to

conquer the highest peak; as he pulls himself over the final rock, he is greeted by a band of theologians who have been sitting there for centuries." Robert Jastrow, *God And The Astronomers*, cited in Subodh Pandit, *Come Search With Me, Book 1 Does God Really Exist? Is Theism Rational? Is evolution Truly Scientific* page 47)

Everything about an ordered and balanced Universe points to one who intended it to be that way

"In the beginning God made the heavens and the Earth."

Moses in Genesis 1 verse 1 (That is, the very first words of the Bible)

4 IN SEARCH OF
THE LOST TRIBE

The universality of morality

L et's try an experiment. What we need perhaps, is a Professor of Anthropology, or maybe an investigative journalist, or an historian. Their qualification for the task must be a scrupulous honesty and a determination to go to the ends of the Earth to find answers, literally to the ends of the earth. Assuming we find a suitable volunteer and have a research foundation to fund unlimited travel, then here is the task. We want our investigator to find a nation or tribe or people group who have no conception of right and wrong and no rules by which they establish right and wrong. In short, they must have no morality at all. They can be a people who have existed in history, or they can be in some obscure part of the world today. The investigator can go anywhere from seeking out lost or uncontacted tribes in the Amazon to the worst neighbourhoods of the most dangerous cities on Earth, to see if they can find such a group. The investigator can interview anyone they want in their quest, follow up any lead, trawl through any archive, visit anywhere, no expense spared and in a year they are to report back. Will they have been able to find a people group, nation or tribe truly without any morality?

Let's think about where they might look, and which groups might fit the description. If we turn first to uncontacted tribes in the South American rain forest, one of the remarkable things about them when they come into contact with the outside world is that the structures of their society differ from others only by a matter of degree. They have roles and responsibilities for different individuals and sub-groups. They have rules on what can and can't be done. They have beliefs about the origin of life and purpose of existence. Even if we consider the head-hunting tribes of Papua New Guinea back in the 19th Century, whilst they engaged in what should rightly be regarded as the abhorrent and evil practice of hunting down members of other tribes and cannibalism, they still had rules which structured their lives and a sense of injustice when they were broken.

Maybe we should turn in a different direction and head to some of the most violent areas of the worst cities. There has been a morbid fascination with which city might claim to be the most dangerous in the world. *National Geographic*, for example, has reported on the topic and it regularly features in news reporting around the world.

Terrible levels of crime are associated with drug gangs. Their members are at once drug fuelled themselves and also ruining the lives of others in the trafficking of drugs. Civilised society tries to stop them. Huge efforts go into policing their activities and trying to disrupt them and stop the violence, often with limited success. But if we look within those groups, then even here, although we find high levels of violence between gang members and between rival gangs, we still find codes of behaviour, although admittedly very distorted ones. Whilst the gang is exploiting, extorting and robbing others of their money and freedom to live without fear, the leaders of those gangs expect to not be robbed themselves! The gang members have a belief that what they have should not be taken from them. They may be considered vile and violent, but they do exhibit a morality, albeit a distorted and corrupted morality.

If we turn to some of the destructive ideologies of the past, we find a similar pattern. The Nazis, the National Socialists of Germany, unleashed such evil on Europe that it is extremely hard to write about. Why take this example? Because it shows how in a civilised society incredible evil can arise; it shows that right and wrong are not distant abstract concepts. The concentration camps and systematic annihilation of Jews, Gypsies, political dissenters, and others was on such a vast scale that it defies comprehension. Anyone who stood up to their plans was liable to meet a premature death.

Yet all that violence and evil was dressed up in a distorted form of morality. They talked of what they were doing as being for the glory of the Fatherland. Hitler wrote of establishing a 1000-year Reich (kingdom). They had a distorted and degraded form of morality rather than an absence of any. They had the charade of a legal basis for their actions. More pertinently, they described doing evil as doing good and attempted to remove all who opposed them at any level in society. Even when total defeat was inevitable, they murdered many who were being held as prisoners for standing up to or criticising Nazi ideology, rather than allowing them to be liberated. Dietrich Bonhoeffer was a Lutheran Pastor who was imprisoned for speaking out against Nazism. He was murdered by the Nazis in prison the night before Germany surrendered. He had been in America but returned to speak out against the growing evil that he saw in Germany and paid the ultimate price. He is representative of thousands of Germans who stood up to Nazism and were killed because they refused to be complicit in such evil. Yet the Nazis claimed they were the ones doing right, and that is the point we can recognise. We are rightly abhorred by what they did but it is still the case that they had a form of morality; a broken, distorted and evil form, but a form, nonetheless.

If we look back through history, no matter how different from our own societies today, every group we come across has a conception of right and wrong in some form. It's simply part of being human. In fact, we can easily see that a society cannot function and prosper without a conception of right and wrong. Past societies may differ greatly from our own, but they still all had some form of morality. This raises some interesting questions. Why is it that there is a sense of right and wrong within people? Why is it that we don't find a total absence of all morality, even where we may be horrified at its corrupted and evil form? The answer seems inescapable; we do live in a moral universe.

Our concern in relation to morality is not as to whether it exists at all, but rather <u>the form it should take</u>. The framework of some form of morality is a given, the crucial issue is to ensure that it is formed around what is genuinely right and wrong rather than being perverted to justify doing evil but calling it good, as did the Nazis and Stalin's and Mao's communists and as have so many others. Whilst the details of the moral codes may vary, the common ground is that they all testify to there being a moral dimension to reality.

In recognising the reality of a moral dimension to our existence, we are recognising one of the ways in which reality is not just a matter of material physical things. It is a simple but profound insight that too many scientists in recent years have tried to deny. For morality to be anything more than an illusion we must recognise that there is more to our existence than just the physical matter we are made up of. And as soon as we do that then we are in a position in common with just about all who have ever lived, to realise that the real question is not whether right and wrong exist at all, but what is it that is right and what is it that is wrong. That is a much more important question. C S Lewis discussed this well in *Mere Christianity*.

Those who believe evolution explains the origin and development of all of reality around us have a serious problem with this question of the moral dimension of our existence. Where did it come from? Why is it universal? Indeed, why does it seem to be part of the very fabric of our existence?

We considered the vast night sky in the last chapter, seeing it point to an ultimate source of reality. In this chapter we have noted the existence of a moral dimension right there within us and permeating the world in which we live. These two aspects of reality compel us to think more about the origins and purpose of life.

John Lennox quotes the philosopher Immanuel Kant,

> "Two things fill the mind with ever increasing admiration and reverence, the more often and the more steadily one reflects on them: the starry heavens above me and the moral law within me." (John Lennox *Gunning For God*, page 230)

To refuse to think further on these questions is to be determinedly committed to limiting our understanding of the world and our place in it.

We do live in a moral Universe, it is an inescapable truth

> "Love the Lord your God... and love your neighbour as yourself."
> Jesus of Nazareth, circa AD 31 quoted in Mark's biography, Mark 12 vs 29-31

5 HOW COULD THEY DO THAT TO ME?

Our inbuilt sense of justice

J ohn headed home as usual. The journey was typical. Work had been better than average with a new commission for an interesting project, an Eco-home that could manage without heating but rely on the warmth supplied by its occupants and appliances. He was mulling over what type of insulation to use. Could he achieve the insulation standard required with some form of natural fibre? When he arrived home and Joanne's car wasn't there, he wasn't worried; she'd be home soon. We all know the routines we have; pick up the post that's come through the letter box and separate the junk mail from the bank statement, put your bag down and head to the bedroom to change out of work clothes, to try to psychologically leave work behind. No matter whether work is interesting or not, this is home, a different place, a place however humble that we need to feel happy to be in, somewhere so powerful that we can sum it up simply as "home".

Joanne didn't come home that evening. It's a situation we all dread, our loved ones no longer being there. Your mind will be racing ahead to all the scenarios; a car crash, a medical emergency. John's sense of unease grew. Something was not right; he could feel it but couldn't put his finger on it. She hadn't messaged him saying she was going anywhere else. Sitting in the kitchen with a cup of tea, he was slowly pondering what he might cook for dinner. If she was delayed at work, he'd start getting something ready and she'd be glad it was there when she came home just as he was when he came in, to the smell of cooking. Food makes home feel like home. It was how they worked things out between themselves. They usually knew who would cook, but if one was delayed the other would start. They had agreed it was good teamwork. Still she didn't come.

Then he noticed it. A small envelope propped up on the fake marble kitchen work top that he had installed, with his name on in her handwriting. Something didn't feel right. As he took the note out the room began to blur. Attempts to catch the emotion of such a situation cannot convey that visceral feeling of your world falling apart. The note simply read:

> John, I've left to live with your best friend Dave. It's been coming for months. I guess I just didn't love you enough. It's hard to know what else to say. Don't come after me. It's over. My solicitor will be in contact about a divorce. I've made my mind up. Joanne

John hadn't seen it coming. He thought he was happily married. He thought Dave really was his best friend, someone he shared everything with since school, but not sharing his wife surely! A cocktail of emotions and rationalisations competed for attention. Anger shouted down the stabbing hurt in his gut; a pain so real it felt as though he had literally been stabbed. Shock suffocated the abyss of loss he was staring at; many emotions were frozen as he failed to compute the future that was now broken. How could he not have known? How could he not have seen it coming? The brutal truth was that he hadn't. Before tears could well up, the competing emotions parted for some thoughts to crystallise. Why me? It's not fair! What have I done wrong? How dare she? How dare they? The two people I trusted most have done that? How dare they?

As evening passed to sleepless night, all his phone calls unanswered by either his soon to be ex-wife or his definitely ex-friend Dave, John felt more than anything that he had been badly wronged. And he had.

Right and wrong aren't trivial matters. We certainly know when we have been wronged by others. That's the easy part. We tend to be less quick to recognise and admit when we have wronged others, when we are at fault. Even so, morality, right and wrong, are not abstract ideas, they are part of the daily fabric of our lives. They may be most obvious when more extreme situations come our way, whether through our own fault or nor, but they are there all the time. Should I speed on the motorway? Should I clean up the mess I have made in the kitchen? Should I relax and watch TV or phone the friend I know is struggling? These choices face us all the time and we recognise and thankfully generally agree on the value of virtue; that doing good to others is the right thing to do and that thinking only of ourselves is wrong. We can in fact only make sense of our world when we experience it in a moral dimension, not merely as if all choices are equally valid. The existence of right and wrong is a real thing and each of us knows it in our hearts.

As John lay there his head whirling, feeling alternately sad beyond words and angry without measure, a small voice reminded him of Anya he flirts with at the gym. He hadn't done anything he shouldn't, but he had wanted to. He thought of online conversations with other women he hankered after from the past. He remembered angry outbursts when he hadn't got what he wanted round the house. None of that justified what Joanne had done to him, most of it she didn't know about anyway, but in between the anger and self-pity he knew he wasn't perfect either. None of us are. He wanted to blame it all on her, it felt easier that way, yet there was still that uneasy insight that it wasn't in truth quite so simple.

It is so easy to see the faults in others but so much harder to admit them in ourselves. Of course, some people are never wrong. They leave a trail of destruction behind them, confident that only others do wrong to them, but they never do anything wrong to anyone else. Their attitude is that whatever anyone might complain about, they deserved it anyway. They simply don't see themselves as they really are. In their most extreme form, they are the dictators and despots, the terrorists and people traffickers, for whom the harm they do to others is always justified by some excuse or ideology or just a perceived need on their part that eclipses any concern for others. Taken far enough they would bring about the end of society and civilisation, behaving worse than any animal that to call them brutes is to be unfair to the rest of creation.

So, have you reached that point of honesty about yourself? You are not perfect either. It's not just that right and wrong are real. It's not just that other people do bad things. It's not just that some other people do things that are wrong, to you. It is that you too will have done wrong to others, whether you always realised it at the time or not. You, like every other person around you are deeply imperfect.

A sense of right and wrong is in every one of us and yet we fail to live up to even our own standards by which we judge others. Then when we judge others as doing wrong, we testify to the existence of objective right and wrong and in doing so we judge and condemn ourselves as well. This is the dilemma of the human condition.

We are all aware that we fail to do the right that we know we should

"We all, like sheep, have gone astray, each of us has turned to his own way".

Isaiah, Jewish exile in Babylon Isaiah 53 vs 6

6 THE DOCTOR AND THE PLAGUE

*Distinguishing good
from bad in nature*

There is a narrow street as old as the town itself that winds down the hill from where the olive groves end, all the way to the river where the old men sit in the shade to discuss and to drink coffee. Centuries of encroachment by plants, and building extensions shade the route. Carpets hang to air, plant pots sit outside doorways, shop doors no wider than a man's shoulders open onto small dark rooms. Railings close off courtyards that cast light across the street. A tethered donkey narrows the passage further. Today it was unnaturally quiet, and we find the doctor making his way house to house on his calls, a heavy air about him, his mind deeply pre-occupied. Should we ask him, he would say he was a progressive man, a rationalist, not given to superstition or religion.

Today what disturbed his mind was the certainty that the next house call would be the same as the last and all the ones before that, and he felt helpless. An anger grew inside him, an aggrieved sense of injustice that could not be quieted. Stooping through a doorway, its low lintel forcing him to bow in greeting, he exchanged the customary salutations, 'Yes he was well, how was the matriarch of the household? how was the father?....' Slipping out of his shoes he was led through the dim light of a well-ordered home to a fevered little boy, abject fear at what was happening to him clear in his eyes. That look was haunting the doctor, patient by patient. Swollen, raging with fever in fact, tossing, groaning, the characteristic swelling or buboes of the plague all too obvious, his outlook was bleak. Moved with compassion the doctor gave instructions on fluids, on keeping the boy cool, on administering anti-biotics and he gave a first injection there and then, the only hope for the poor child. Yes, he would call again tomorrow. They must quarantine the boy, avoid all contact outside the house until it was clear if he might start to recover. No visitors, no contact, no rubbish in the courtyard; burn it all immediately etc. The doctor gave all the best advice he could, then deeply saddened took his leave. Would the boy still be there tomorrow when he called again?

Back on the street the doctor struggled to make sense of the unfolding disaster. He was a rational man. He believed in science and progress. He had had enough of religion at church school where the priest's hypocrisy was sufficient to put him off for a lifetime. It was to him, mindless subservience to be told what to do or how to live by an imaginary higher being, although in his experience it was his surrogates in religious clothing who did the telling what to do. In his self-assembled package of views on the world he saw evolution as the highest "truth" yet discovered, he held it with almost religious devotion in his pantheon of ideas that were the deities of his existence, though he would never have called them that. Here is the doctor's dilemma, can he fight the Bubonic plague in North

Africa and be true to his evolutionary beliefs? To do so is to recognize that there is both good and bad in nature, which as we will see is something he can't explain, since if everything evolved then surely it is all equally valid, equally good? As he saw it, this outbreak of the plague proved that there was no benevolent god. How could God create a plague that caused such terrible suffering and painful death?

At the next home it was the same, another victim. The town authorities needed to act fast to try to contain the problem presently only in one neighbourhood. The truth was that they needed money and resources and outside help to form the right strategy and of course they needed a lot more medicine immediately.

Yet much more than this unfolding disaster, a spectre from the Middle Ages visited on the present, what troubled the doctor most was that he could not resolve his understanding on this problem. He believed in evolution as indisputable fact, so surely the plague had evolved too. Therefore, on what basis could he call it bad and seek to eradicate it? Why should he fight what was only natural? Was it just misplaced sentimentality to fight the disease and try to save lives, after all "survival of the fittest" surely meant death of the weakest? Being logical and consistent with his beliefs he had no basis for helping these desperately ill people.

He ran the conundrum round his head another way. If God had made everything then he had made the plague too which meant that he intended for it to kill people. Whichever way he looked at it, he had no basis to distinguish good from bad in nature, which meant that he had no rational basis for what he was doing, so why did he do it? Was he just living out the echo of the Christian worldview he had rejected as a young man? He seemed to be acting on the cultural memory of a more certain past where people were sure that this medical work was the right thing to do. Sadly, the doctor never solved that problem.

I have painted this scenario loosely based on Albert Camus' book The Plague[3]. As I see it, Camus presents the problem as being that if God made everything, he must have made the plague too, so it was intended to be, so why fight it? It would be tantamount to fighting God himself. There is a certain apparent logic to that. If everything evolved, then the plague evolved too, so why do people take precedence over the plague? Why are people more important? Indeed, why fight something that is eliminating the weak and enabling the strong and fit to survive thus furthering evolution?

This is a fundamental problem. In Camus' argument, he makes the assumption that everything as it is now, is exactly as God made it originally. Many others supporting evolution have made the same assumption and used it to try to dismiss the idea of God. They point to a parasite for example and then say how could a good God have made such a thing? They assume that everything is now as it was originally intended to be. They then feel safe to dismiss God out of hand, job done, move on.

The Christian world view is completely different. In the beginning God made a perfect creation, but rebellion against him by the first people (Adam and Eve) brought death and suffering affecting not only people but all of creation around us. That rebellion brought death on them and their descendants. Now all people die, and nature is 'red in tooth and claw'. So, to the Christian, other people are valuable because they were purposefully made by God. And the plague is not something he originally created but a part of the malfunctioning of what was once perfect. This makes it reasonable to value people and fight the plague, whilst being consistent when doing so.

So, the Christian has a basis to recognise both good and bad in nature, for they are both truly there. A disease like the plague is a symptom of a world gone wrong, not part of the original plan.

If we flip the coin over, so to speak, then if everything evolved then everything that exists has an equal right to exist, viruses and harmful bacteria included. There is then no coherent and consistent way to reconcile that belief with fighting the plague since it is just part of the natural world. We don't find many people following that through to its logical conclusion and doing nothing about their own health or others'.

Many forms of this logical fallacy have been published by a range of authors over the last century. On the one hand they insist that everything has evolved. On the other, when they see bad in nature, they blame God. But what they aren't willing to do is to consider that the bad they see wasn't there in the original creation but has arisen later and is not from God.

If, like the doctor, you are moved by compassion to help the sick and needy then you are agreeing with a core insight of the Judaeo-Christian world view, but one which is incompatible with secular humanism and evolution; namely that there is both good and bad in this world including in nature around us and that it is entirely possible to know the difference, with a solid basis for doing so. The way in which bad came into our world is known as "the fall", that is a fall from an original perfect state. Without recognising the fall, everything in our world has to be accepted as equally valid. In fact, in the final analysis, the very concepts of good and bad then break down.

If you wish to reject the Christian world view on this point, then an evolutionary and secular world view simply does not give the basis for making those distinctions as to good and bad in the world around you, and the consistent outcome would be to have no concern to tackle disease or anything else bad arising in nature. That is a very bleak position. Maybe now you can see why many people have suggested that secular western culture is operating on the memory of what, ironically, it thinks it has rejected.

People do make distinctions between good and bad in nature, in the world around us, thus agreeing with the Christian world view whether they realise it or not.

The bad we see in nature is not what God originally made. It is meaningful to distinguish good from bad

> "God saw everything that He had made and it was very good."
>
> Genesis 1 vs 31

> The came rebellion (the fall from the original perfect state),
>
> "Cursed is the ground because of you."
>
> Genesis 3 vs 17

7 IS IT WORKING FOR YOU AND WHAT HAPPENS WHEN IT DOESN'T?

The cost of secular discipleship

"Life, liberty and the pursuit of happiness."

These famous words from the American Declaration of Independence not only have a special meaning for Americans, they resonate with hearers around the world. Yet what is happiness? Is it having all we want? Is it the absence of pain and suffering? Is my happiness the same as yours? What if pursuing your happiness takes away mine? Can happiness be meaningfully understood in only physical and material dimensions? Let's consider how people try to make themselves happy and whether happiness can really exist without a spiritual dimension.

What will make you truly happy? What will give meaning in

your life and purpose to your existence? We look for answers in a million directions and many potential answers are trying to grab our attention. Here are some of the types of answers being pushed all the time that tap into this basic desire.

If only I were richer, I would be able to make myself happier. The popular TV show *"Who wants to be a millionaire?"* plays to this inbuilt desire we have, to find happiness through wealth.

If only I had a better body, I would feel better about myself. Multiple different diets compete claiming success at weight loss and giving people a better figure and raising self-esteem.

If I had a bigger house in a better neighbourhood, life would be better. Having the right people around us will surely make us happier.

If I had a better-looking woman/ a more attractive man, life would be more satisfying. A better-looking spouse would be definitely more satisfying and I'd feel better about myself, especially since other people would see how well I had done.

The themes that come up repeatedly include the following: relationships, money, travel, power, success, approval, status, homes and more.

You might be guessing that what is coming next is a neat answer that says one of the following:

You will only be really happy with a religious experience. (TV evangelist?)

You will only be really happy if you stop desiring these things. (Self-help guru?)

You will only be really happy if you are shown how to be successful at getting many of the things mentioned above. (Glossy magazines?)

You will only be really happy if you stop worrying and buy a particular self-help book/ manual. (More gurus?)

You will only be really happy if you attend a particular course/ church/ therapy programme. (Too many potential providers to list!)

I don't believe any of those categories of answer and there are good reasons why you shouldn't either. It probably won't surprise you if I said that wanting a nice house or great partner is not of itself a bad thing in any way. However, would it surprise if I also said that absolutely no-one can guarantee to make you happy because we live in damaged world? We all get caught up in things beyond our control. <u>Anyone who claims to have a neat answer for how to make you happy is either deluded or dishonest.</u> Other people do bad things to us even when we haven't done anything bad to them. This is so obvious it almost shouldn't need saying, yet a whole self-help industry lives in denial of this simple point. Religion is often presented as being the exception that will be the real answer to make you happy. What if it isn't either?

Consider instead, if what each of us is needing is something more fundamental than the external things that make us happy or unhappy, or any internal change we can bring about by ourselves from our own efforts? There is a place for what we can do to help ourselves and for what others can do for us and we can do for them. It is perfectly reasonable to want to house your family. It is sensible to seek help from doctors for illness. It is entirely right to want a loving wife or husband. But here is where it starts to get tricky. What do you do when the things you legitimately want, go wrong, or don't satisfy, or let you down, or are taken away? In short what do you do when it's not working for you?

This is not an abstract discussion. It is a painfully real matter for every one of us. What do you do when divorce overwhelms you? Or you lose your home? Or you become seriously or terminally ill? Or lose your job with a family to support? Or you finally admit you have an out-of-control addiction?

Apart from your own challenges, what do you do when others close to you are caught up in addiction, for example, and you somehow just can't help them? What do you do when conflict comes to your neighbourhood, and you are caught up in something beyond your own control? For Christian belief to be worth something it has to stand up to the challenges of life; when we are happy and when we aren't. It can't just be a quick fix or a panacea. It can't just be glib answers or a means of generating happy or positive feelings. I would suggest it has to be of a fundamentally different order from the other answers available.

We could go on and on listing the trials and difficulties of life. Here lies one of the great tragedies of the human condition. We hope for good and constantly seek it but are repeatedly disappointed in our quest. If belief or faith is to be of any real value, it must offer something more substantial than the other answers we are offered because they are not enough to sustain people on their own. We also need to be sure that the answers we find are the right answers.

It is surely no coincidence that as society has turned away from believing that Christian belief is plausible or meaningful and has turned to other answers it has reaped a terrible harvest. Suicide rates stand at all-time highs across the developed world. Divorce is at record levels with endless hurting people left in its wake. Bewildered children turn to self-harm.

Considering what children in secular societies are brought up with, it's no wonder there is a growth of despair. They are told that they and all life arose from a cosmic accident. That everything evolved through an endless cycle of pain and suffering and death all by Random Chance. That when they die that's it, or that they float off to some vague unlocated heaven to sit there watching us suffer here. That there's no real right or wrong, that everything is relative. All boundaries are questioned, nothing is reliable. They are encouraged to seek material success, but increasingly see through it. Their sense of their very self is distorted by the messages preached at them by secular culture. Their minds are pumped with images of violence and pornography, degrading their ability to develop healthy relationships. Even the concept of healthy relationships is too often drowned in cynicism and scorn by the media. They are offered no hope, no meaningful measure of their own worth or that of others. And yet commentators still wonder why there is a surge in drug abuse, self-harm and violence in the young.

If we look away from the personal struggles people face when their worldview turns out not to have the power to help them and instead look at what has been going on with societies as a whole, it is no better. When we look back over the Twentieth Century one of its defining characteristics is that it was the century when people tried to live without God with terrible consequences.

Atheistic communism set out to remodel Russia, Eastern Europe, China and other countries. The results are so appalling they are almost incomprehensible. It is estimated that at least 40 million died in Mao Zedong's China. At least 9 million died in the Russian civil war and 20 million under Stalin. The second world war took 55 million away. (See David Berlinski, *'The Devil's Delusion, Atheism and its Scientific Pretensions'*). Other estimates suggest that Communism was responsible for a death toll estimated to be at least 94 million in the Twentieth Century (including at least 85 million in China and Russia). (See for example, Stephane Courtois et al, *'The Black Book Of Communism'*).

Is this immense human misery genuinely unrelated to a desire to live life without reference to God? As David Berlinski puts it,

> "What Hitler did not believe, and what Stalin did not believe, and what the SS did not believe, and what the Gestapo did not believe, and what the NKVD did not believe and what the commissars, functionaries, swaggering executioners, Nazi doctors, Communist Party theoreticians, intellectuals, Brown shirts, Blackshirts, Gauletiers, and a thousand party hacks did not believe, was that God was watching what they were doing. And as far as we can tell, very few of those carrying out the horrors of the Twentieth Century worried overmuch that God was watching what they were doing either. That is after all the meaning of a secular society."

> (David Berlinski, *'The Devil's Delusion, Atheism and its Scientific Pretensions'* page 26).

Other authors have responded with the wrongs they claim Christianity has caused. People claiming to be Christians have done some terrible things (though on nothing like the same scale), but I see a crucial difference. Jesus, the person Christians claim to follow and claim to base their beliefs on was very frank,

> "Every good tree bears good fruit, but a bad tree

bears bad fruit….. Thus by their fruit you will recognise them." (Quoted in Matthew's biography of Jesus chapter 7 vs 17-20)

He couldn't be more blunt. We can measure what they did against the teachings of Jesus and the apostles and say that whilst they were claiming to be Christian, they were not acting in the way Christians should. It is fair to ask whether they were Christians at all. But isn't David Berlinski on to something with atheism? It is worth noting that he is not a Christian, he is not making a partisan point, he is just pointing out the flaws in secularism and its consequences. If people do evil and it is <u>consistent</u> with their worldview, don't we have a serious problem? Isn't it fair to question their worldview?

The individual pursuit of happiness in a purely secular and materialistic way is letting down millions all the time. It promises everything but delivers little of lasting value. At the same time the pursuit of the secular dream at the level of whole societies has delivered unprecedented violence, suffering and death, all in the name of "building a better society".

What do you do when you finally wake up and realize that the cost of secular discipleship is simply too high, that the personal and societal cost of trying to live without God is simply too great?

Many people have testified to something deeper and more powerful than could ever be described as just "happiness", that sustains them through the happy and unhappy experiences of life. They find it in surprising ways.

Take for example the drug addict or alcoholic. There is a journey for them to go through before they will ever find freedom from their addiction; without that journey they will never escape. They will go through many typical stages of denial of reality. They will deny they have a problem. They will delude themselves that they need a bit of help, but if they try harder, they will be able to overcome it. They try to control it, they fail. They try to find a medicine or therapy that will fix it. They become totally discouraged and give up hope of ever changing. Then finally, the first step to recovery that starts setting them free from addiction, is to recognize that they absolutely cannot overcome their addictions and need help from a higher power than themselves.

In many ways the addict who gets help and recovers, but in the process finds that God is real and powerful, is the fortunate one. Most people go through life still trying to convince themselves that if they just get this or that new thing or try some other strategy, they will be OK, and they are still denying the need of help from a higher power till the day they die. Sorry to be so blunt.

How bad does it have to get before you are willing to ask for Jesus to begin changing you from the inside out? This is what Jesus meant when he said, *"You must be born again,"* and it is the only way to lasting peace.

It is in the final recognition of powerlessness, that human pride is put aside, and the power of God is allowed in

> "What good is it for a man to gain the whole world, yet forfeit his soul?"

> Jesus of Nazareth in Mark's gospel 8 vs 36

Real peace of mind is from God

"You should not be surprised at me saying, 'You must be born again.'"

Jesus of Nazareth in John's gospel 3 vs 7

8 THE CURIOUS CASE OF THE ATHEIST WHO CEASED TO EXIST

Following the argument wherever it leads

O ne of the most curious phenomena of in-depth investigations is that the thing you set out to look for sometimes turns out to not be there after all. Sometimes when you look for something it ceases to exist. History has been full of examples of things that people were sure existed, but then turned out to not be there when they looked more carefully. Unicorns were sought but remained elusive until "Unicorn" tusks were found to be from Narwhals in the Arctic Ocean. It explained where the "Unicorn" tusks had come from solving the mystery of the unicorn and simultaneously making the unicorn extinct, so to speak. New evidence comes to light and makes it clear that what we thought we knew was just assumptions, or misinformation, or plain myth. It can be real fun checking out things people think they know and then proving or disproving their preconceptions, when all that is at stake is say the existence of unicorns; but it becomes a whole lot more serious when it concerns the foundation of your entire worldview.

Imagine building your entire career and reputation on one position, to then come to the view that you were wrong all along. Anthony Flew was a Professor of Philosophy. He was also a famous atheist. In 1950 he wrote a paper *"Theology And Falsification"*, that was a seminal publication in defence of atheism that has been reprinted many times. For the next 50 years he defended atheism vigorously and eloquently, but then to the surprise of just about everyone familiar with his career, he changed his mind.

He quotes Plato (in his work 'Republic') as attributing to Socrates the following maxim:

> "We must follow the argument wherever it leads." (Anthony Flew, *There is a God; How the World's Most Notorious Atheist Changed His Mind,* page 132)

In doing just that, Anthony Flew changed his mind and came to a belief in God. He wrote a book of his journey from atheism to believing there is a God; *'There is a God; How the World's Most Notorious Atheist Changed His Mind'.* That "conversion" caused a storm and it can't have gone down at all well with some of the recent popularisers of atheism.

When most people hear the word philosophy it turns them off. They think of clever people arguing about things they probably don't really understand, to come to conclusions that ordinary people often regard as nonsense. Philosophy has a fairly bad name. So, I must ask you not to be put off. I would suggest that philosophy at its best is simply thinking clearly and following the evidence or argument wherever it leads. Anthony Flew does that brilliantly in his book. He very clearly and in plain language, sets out the evidence that built up to the point where he changed his mind and admitted that he had been wrong. That takes courage and honesty, as well as a rigorous intellect. Anthony Flew looked at several lines of argument and evidence. Here is some of what convinced him.

When considering the advances in our understanding of DNA and what constitutes life itself, he concluded,

> "The only satisfactory explanation for the origin of such "end-directed, self-replicating" life as we see on earth is an infinitely intelligent mind."

> (Anthony Flew, *There is a God; How the World's Most Notorious Atheist Changed His Mind* p132)

This includes that such phenomena as the chemical information coding system, DNA, could not have been self-creating and self-organizing. He argues that we now know that DNA is a language and as such it must have had its origin outside the chemicals that encode it, just as the letters on this page encode ideas based in language that I am using to communicate with you. The ink on the page or the LEDs in your computer screen did not write this book, the language and meaning originate elsewhere.

At a different scale, when thinking about the very origin of the universe, to put it in colloquial terms Anthony Flew quotes the lyrics of *The Sound Of Music*,

> "Nothing comes from nothing, nothing ever could." (Anthony Flew, *There is a God; How the World's Most Notorious Atheist Changed His Mind*, page 133)

To postulate that the universe just created itself is simply absurd. Indeed, a primary thing that needs explanation is the fact that the universe exists at all (including us within it). It is real. Anthony Flew quotes Richard Swinburne,

> "It is very unlikely that a universe would exist un-
> caused, but rather more likely that God would exist
> uncaused. Hence the argument from the existence of
> the universe to the existence of God is a good... argu-
> ment." (Anthony Flew, *There is a God; How the World's
> Most Notorious Atheist Changed His Mind*, page 144)

This line of argument (the so-called cosmological argument)
has been fought over back and forth for a long time, but what I
find interesting with Anthony Flew is that having spent a career living with the debates he was finally persuaded that this
simple argument if carefully set out, is compelling. His understanding developed further, coming to the view that there is
no good argument to deny that God <u>does</u> exist outside time and
space and that He is capable of and chooses to intentionally act
into it.

As David Berlinski puts it,

> "The hypothesis of God's existence and the facts
> of contemporary cosmology are consistent." (David
> Berlinski, *The Devil's Delusion, Atheism and its Scien-
> tific Pretensions*, page 80)

I cannot do justice to Flew's arguments in a few short para-
graphs, but we can note his conclusions and you can read more
of what he and others have written to explore further. His con-
cluding chapter is particularly clear. He sums up the evidence
he discusses in the book.

> "The three items of evidence we have considered in
> this volume – the laws of nature, life with its teleo-
> logical organization, and the existence of the uni-
> verse – can only be explained in the light of an Intel-
> ligence that explains both its own existence and that

of the world."(Anthony Flew, *There is a God; How the World's Most Notorious Atheist Changed His Mind*, page 155). (note: Teleological in this quote, means having purpose, function and design).

A Mind or Intelligence is a necessary precondition for the existence of reality, both physical reality and non-physical reality (We will return to the issue of non-physical, or supra-physical, reality shortly).

Flew sums up his decades long journey and reversal of position, saying,

> "I have followed the argument where it has led me. And it has led me to accept the existence of a self-existent, immutable, immaterial, omnipotent, and omniscient Being." (Anthony Flew, *There is a God; How the World's Most Notorious Atheist Changed His Mind*, page 155)

In short, he had found God!

His book, very honestly, concludes with issues he was still working on towards the end of his life including,

> "the question of whether the Divine has revealed itself in human history."

(which we will look at in a later chapter) and he reminds us that,

> "You cannot limit the possibilities of omnipotence except to produce the logically impossible. Everything else is open to omnipotence."

However, in relation to the Christian claim that,

> "God became man in the person of Jesus Christ",

he concludes,

> "As I have said more than once, no other religion

enjoys anything like the combination of a charismatic figure like Jesus and a first-class intellectual like St. Paul. If you're wanting omnipotence to set up a religion, it seems to me that this is the one to beat!" (Anthony Flew, *There is a God; How the World's Most Notorious Atheist Changed His Mind*, page 157).

Just because atheism has become popular again in some circles, does not prove it right. Fashions come and fashions go, but the truth remains. One of the great ironies of the recent "New Atheists", like Richard Dawkins and Sam Harris, is that they effectively argue that physics and chemistry are all there is, (so called strict materialism) which is a reinvention of the arguments of the Logical Positivists of the early Twentieth Century, that Anthony Flew was influential in demolishing in the 1950s. Flew's arguments for the existence of God, in the Twenty-First Century , offer an eloquent demolition of attempts to resurrect those materialist atheistic ideas.

At the end of his book "*There is a God; How the World's Most Notorious Atheist Changed His Mind*", there is an excellent appendix by Roy Abraham Varghese, who discusses some of the arguments set out by Anthony Flew. He summarizes,

> "five phenomena in our immediate experience that can only be explained in terms of the existence of God." (Flew, *There is a God; How the World's Most Notorious Atheist Changed His Mind* Page 161)

I'll quote selectively from some of what he discusses to give the outline. He states that,

> "God is the condition that underlies all that is self-evident in our experience."

The way he sets out his argument is simple, but compelling. He says, "the approach taken is, that we have all the evidence we need in our immediate experience and that only a deliberate refusal to "look" is responsible for atheism of any variety." (Flew, *There is a God; How the World's Most Notorious Atheist Changed His Mind,* page 163).

In other words, there are some things about ourselves, and our experience of reality around us, that are in themselves convincing evidence for the existence of God. He discusses several areas that are not explained without the existence of God: rationality, consciousness, the self and the origin of the supraphysical (e.g. non-material reality).

Rationality

The fact of our existence and a rationally ordered world around us that we can comprehend and interact with predictably, leads us to believe that reality is more than simply matter and that it has a rational cause. We also know and experience more than just a physical reality in being conscious, thinking beings,

"It is incoherent .. to suggest that consciousness and thought are simply and solely physical transactions." (i.e. not just neurons firing in our brains). (Flew, *There is a God; How the World's Most Notorious Atheist Changed His Mind,* page 164)

As for whether a God need exist prior to the universe he puts it very simply.

"Take your pick: God or the universe. Something always existed," and, "God is not an ultimate brute fact, but the ultimate Rationality that is embedded in every dimension of being." (Or one might say, the source of that rationality) (Flew, *There is a God; How* the World's Most Notorious Atheist Changed His Mind page 165)

As for the idea of a Big Bang making the universe out of nothing, he reminds us that it is a simple mistake to think that "nothing" is some kind of "something".

> "Absolute nothingness cannot produce something given endless time – in fact there can be no time in absolute nothingness!" (Flew *There is a God; How the World's Most Notorious Atheist Changed His Mind*, page 170)

We can add to this point that Einstein claimed that space and time are inextricably linked in what he called space-time, so it makes no sense to talk of time before the universe existed because without space there is no time!

These are, on one level, surprisingly simple arguments to grasp, yet on another utterly profound and most people need to take their time to consider them and think them over for them to sink in. So, don't be put off if you have many questions arising from such a brief overview. I simply suggest you read more and let it come clearer. The suggested reading at the end of this book gives some places to start.

Do however, take from these discussions one important thing. Do not be brow beaten by teachers, the media or bestselling books or popular culture, into thinking that all right-minded well-educated people don't consider belief to be credible. Minds as fine as any in the last century are firmly on the side of belief in the existence of God.

Consciousness

Varghese argues,

> "We are conscious, and conscious that we are con-

scious. No-one can deny this without self-contra-
diction – although some persist in doing so." (Flew,
*There is a God; How the World's Most Notorious Atheist
Changed His Mind,* page 173)

In other words, we know that there is more to reality than just
the physical and material.

"The power of thinking in concepts is by its very nature something that transcends matter." (Flew, *There
is a God; How the World's Most Notorious Atheist
Changed His Mind,* page 177)

This argues powerfully against any idea that we are just physics and chemistry driven by our genes.

"For Dawkins, the main means for producing human
behaviour is to attribute to genes characteristics
that can significantly be attributed only to persons." (Anthony Flew, *There is a God; How the World's
Most Notorious Atheist Changed His Mind,* page 79)

Or as John Lennox puts it so well,

"If DNA neither knows nor cares and we dance to
its music, how is it that most of us both know and
care?"! (John Lennox, *Gunning For God, Why The New
Atheists Are Missing The Mark,* page 114)

David Berlinski points out that even the most ardent proponents of evolutionary determinism (i.e. that we are controlled
by our genes) are not prepared to follow it to its logical conclusion.

"What is remarkable in this is that no-one taking
selfish genes seriously takes them seriously. Richard
Dawkins has gone out of his way to affirm that he, at
least, is not under the control of his genes. 'I too am
an implacable opponent of genetic determinism' he

has written. His genes are not so selfish as to tell him what to do." (Berlinski, *The Devil's Delusion, Atheism and its Scientific Pretensions*, page 176)

Strict materialism is an idea that no-one can live with consistently. The very act of deploying a mind to argue for evolution against other minds that think otherwise, displays human agency that cannot be explained by an insistence that everything is controlled by our genes. The idea that we are controlled by our genes is a popular idea, but it is still incoherent. If genes control everything, why do some people's genes argue for that position and others against it? And if they don't, then a materialistic explanation which is what evolution limits itself to, has no basis for any explanation of the existence of the mind. This is a serious problem.

Berlinski again,

"We do not have a serious scientific theory exploring the powers and properties of the human mind. The claim that the human mind is the product of evolution is not unassailable fact. It is barely coherent." (Berlinski, *The Devil's Delusion, Atheism and its Scientific Pretensions*, page 174)

The self

"The cells in your body keep changing and yet "you" remain the same." (Flew, *There is a God; How the World's Most Notorious Atheist Changed His Mind,* page 180)

Over our lifetime we eat and breathe and build and then renew the physical substance of our bodies yet remain in every sense ourselves. Our "self" is clearly more than just cells and tissues and organs. Varghese writes,

"The most fundamental reality of which we are all aware, then, is the human self, and an understanding of the self inevitably sheds insights on all the origin questions and makes sense of reality as a whole. We realize that the self cannot be described, let alone explained, in terms of physics or chemistry: science does not discover the self; the self discovers science. We realize that no account of the history of the universe is coherent if it cannot account for the existence of the self." (Flew, *There is a God; How the World's Most Notorious Atheist Changed His Mind*, page 181)

As you read that quote you are validating its truthfulness by evaluating it yourself! There is no convincing atheistic, materialistic explanation of the origin of the self because such explanation is trapped in trying to explain everything in just the laws of physics and the chemistry of our bodies, in a deterministic way.

The origin of the supra-physical (or non-material reality)

Where did such realities as life itself, rather than just inanimate matter come from? Where did thought and the ability to think in concepts, and the existence of the self come from? They are clearly more than just physical, material phenomena, that is they are supra-physical (or sometimes described as 'non-material reality')? Varghese argues,

"The answer to the question of the origin of the supra-physical seems obvious; the supra-physical can only originate in a supra-physical source. Life, consciousness, mind, and the self can only come from a Source that is living, conscious, and thinking." (Flew, *There is a God; How the World's Most Notorious Atheist Changed His Mind*, page 183)

He goes on,

> "Matter cannot produce conceptions and perceptions. A force field does not think or plan. So, at the level of everyday experience, we become immediately aware that the world of living, conscious, thinking beings has to originate in a living Source, a mind." (Flew, *There is a God; How the World's Most Notorious Atheist Changed His Mind,* page 183)

This is not an abstract discussion. Core parts of our experience of reality are not explained without accepting that the supra-physical exists. As John Lennox observes,

> "the ability to love is intimately linked to what we call "free will"."

> (John Lennox, *Gunning for God, Why The New Atheists are Missing the Target,* page 140).

If it is not free at all, but merely determined by physics and chemistry within us, then it is not really what we call love either. That is an absurd position to take that denies an essential part of our experience and of what it means to be human. Love is a supra-physical (non-material) concept we all understand and know to exist, that relies on genuine free will and is not explainable by physical, material means alone. We all know and relate to this reality. Therefore, where does love originate from?

So, if philosophy is about clear thinking and following the argument wherever it leads, then atheists and with them, those who think evolution explains everything, have some serious problems. There are fundamental aspects of reality that evolution and science simply cannot explain. These are not matters that can be set aside as problems to solve later. They are in fact powerful evidence that the important question is not whether

God exists and is the source of all reality, but rather that the real and more important question is, 'What is God like'? In that sense philosophy in the last two hundred years has been fatally side-tracked and one reading of Anthony Flew is that he thinks it should return to its classical heritage and not be led down the dead end of atheism.

Anthony Flew's intellectual conversion though remarkable, is far from unique. He had been on an incredible journey from arguing powerfully for atheism to writing one of the best defences I've come across that there is a God, indeed that there must be a God. Many others have set out to disprove the existence of God and demonstrate the futility of Christian belief and have ended up achieving exactly the opposite, simply because that is where the evidence and argument leads. We will look at some other unlikely conversions in a later chapter.

In addition to Anthony Flew's book *There is a God; How the World's Most Notorious Atheist Changed His Mind*, a systematic and highly readable and compelling case for the existence of God is built up through J. Warner Wallace's book *God's Crime Scene, A Cold-case Detective Examines the Evidence for a Divinely Created Universe*. He identifies that the cause of the universe, must have the following attributes:

1. "External to the universe
2. Non-spatial, atemporal, and non-material
3. Uncaused
4. Powerful enough to create everything we see in the universe
5. Specifically purposeful enough to produce a universe fine-tuned for life
6. Intelligent and communicative
7. Creative and resourceful
8. A conscious Mind
9. Free to choose (and create) personally

10. The personal source of moral truth and obligation
11. The standard for good by which we define evil."

Summarising the case that he presents he concludes:

"We're not inferring God's existence on the basis of a negative case against naturalism. Instead, we're inferring supernaturalism on the strength of a positive case, given the cumulative evidence. In fact, the universe displays the very characteristics we would expect to find if it had been created by the Divine suspect we've described in our profile."

(J. Warner Wallace, *God's Crime Scene, A Cold-case Detective Examines the Evidence for a Divinely Created Universe,* page 193 and 197)

Are you afraid that if you follow the argument wherever it leads, you too will end up believing?

The evidence leads to God

"The heavens declare the glory of God; the skies proclaim the work of his hands. Day after day they pour forth speech; night after night they display knowledge. There is no speech or language where their voice is not heard. Their voice goes out into all the earth, their words to the ends of the world."
Psalm 19 vs 1-4

PART 2 IS EVOLUTION THE ANSWER?

9 IT LOOKS LIKE SOMEONE DESIGNED IT, IT WORKS LIKE SOMEONE DESIGNED IT...

We recognize Design when we see and experience it

A t the time of writing, another lost city has recently been discovered in the jungle in Central America. Huge stone structures had lain hidden in thick jungle for hundreds of years only to be rediscovered by archaeologists. The large cut stones show careful working. The whole city has a functional structure with different buildings for living in, food storage and religious or ritual purposes. Across central and south America many such cities have been found in the last two centuries. In each case we can infer intentionality. The buildings, though ruined, were clearly planned and intentionally built. In none of the cases of these hidden cities being re-discovered, does anyone consider it plausible to argue that they just happened as a "natural" phenomenon, with no Design input. In fact, to insist there was no Design intent, would be considered plain stupid, because we recognise Design when we see it and experience it.

In 1902 a wooden box was retrieved from a wrecked ship off the coast of the Greek island of Antikythera. When it was opened by archaeologist Valerios Stais a curious clock like artefact was revealed, encased in corrosion and dirt. It looked like a complex time keeping device of some sort. With time and care it has been analysed sufficiently for working replicas to be produced and its function deciphered. It turned out to be an astronomical computer from some time probably in the first or second centuries BC. The gears inter-mesh to assist in the calculation of astronomical movements. It is an elegant and impressively complex computing or calculating device. Such complexity was not seen again in Europe until the fourteenth century. When looking at heavily corroded and disrupted components of the Antikythera Mechanism it was immediately apparent from the parts that were visible that they were designed and intentionally constructed. They were not natural items from the seabed. (See http://www.antikythera-mechanism.gr/). Again, Design spoke for itself[4].

In both examples, an ancient computer and an ancient city, we recognise Design when we see it. Then having done so we can set about trying to figure out more details about what has been discovered. In both cases not everything is known or will be known about their construction and use, but we can be sure they were designed, carefully and intentionally constructed and the remains, though incomplete, testify eloquently to this.

When we turn to nature, the story of scientific discovery over the last couple of centuries has been one of unveiling breathtaking complexity and organisation that goes from the sub-atomic level, through single cells and more complex organisms, up to ecosystems and on out to the solar system and galaxies beyond.

Simple cells?

We will focus on just single cell organisms and DNA at this point in the discussion. If we look at what has been discovered about DNA and single cell bacteria in the last few decades, then two incredible stories have emerged. First, DNA the code of life in every living cell is immensely complicated and its replication involves precise mechanisms. Second, even "simple" single cell organisms are actually complex beyond anything that anyone guessed at 150 years ago.

> "We live in a golden age for the study of biology... the overarching picture is one of fathomless elegance – a seemingly never-ending parade of sophisticated structures, brilliant organizational arrangements, and well-nigh incomprehensively complex systems. In fact, stunning breakthroughs come so thick and fast in our times that a danger is to become jaded." (Michael Behe *Darwin Devolves, The New Science About DNA That Challenges Evolution*, page 43)

Irreducible complexity

Michael Behe in his book *'Darwin's Black Box: The Biochemical Challenge To Evolution'*, discusses what he calls Irreducible Complexity. In engineering systems diagrams, a "Black box" is a part of the system where we do not know the detail of what is going on inside it. That was how it was for Darwin with cells, in his day virtually nothing was known of what went on inside cells, hence being a "Black box" to Darwin.

Today we know a vastly more. There is an incredible amount

going on within every living cell and interestingly at the level of the single cell we find structures that cannot function unless they are complete. If any essential part is missing, they don't work. If key parts are missing, the cell can't function and ultimately dies. This has become known as irreducible complexity. If you take one part away, the whole thing becomes useless. This is the case for structures within cells and for cells as a whole.

Michael Behe looked at the flagellum in single cell bacteria, a hair on a bacterium that can rotate to propel the bacterium about. It looks like a biological equivalent of an outboard motor. It needs multiple parts all in their correct relationship to one another to function, and the bacteria needs it to work to move about. Take parts away and the flagellum ceases to work. All the parts had to come together at the same time to be functional, otherwise there was no advantage to having them since they would be non-functioning. Such a Design would not accumulate in stages by chance since at each of the multiple steps towards a finally functioning and useful flagellum, the parts would always be non-functioning and confer no evolutionary advantage and thus not be passed on. (Michael Behe, 'Darwin's Black Box: The Biochemical Challenge To Evolution').

This type of Chicken and egg problem exists in biology in so many ways that it cannot be avoided. Michael Behe discusses it at length in his books.

> "The machinery of the cell ... is very elaborate indeed. Therefore it too is irreducibly complex. Since irreducibly complex systems are quite resistant to gradual construction by an unguided process such as Darwin's mechanism, and since there is not plausible evidence to show they can be so constructed, it is reasonable to conclude that random mutation and natural selection did not produce the molecular ma-

chines of the cell." (Michael Behe *Darwin Devolves, The New Science About DNA That Challenges Evolution,* page 233)

Where did the information come from?

It is not possible to meaningfully separate the irreducibly complex structures of the cell from the information that produces and controls them. Every process and structure in the cell requires information to build it and operate it, which is contained in the cell's DNA. (Even this is a simplification since RNA also contains information and recent understanding of epigenetics is showing information stored in cells in other ways than just the DNA coding, which just amplifies the information problem). Without the DNA the cell is dead. But without a cell to sustain it the DNA degrades quickly. There is a very high level of inter-related complexity that must be reached as a minimum, for a viable cell to exist and it must include the information in the DNA. The information cannot evolve separately since it is only carried within cells. At any stage of evolution of the first cell, it would have needed to hold the necessary information for its formation and function and successful replication, within itself, without significant mistakes, otherwise it would not be able to live and reproduce. You can't have half the code and have a living reproducing cell. This is serious problem for evolutionary explanations of life. It has also turned out that what was thought of as "junk DNA" is no such thing after all and has a purpose.

In fact, without a complete cell the DNA would not be able to assemble proteins or any other basic building blocks for life to keep the cell alive. The cell is like a factory that makes more of the materials from which it is itself constructed. Without a fully functioning complete cell (which requires its DNA to function), the DNA in a cell can't make anything. This point alone has caused many to conclude that evolution from nothing to all life today is not possible.

There is no conceivable way to overcome this problem with partial cells formed by Random Chance. The only proposal evolutionary theory has to deal with this problem is to claim that endless small changes somehow got us to where we are now. But if there is no means to capture and reliably store and use the information necessary for life, then no amount of time will change that, and no small change can be beneficial or passed on. Non-living things are inert. A rock is a rock. If you stare at it for hundreds of years, or millions or a few billions of years it will remain just a rock[5].

If what we see at the level of each cell, is a high level of apparent intentional Design not randomness and we also see endless examples of irreducible complexity it begs the question, is this Design? If at the level of DNA within the cell, we see a highly organised complex code for life, then we must again ask the very basic question; if it has all the attributes of a Design code, then surely wasn't it designed? This code or programming language has to come from somewhere before the cell can exist, and it must originate in someone designing it. Very many scientists look at this evidence and are convinced that it does have all the attributes of Design and thus there must be an intentional cause to its existence. In other words, there must be a designer.

> "Coded language structures are non-material in nature and absolutely require a non-material explanation." (John Baumgardner in *In Six Days, Why 50 Scientists Choose to Believe in Creation*, page 213)

There has been a spate of books on this theme in the last 30 years, from biochemists, micro-biologists and others, such as: *'Darwin's Black Box'*, by Michael Behe and *'Signature in the Cell'*, by Stephen Meyer, and they have caused a storm. This was part of the evidence that convinced the atheist philosopher Antony Flew that there is a God.

An engineering analogy

Several European car manufacturers have claimed that they have suffered from Chinese companies reverse-engineering their cars and then producing copies. Now, if the copy that was produced had wheels without bearings, the car might look the same, but the wheels couldn't turn, and it would be useless. It must not only look the same it must also function in the right way, or it becomes a very large model car to put on a stand rather than to drive. If the car had an engine and a fuel tank but no fuel line to link the two it would never move. If the engine block was a perfect copy on the outside but had no pistons, cranks, camshafts etc on the inside, the car would be utterly useless. It goes further than this, because even if all the right physical parts are included, but there is no software in the engine management computer, the engine still won't run. It is only with the integration of all the design elements that we have a viable car. Now some parts might prove to be dispensable. A car copy without opening electric windows would be less convenient but would still be useable. But a car with no brakes isn't and a car with no power in the battery and no software in the engine management is still a non-functioning car.

This is exactly the situation with the "simplest" single cell organisms. Not only do all the parts need to be together in the right relation to one another, but the cell must be "programmed" to operate in the right way and that requires the right information to be stored in its DNA. No information equals a dead non-functioning cell. This point is so straight forwards and clear, it is quite incredible that anyone should try to pretend that this insurmountable problem for evolutionary explanations doesn't exist.

Whilst critics of the idea of irreducible complexity might point out a similar cell with one bit less, what they can't show is a cell without most of the essential parts, which must include some form of cell membrane as a wrapper to keep all the parts together, some form of fluid inside the cell, a place for information to be stored and a means to copy that information and act upon it, a place to store energy etc. Even the minimum level of inter-connected and inter-dependent complexity necessary to sustain any form of life is immense. There simply isn't a way to get there from randomly associating pieces of stuff near one another and hoping they will organise themselves into such a mutually dependent form. It's like putting a few billion bits of plastic and metal into a large tombola and turning it endlessly expecting a supercomputer to accidentally form itself by chance.

Yet that is a reasonable analogy. There are about 3 billion letters in the code making up human DNA. If we print out the human genome (whole DNA record) in normal text it will fill about 850 Bibles in volume. We inherit one copy from each parent therefore there is 2 x 850 Bibles worth of letter code in every cell within us, but it occupies just a microscopic dot. If the strings of DNA in our cells are strung out, they are about 2 metres long, yet they are bundled so small that you need a microscope to see them. Each "letter" in the code is only a few billionths of a meter tall. DNA is quite fragile and doesn't stay intact outside a cell, but the cell needs a complete functioning DNA to regulate it and keep it alive. (Robert Carter chapter 2 *Evolution's Achilles Heels,* page 53).

Every part of that code has a function and needs to be in the right place. Randomness doesn't even begin to look like a reasonable mechanism for that level of complex information to be assembled. John Lennox observes that,

"The point is that when we see anything that involves language like information, we postulate the involvement of a mind."(John Lennox *Can Science Explain Everything?* Page 50). He also notes that,

"Science has revealed that we live in a word-based universe." (*Can Science Explain Everything?* page 51)

We must repeat a point because it is so fundamental. To get from an inanimate object to life, a cell would have to develop DNA to a high level of complexity, capture information (though no-one knows how), protect it and keep it stable and simultaneously use that information to function itself, because there is no other information to fall back on. Then it must reproduce and accurately pass that information on. Otherwise, the information died with that first functioning cell; and that's just the first supposed steps to life.

It turns out however, that the problem is even greater than this. DNA is not a static printed code but effectively a living operating entity. There are up to 1 million lesions or breaks in the DNA in each cell in your body per day[6]. These breaks have to be found, checked and repaired every day to keep the cell working properly. And there are 30 to 40 trillion cells in your body (see for example, Sender, Fuchs, Milo (2016) *Revised Estimates For The Number Of Human And Bacteria Cells In The Body*). So, DNA acts like a self-fixing supercomputer operating system. It finds and fixes its own problems to maintain a stable and functional cell for it to remain in. It maintains the cell that hosts it and fixes itself. DNA also regulates the function of individual cells within larger tissue structures and organs and systems, as well as within the body overall. It does this whilst being capable of accurately passing on this information to the next generation. (See Robert Carter, chapter 2 *Evolution's Achilles Heels,* page 53).

DNA also operates in a further dimension; time, whereby different parts fold and unfold to function and express themselves at different times. It is not just a 3-dimensional structure, a helix, but different parts function at different times. The information density and the layering of information are beyond any other information carrying mechanism in existence. There are multiple overlapping codes in the genome, as though, by analogy, the letters of a page could be read in different orders at different times for different messages to express themselves. (Robert Carter, chapter 2 *Evolution's Achilles Heels* page 60).

There is no known mechanism to genetically accumulate information and complexity. Mutations are leading to accumulation of errors and faults in DNA, not improvements. The genome of all living things is <u>degrading</u>, not improving. (See Robert Carter chapter 2, *Evolution's Achilles Heels*). Which of course takes us back to the question of, where did the information come from in the first place?

No one would believe that random sections of computer code would be able to self-assemble into a complete operating system, then program a computer, all the time <u>with the power source switched off</u>. Someone had to put the parts together, add the software and power it up. Yet DNA is massively more complex than any computer operating system. There is no route from random pieces of code to a functioning cellular programming system (DNA) by Random Chance. That's not how coding languages work. They are not built from the bottom up by Random Chance.

Since there is no known mechanism to add information to the genome, only to vary it or lose some of it, some mind had to have conceived the whole picture to have created the functioning whole.

When talking about DNA Phillip Johnson observes that,

> "Everyone uses the vocabulary of intelligent communication to describe protein synthesis, programmed instructions, languages, information coding and decoding, libraries.

> Why not consider the possibility that all life is what it so evidently seems to be, the product of creative intelligence? Science would not come to an end."

> However,

> "They would face the possibility that beyond the natural world there is a further reality which transcends science." (Phillip Johnson, *Darwin on Trial*, page 140)

The Designer's signature

In *Signature in the Cell*, Stephen Meyer points out that the chemicals that make up the information code in DNA (referred to in short-hand as A,C,G,T) are free to associate in any order. Computers are programmed with a binary code of 1 and 0, and the combination of 1s and 0s allows all the astonishing complexity of the digital world. In biology the four-letter code of A,C,G and T permits the existence of all life as we know it. Just as there is nothing in the computer itself that determines the order of those 1s and 0s, they are programmed into it by an outside intelligence, so with As, Cs, Gs and Ts, there is nothing about their chemistry or the chemistry around them in the DNA helix that determines their order. Therefore, since they carry information, something outside the DNA determined the order of those chemicals and hence the information they covey. Their ordering is not random and is meaningful and thus intentional.

When many people have let that fact sink in it has rocked their world. Here at the heart of the DNA in every living cell is compelling evidence of the existence of the non-material cause of the information that gives life; truly a signature in the cell. If the code is essential for life, cannot have arisen by chance and is not determined by the physical chemistry of its constituent parts, then the most reasonable inference is that it is the handiwork of an infinitely intelligent mind who can see the end from the beginning, a Designer: in short God.

When Crick and Watson completed their model of DNA, the double-helix. Watson is reported to have said, "It has to be right; it is so beautiful."[7]

As we feel awe at the complexity of DNA and yet also admire its beautiful simplicity, the world of concepts (Mind) and the world of physical things touch one another, and we know the reality of both, and are convicted that the one arose first of all in the other.

> "Intelligence is the most causally adequate explanation of the origin of the information necessary for life." (Stephen Meyer, 2020[8], see; *Signature in the Cell*).

The world around us looks Designed because it was Designed

> "I praise you because I am fearfully and wonderfully made; your works are wonderful, I know that full well."

> David, King of Israel, writing poetically in Psalm 139 vs 14

10 BACK TO FIRST PRINCIPLES

Design vs Random Chance

Evolutionary explanations of life have been fundamental to destroying the faith of millions, so we must look carefully at their adequacy. Then in the last section of the book we move on past dealing with evolution as a barrier to belief in God and look at other aspects of the Christian worldview.

If you find these discussions about evolution difficult, I hope you can pick up on the key points and carry them into what follows. Some readers will want a lot of detail and reassurance when discussing evolution's claims, others won't need so much. I have tried to keep it as non-technical as possible throughout. The main conclusions we can draw are, however, very clear.

What do we mean by Random Chance?

Games of chance like roulette are a good place to start this discussion, so that we can come to terms with what Random Chance is and what it can achieve and what it can't (John Lennox, *Can Science Explain Everything?*). Picture a large roulette wheel made of wood and brass and other materials, and picture also small balls to be used on the wheel and a croupier standing in attendance. If we take a hypothetical spin of the wheel and play some balls, then if it is well made and well balanced there should be an equal chance of any outcome. Any individual ball can score between zero and 36 (or a similar number if the wheel is one of the common variants). What the ball can't score is 243 or 10,000,000,000. Similarly, if no-one plays the ball nothing is scored. (John Lennox, *Can Science Explain Everything?*).

Random Chance can only explain, at the very most, a small part of the game of roulette and the operation of the wheel. Someone has to make the roulette wheel and the balls that go on it, then spin the wheel and play a ball. Then Random Chance operates within the constraints set for it. Random Chance alone does not explain the whole of the game of roulette, it does not make the roulette wheel, or the balls and thus the parameters within which it can operate or provide the input to the system that sets it running.

Here is another example. You know I *chose* to write this discussion. I used a computer, I typed on keys on a keyboard. I saved a file and later published a book. You *chose* to download it or buy a physical copy, or were given one, and chose to read it. In doing so you and I are interacting within so many layers of a structured reality that we would consider it utterly absurd to claim that the ideas thus conveyed are the result of Random Chance and are merely natural phenomena rather than intentional and the result of a human agent. There are nearly 100,000 words and 481,100 characters in this book and consider what range of ideas and concepts they address. In contrast there are

3 billion letters in the DNA in every cell of your body. How is it reasonable to accept that this book is not the result of Random Chance and yet claim that the human genome is?

Random Chance can have no ultimate explanatory power because it presumes a fundamental structure to reality within which it can operate, from the laws that govern the structure of the universe down to the chemistry in every molecule in our bodies as well as the rules of the game so to speak (of roulette or anything else for that matter): the world of concepts and the world of physical things. That structure to reality came from somewhere and must precede the operation of Random Chance in any context. It sets boundaries within which Random Chance can operate and potentially achieve anything, yet Random Chance can offer no explanation for the existence of that structure in all its dimensions, or the existence of those boundaries.

Thus, any appeal to Random Chance to *achieve* any outcome presumes that there is a sphere within which it can operate that has certain fundamental properties already in place prior to its operation:

> Ordered laws as opposed to chaos
>
> Cause and effect as opposed to genuinely random outcomes
>
> Being as opposed to non-being
>
> Agency and end-directed processes as opposed to continued randomness

The very non-random nature of all of reality is one of its most striking characteristics. These properties do not emerge from randomness. On what basis is it reasonable for the evolutionist, who is committed to finding an explanation based on natural causes alone, to assume they pre-exist the operation of

Random Chance, even if chance could somehow achieve any constructive outcome?

How can randomness give rise to structure, order and stable categories? This requires something non-random preceding it, or directing it, at which point it stops being truly random. If it precedes it, then the Universe and life did not arise in an undirected explosion. If it directs it, then end-directed outcomes require an intelligence to steer events towards a non-random result. Either way, for randomness to lead to stable non-random outcomes that contain information, would require intelligent action to direct it in some way, otherwise randomness will always produce more of the same. Since we have a structured reality that we are a part of and can observe and rationally comprehend, we know that there is Design within it caused by an intelligent agent, because no other cause produces such phenomena.

This is about more than just different types of plants and animals being categorised, it is about the most fundamental phenomena that we all experience and rely on to be able to exist and make any sense of the world. The existence of many aspects of reality including the existence of concepts and language, as well as the amazing physical world of nature, all point to an intentional designer. A blanket denial of Design in physical nature has the immediate implication of a denial of so much more of the reality we exist within, including the world of concepts and ideas and the categories we use to function within it. That is inevitably incoherent, and thus self-defeating.

Thus, there is a deeper structure to reality than just the physical and material, and that structure sets the framework and boundaries within which the physical and material can exist and be what they are. There are multiple elements of that structure that we all experience and know to be real.

Philosophers, theologians, novelists and poets have all sought to understand more of that deeper reality, seeking meaning, beauty, truth and hope. The strict materialism of evolutionary explanations insists that all of those things are in effect not real and thus don't mean anything or truly exist, that they are "epi-phenomena". It impoverishes us and reduces people to machines explained only by their constituent parts (which we must remember we don't understand fully either). Yet as we shall see from various angles there is a deep inconsistency and ultimately a total incoherence in that attempt.

What can Random Chance not do?

Random Chance, that supposedly drives evolution, should have no structure or categories within it because that admits limits and organisation and hence intent and Design which we know from our consistent experience only occur when another agent has caused them to be there. As soon as there is any element that cannot be accounted for by Random Chance alone there is Design at some level, whether evolutionists like that idea or not.

On what basis is it possible for the operation of randomness to produce multiple layers of interdependent complexity and organisation and non-randomness? Nature around us does have these properties which is *prime face* evidence of Design, and if there is Design in any part of it, then it is not random. The inference goes much further because if it is not random it necessarily had a cause, and all causes necessarily had a first cause.

Genuine unstructured unguided randomness would also always be its own undoing. A reality built from complete randomness would always destroy any apparent structure, categories, limits, organisation, or Design by the continued operation of randomness and if it does not it isn't truly random because someone set the boundaries within which it can operate.

Some objectors will point to what they perceive to be randomness in nature and claim it undermines this argument, but that randomness, as they perceive it, always occurs within clear boundaries and categories and that begs the question; where did they come from?

Others point to the models of sub-atomic particles that appear to be built on randomness rather than a fixed order, a probabilistic rather than deterministic reality. Two things are worth noting.

First, they are models, not directly observed reality. Models and what actually exists are never quite the same thing. Newton's laws are perfectly adequate for many purposes and where they are applicable, they are perceived to be "true", but they have their limitations. Einstein's theories can be applied in other situations and again there are circumstances where they hold true and are thus seen as "correct", but they too have their limitations and there are situations where their explanatory power breaks down. Both remain models. Similarly, no-one has bridged the gap between quantum mechanics and general relativity.

Second, any apparent randomness at the sub-atomic level still occurs within certain boundaries and those bounds, or limits, also have to originate somewhere, thus underlining the fundamental point that reality from the sub-atomic level upwards is not truly random and there are clear categories which we can observe, and which hold true.

We also cannot attribute agency to randomness, (in achieving intentional outcomes) because Random Chance is not a being and thus cannot exercise agency (more on agency in a moment).

The way we recognise Design is consistent with how we derive scientific knowledge and common-sense knowledge

We observe Design around us all the time because reality has attributes that we know from all of our prior experience cannot be attributed to randomness/ Random Chance, such as consistent structure, goals or end-directed outcomes, complex chains of events that must occur in the right order, information, symmetry and much more.

We can recognise such attributes of Design on the basis of inductive reasoning, which is also how much of science operates; every time we observe phenomena X, then Y happens or is believed to be the cause of it. It can only be a probabilistic claim based on our repeated observations and experience, even if that observation is taken as the confirmation of a prior formulation of a hypothesis or law. It is always conceivably possible that there are exceptions to the rule we derive, but operationally we accept it as an accurate picture of reality, even though it is not absolute proof in logical terms. That of course is why scientific knowledge is always contingent and never final.

It is worth mentioning that exactly what is science has been the subject of intense debate. Various types of reasoning are put forward as science. Repeated observation (inductive reasoning) is what most people will think of as what science is. A different type of reasoning is also often put forward as science, namely testing multiple competing ideas (hypotheses) against the evidence to see which is best supported by that evidence. This is called inference to the best explanation. It is how detective work proceeds. It is something which we are quite familiar with in everyday life and again it cannot lead to absolute final answers, it just leads to the best explanation we can find from the evidence available.

There is no conflict between Design as the explanation of what we observe around us and the scientific method of inference to the best explanation. When we find evidence that cannot fit to an evolutionary explanation, but which is what we would expect with a Design explanation, we can safely say that the inference to the best explanation is to a designer: God.

We can of course also accept Design as something revealed to us and that need not conflict with any knowledge we can derive from reason. The two are not opposed to each other. (John Lennox, *Cosmic Chemistry*).

To overturn this argument, (philosophically and logically) and to claim that Random Chance is the better explanation than Design you must either claim that Random Chance is the more convincing first principle, or you must argue that all our inductive experiential and scientific knowledge of reality (derived by any form of scientific reasoning) is better aligned with randomness and Random Chance than Design. That case is simply not proven.

Indeed, such a case cannot be proven because it is the nature of inductive arguments that they are not absolute proof either way. Similarly, arguments offering an inference to the best explanation can be convincing but are also not absolute proof. Science cannot validly make any absolute knowledge claims, even though some scientists like to do so. We must recognise the fundamentally contingent nature of all scientific knowledge claims. Thus, no matter how sophisticated the scientific models, or how useful they are, reality is more complex and there is always more to discover and understand.

We are left therefore with no alternative but weighing evidence and making the inference to the best explanation (see

Stephen Meyer, *The Return Of The God Hypothesis,* for a fuller discussion of inference to the best explanation). Science keeps producing evidence that points firmly in the direction of Design, and we keep discovering more and more evidence that has no prospect of ever being integrated in an evolutionary model. The weight of that evidence becomes more and more compelling as it builds.

It is thus completely reasonable and rational to accept the argument from Design to a designer, because such a claim does not conflict with how we derive much scientific knowledge, or everyday knowledge, in any way at all.

The chapters that follow essentially explore the inference to the best explanation by setting out evidence that is best explained by Design as well as evidence that does not fit an evolutionary explanation. You must weigh that evidence.

To be ready for the further discussions we must remember not to fall for one of the fallacies that regularly surfaces in scientific debate, the idea that somehow the methods of science prove some claim beyond any doubt. Hopefully by now you can see that is not logically possible.

You will also see that the judgements made as to what is the best explanation are inevitably made by scientists and others, with a worldview whether they are up front about it or not, and that worldview affects the judgements they make. It is just not possible to take the scientists out of the science and it is not possible to take the worldview out of the scientists.

That is why these discussions on evolution take a very broad view of the relevant data about the nature of reality and of ourselves, as well as the evidence that is put forward to support evolution or Design. We cannot accept a very tightly constrained definition of what is relevant to the science around origins because as we will see shortly, science and scientists are unable to operate without many things that evolution cannot explain.

Being able to recognise Design means we are also able to acknowledge other concepts including persons and agency, cause and effect and intentional end-directed outcomes or goals

Recognising Design, also means that we recognize the necessity of a mind behind nature and a purpose to it. As a bare minimum we can recognize the existence of the phenomenon of mind and as soon as we do that we must then consider where that leads us, which is probably why so many people have tried strenuously to deny either or both. Even the atheist philosopher Thomas Nagel recognises the inescapable phenomena of mind.

> "My guiding conviction is that mind is not just an afterthought or an accident or an add-on, but a basic aspect of nature." (Thomas Nagel, *Mind and Cosmos, Why the Materialist Neo-Darwinian Conception of Nature is Almost Certainly False*, page 16)

What he fails to do is follow this on to the inevitable next step and recognise that the existence of mind implies purpose and intent and hence an actor to make it that way. We will return to the matter of mind in another chapter.

There are other whole areas of knowledge and categorisation of reality that a strictly materialistic evolutionary explanation built on Random Chance must in effect deny. Let's look at some examples. We know these things unmediated by culture, education, philosophy, religion or indeed anything at all. We accept them and use them to think and live whether we are self-consciously aware of them or not.

For example, either you exist or you don't, and you ought to be clear on which of those options is correct! So, we accept existence and non-existence as distinct categories of physical reality and also know that in the world of concepts non-physical things can exist.

Similarly with cause and effect, either we understand causes as having effects or we know nothing because if we cannot identify correctly causes and effects, we have no basis for establishing the relationships we need to make sense of the world around us or crucially to act within it. Some have argued against this philosophically, but even they won't step straight in front of a moving bus. We identify causes and effects intuitively from a very early age because there is no other way to exist and the capacity to undertake such reasoning seems hardwired into us.

Then there is the concept of agency: either a being has agency, with the potential to act and effect change, or it is not a being and cannot do so. Rocks do not have agency, but people and animals do. They undertake actions with intent and achieve desired outcomes. They are not merely helpless victims of random events like leaves blown on the wind. People exhibit agency by picking up a broom made by another human being for a purpose (i.e. it was designed) and intentionally sweeping up the leaves for example.

These fundamental phenomena do not need elaborate justification, they just are. Hence, one could suggest, God's description of himself to Abraham, "I am". There can be no further justification to eternal self-existence!

There is no halfway ground on these points; either you can categorise reliably, or you can't. Either something is fundamental, or it is not. Either you have agency, or you do not. (As a start on Aristotle's arguments, you could try Josh McDowell, *Evidence*

That Demands a Verdict, chapter 33).

From the simplest of actions to more complex goals, people are also end directed. They have goals, make real meaningful choices, and undertake actions to realise those goals, from deciding what to shop for dinner to choosing an education to pursue a particular career. We need purpose and hope. When they are absent, we must find them or the consequences are extremely serious for us. Viktor Frankl who survived a Nazi concentration camp wrote about this in his book *Man's Search For Meaning*. In the concentration camps those with no hope were unable to survive the horrors of their utterly cruel and degraded treatment. Hope is essential to life.

Thus, the worlds of concepts and physical reality both exist and there can be a meaningful correspondence between them, although our scientific understanding of physical reality, held as it is in the world of concepts, will always be incomplete and contingent. (Even recognising this completely undermines the evolutionist's assumption of naturalism or strict materialism i.e. that the physical is all there is).

Evolutionary explanations are entirely inconsistent in relation to this. A pillar of western secular thought has become a commitment to the claimed creative agency of Random Chance in driving evolution. How can Random Chance have creative agency? How is that even possible? So, a rhetorical sleight of hand must be deployed assigning to Natural Selection a creative role that it cannot have since it is not a being (person) and does not have agency or even consciousness.

Is Design an illusion?

Scientists proposing evolution as the explanation of the reality we live in and experience, propose it on the basis of two assumptions. One, that the physical world is all there is, that is naturalism (sometimes called strict materialism). Two, that Random Chance is the originator of everything that exists (i.e., Random Chance operating through Natural Selection). They also dismiss Design as an illusion, or unwarranted assumption. Therefore, any explanation that they seek must be achieved in purely naturalistic terms on the basis of Random Chance alone. This is the basic foundation of their position.

The best explanation that evolutionists can offer for the existence of the Design we see in nature, is to say that it isn't really Design at all, it only looks like it. Richard Dawkins the well-known apologist for evolution, dismisses this Design as all an illusion. He says it merely looks designed but is in fact the result of Random Chance with absolutely no Design input whatsoever.

> "Biology is the study of complicated things that give the appearance of having been designed for a purpose." (Richard Dawkins, *The Blind Watchmaker*, chapter 1)

If you stop to think carefully about that for just a moment, he is maintaining that there is absolutely no Design input into anything we see in nature whatsoever, at any level from the existence of cause and effect to the stable categories we consistently observe in nature; that gravity works all of the time, that donkeys are different from blue whales, that apples and pears are both edible but different. If we take the book writing example again, when Dawkins sets out to write a book, his end-directed activity does indeed result in a book conveying concepts; he has goals and achieves them (or at least some of them!). He has to exhibit human agency, operate within the world of concepts and convey information through a range of physical media to be able to communicate anything, but where did all that structure to reality come from. Why is it possible that he can do any of that?

The only way to escape the conclusion of Design is to look at the whole of reality around us and insist against all logic and evidence and prior experience that it isn't Design at all; or even to deny the concept of Design itself. The only area of scientific endeavour that I am aware of that consistently tries to make such an incoherent denial of Design is the scientific community working on the origin of life, on evolution and cosmology, but it is self-contradictory. The world of ideas that the evolutionist operates within allows them to impose a categorisation on the reality they observe with multiple layers of structure from cells to organisms to species to genera etc. They know life around them exhibits stable categories that they can identify, but they have no basis for how any stable categories can arise from randomness.

When seeing the crushing inevitability of the victory of Design over Random Chance as the most plausible explanation of our origins, some scientists then try to invoke laws as directing evolution rather than Random Chance. This simply gets us nowhere and leaves us with the same basic problem. Laws must exist before what they control; but where did the laws originate from? And we come back round the loop to a designer.

Design and Random Chance are distinct categories of explanation

If all of reality, in all of its dimensions including physical nature, is not designed in anyway, why is it not random, and only random, and nothing but random for all time because Random Chance is the explanation that evolutionists offer us as the alternative to Design? Even if some structure coalesces from something random it still isn't necessarily information, although it may be evidence of intelligent input to the system to set the boundaries within which it can operate and within which that structure can arise. Hence when we see stable, functional, non-randomness including information we are seeing Design.

If what is claimed to be Design in nature is just the result of Random Chance let's be clear, it must have only the attributes of randomness in all dimensions and all the time. If it does not, then it exhibits Design at some level.

Random Chance and Design are distinct categories of explanation and distinct phenomena. When we see Design in something it is not a weak claim to knowledge but a fundamental one. To deny that there is any evidence of Design or intent in nature whatsoever, seems to me to be a fundamental claim to not knowing, a kind of anti-knowledge. If we are not capable of categorising reliably, then we are not capable of knowing.

Recognition of Design can be thought of as properly basic knowledge

Everyone's knowledge starts somewhere, otherwise we have an infinite regress of proof, as Aristotle pointed out, and no knowledge is then possible. Hence the inevitability of accepting some first principles or properly basic knowledge as a starting point.

In his book *Undeniable, How Biology Confirms Our Intuition That Life is Designed,* one of Douglas Axe's key points is that what he calls our universal Design intuition is valid. We assess the world around us, recognise Design from our experience of Design and thus know that anything that is designed had a designer. He suggests that it takes a lot of "education" (some would say brainwashing) to knock that out of us.

We know that we exist. It is a first principle; being as opposed to non-being. It is directly experienced and known. There needs be no chain of inferences or contingent claims. We exist and we know that we exist. We also recognise Design when we see it. That is not quite the same as saying, "It's just obvious, or self-evident." It may be, but the more important point is that there is a reason for that being the case and why we recognise it for what it is.

Thus Design, is not an explanation of nature or an interpretation of it, but rather *a fundamental property of it* and if there is Design, there was a designer. That people have known this for millennia does not make it out of date or wrong.

Remember that the vast majority of human beings who have ever existed have taken the same view, however sophisticated their ability to express it, that the Design they see around them means there was a designer.

William Paley argued that if we should find a watch on the floor when out walking, we would infer from its properties that it was designed. He held design to be evident from the observable properties of things that are designed. Over the succeeding 250 years to the present, discussion and argument has gone back and forth over the design argument for the existence of God as creator. Darwin was initially impressed with Paley's design argument then later thought he had found a scientific explanation that did away with the need to invoke a designer. As we shall see in various ways, that was a mistaken belief. However, a critical change has been occurring in the last 20 to 30 years because science itself has been reinforcing the view that there must be a designer. That may not be the story you have been told, but I am entirely with Anthony Flew, that the argument is persuasive and the outcome inescapable: there is Design and thus a designer, God.

> "Those scientists who point to the Mind of God do not merely advance a series of arguments or a process of syllogistic reasoning. Rather, they propound a vision of reality that emerges from the conceptual

heart of modern science and imposes itself on the rational mind. It is a vision that I personally find compelling and irrefutable." (Anthony Flew, *There is a God; How the World's Most Notorious Atheist Changed His Mind*, page 112)

It is not possible for evolutionists to be consistent with their denial of Design

Evolutionists may deny Design because they don't like where that leads, but remember, every time that you hear someone such as the naturalist David Attenborough (in a BBC nature documentary) intone that nature *intended* something or that evolution *caused* something, he is simply demonstrating how his attempts to find an evolutionary explanation are always undermined by reality. Evolution cannot intend anything or cause anything or direct it to an outcome. Random Chance cannot do any of those things.

It is beyond credibility to say there is no Design in living creatures. Don't be intimidated by the qualifications and impressive titles of people like Richard Dawkins claiming this could somehow have been gotten around by Random Chance, long time spans and endless small changes. Wishful thinking is wishful thinking, whoever indulges in it.

What can we conclude on Design versus Random Chance?

We can now follow the argument from Design in the other direction.

God exists, has agency and is the ultimate cause of the effects we see in nature including its structure and organisation at every level, the parameters within which life can exist; He is the designer behind the Design that we recognise.

Wow, it really is that simple! The existence of one transcendent, omnipotent God is the simplest and most coherent and sufficient explanation for the structure of all of reality including the Design we see in the physical world as well as the world of concepts and the information necessary for life.

We will consider several aspects of the evidence in favour of Design and against Random Chance in more detail.

First, we will look at some more detail of the evidence of Design that keeps emerging from science and does indeed seem undeniable.

Second, we will look at some evidence that does not fit evolutionary explanations of reality.

Third, we will demonstrate the very severe practical limits to what Random Chance can achieve within the decidedly finite limits of the time and space available to it. (Building on the work of Douglas Axe, *Undeniable, How Biology Confirms Our Intuition That Life is Designed*.)

On route we will note once again how the assumption of strict naturalism is easily falsified, which removes another pillar of the evolutionary explanation of life.

If you want to test the ideas introduced here against the extensive attempts to argue differently, the following suggested books will help.

The discussion around agency and cause and effect is covered well by Anthony Flew in *There is a God; How the World's Most Notorious Atheist Changed His Mind*.

The question of whether our Design intuition is valid and whether it constitutes properly basic knowledge is explored by Douglas Axe in *Undeniable How Biology Confirms Our Intuition*

That Life Is Designed.

Stephen Meyer considers at length how science makes knowledge claims, what inference to the best explanation is, and how that relates to these debates in his books:

1. *Signature in the Cell;*
2. *Darwin's Doubt, The Explosive Origin of Animal Life and the Case for Intelligent Design;*
3. *The Return of the God Hypothesis, Three Scientific Discoveries That Reveal the Mind Behind the Universe.*

Cosmic Chemistry by John Lennox is another excellent in-depth discussion of many of these issues, and his book *Can Science Explain Everything?* is a shorter and more accessible start on the same material.

We know Design when we see it and we do see it in nature at many levels and everywhere we look

Science does not prove the absence of a designer, in fact quite the opposite. The more that scientists look, it is the same story of continually unfolding complexity and Design, from the single cell to far reaches of the universe, calling out to us the existence of a designer: God.

You can accept this argument from Design to a designer at many levels of understanding, but it does not become 'more true', the more sophisticated the argument that is used to defend it. A child's understanding of Design as an inherent characteristic of reality around them is as valid as the philosopher Anthony Flew's, or scientists such as Douglas Axe, Stephen Meyer, Michael Behe, John Walton, Robert Carter and others referenced in this book, along with thousands of others who are convinced by the evidence in their fields.

The Design in the world around us points unmistakably to its Designer

The Apostle Paul states this in just one sentence.

> "For since the creation of the world God's invisible qualities – his eternal power and divine nature – have been clearly seen, being understood from what has been made, so that men are without excuse." Letter to the church in Rome; Romans 1 vs 20

With such economy he rules out atheism, and in the context of our discussion, evolution as an explanation of where all life came from.

11 ONE SMALL STEP FOR SCIENTISTS

One giant leap for evolution

Science fiction can be fun. I have enjoyed Star Trek, Red Dwarf and other science fiction series and films (movies). In our imaginations almost anything seems possible and increasingly, it can be rendered digitally with astonishing realism. In our imaginations people can travel faster than the speed of light. They can be tele-ported to other locations. They can be blended with robots and continue living after their death as holograms. A favourite episode of Red Dwarf had Lister become the luckiest man in the universe. Everything he did or tried was possible because well, he was the luckiest man in the universe; opening a door with a multi-digit combination at the first guess, no problem, because he was the luckiest man in the universe. No odds were impossible for him to beat. It was funny and entertaining because we know it is not true. The laws of nature, and our disbelief, can be suspended for entertainment; but science fiction is not science and wishful thinking is not real life.

It is easy for evolutionists to make a quick jump over a gap in their understanding, it is another thing altogether to try to find the real evidence that will fill that gap in the purely naturalistic terms by which they demand it must be filled.

Science is popularly projected as having answers to all the big questions about where we came from and why we are here. Nothing could be further from the truth. Just as an illusionist succeeds in making you believe something impossible by keeping your attention away from seeing something else, so the proponents of evolution want you to believe that all the difficult questions have been answered or will be shortly; that there will be no insurmountable gaps. This amounts to nothing short of a conjurer's illusion. It is possible to become lost in the vast scientific literature on evolution without seeing the wood for the trees, for a whole career in fact.

In this chapter we will continue to look at some of the evidence coming from science itself that demonstrates these problems. I have sought to keep the discussion as non-technical as possible and to refer extensively to where you can follow up the evidence in more detail. Too many discussions of evolution get lost in terminology and assume too much specialist knowledge of maths, physics, biology and chemistry making them impenetrable for the lay reader, so technical language is kept to a minimum. Describing something in complicated language does not make it "more true", and indeed often hides where it is wrong.

Let's take another look at one of the gaps in evolutionary explanations: attempts to answer the question of where everything came from without invoking God as part of that explanation.

From nothing to something

The present scientific consensus is that the universe began at something like 13 billion years ago. There is a very obvious logical connection from that idea to the idea that God brought it into existence from nothing.

In contrast, the proponents of the Big Bang theory of the origin of the universe, want you to believe that the universe created itself from nothing. There is no logical reason to accept that as a more reasonable explanation of the origin of everything than to believe that God created it.

We must not get carried away however, because whilst this is a powerful indication that there is a God, it does not prove the point because the Big Bang theory is like all scientific theories just a model of reality and not reality itself. Like all scientific theories it has some problems. There is a further complication to remember. Some scientists not liking the idea that the universe had a beginning because it lends such obvious support to the existence of God, have tried to model the universe in other ways than the Big Bang, either without a single absolute beginning point or multiverses and other such exotica. All of which reminds us that science is mis-sold to the public all the time. Scientists are portrayed as knowing things for certain and having discovered the truth of some matter in nature. The real truth is that scientists do not discover truth in nature, they merely model nature and make theories about it. Scientific knowledge is never final or absolute because it can't be.

Let's look briefly at some of the problems with the Big Bang theory. The Big Bang theory holds that the universe expanded from an infinitely small dot to a vast universe in an incredibly small fraction of time. This goes against all the laws of physics which now govern the universe. So, for reasons unknown, those laws had to, in effect, be switched off until the universe was hugely expanded, then suddenly switched on. Just because someone can make a mathematical model with that assumption built into it does not mean it is true, simply because it is in a model. As a minimum, all it means is that someone made that assumption.

Physicists have no ultimate means to explain how we could go from absolute nothing to matter existing and from an explosion to an ordered, finely tuned universe. And remember as was noted in a previous chapter, nothing is not some kind of something which presents a serious problem for all such explanations

If the universe behaves according to precise laws of physics, those laws must have predated what they control. Ordered laws don't arise from and within the random chaos of an explosion. Ordered laws do not emerge from the things they control but must be pre-existent to be able to achieve any effect. We should also note the nature of scientific laws:

> "The laws of physics represent only our descriptions of nature. Descriptions in themselves do to cause things to happen." (Stephen Meyer, *The Return of the God Hypothesis, Three Scientific Discoveries That Reveal the Mind Behind the Universe*, page 371)

Similarly, if there is cause and effect in the whole universe and it had a beginning, then it necessarily had a first cause. That is really not hard to understand.

Astronomy and cosmology run other conjuring tricks here. Evidence is pointed to that is claimed to fit the Big Bang model, but evidence that doesn't fit it is brushed aside to work on later. For example, Cosmic Background Microwave radiation is held to be "the afterglow of the Big Bang", but there is a significant problem with that. It is measured as coming towards the earth from every angle at the same temperature. That would mean that following the explosion of the Big Bang, that radiation would have to have interacted across the whole universe to have evened out its temperature, a bit like warm and cold air in a room mixing and evening out to a consistent temperature. However, if we can see into the Universe, as is claimed, to about 13 billion light years in all directions, then the universe hasn't had enough time over its claimed 13 billion years of existence for the cosmic microwave background radiation to have interacted across the whole universe to even out its temperature. Yet that is what we observe. This is the so-called Horizon Problem and there are significant problems with attempts to explain it away. (See John Hartnett, chapter 7 *Evolution's Achilles Heels,* page 229). It seems it is too easy put to this to one side as a problem to solve later.

One thing we can be sure of is that scientific models and theories will always be revised at some point, it is the process science operates under. We should also recognise that there are limits to what science can know, or ever know; indeed, that its methods might have limits that we might be able to identify and yet not go beyond. (John Hartnett, chapter 7, *Evolution's Achilles Heels*).

Anyhow, the illusion of "knowing" with certainty how the universe was formed is maintained by not worrying too much about what doesn't fit current the model. The attitude appears to be that the model must be right, so we'll find a way to make the data fit in the end. So, we must repeat that what is offered as certain scientific knowledge and beyond question, is still just models and theories. They may prove quite useful in some contexts, but they are not reality itself, just models of it, and those models will have limits and will inevitably be revised at some point.

If we turn now from the Big Bang theory to other attempts to explain the origin and existence of the universe we head into even greater problems. If you have the appetite for an in-depth discussion of these ideas, I thoroughly recommend Stephen Meyer's book *The return of the God hypothesis*.

Something that has struck me strongly over many years has been that all scientific models of the origin of the universe have at some point assumed something that they can't explain or rely on some prior entity, laws or phenomena which they take for granted. If they are purporting to explain the origin of the universe from nothing, that is clearly a severe case of mis-selling. They end up thus not being a true explanation of origins but rather an attempted explanation of the development of the universe following some specific foundational assumptions made by the scientists. They may be fascinating models, but they don't answer the question of ultimate origins. These theories and models are often not clear or up front about the assumptions they make, but it is a serious limitation to all such explanations.

In 2021 I was delighted to see that Stephen Meyer has followed that critical weakness through very systematically and exposed how it is a problem for various attempts to explain the origin of the universe. In *The Return of the God Hypothesis*, he looks at various attempts to develop scientific models of the origin of the universe and repeatedly exposes those same weaknesses. For example, with Quantum Cosmology he concludes,

> "In so far as quantum cosmology models the origin of the universe, it implies the need for prior intelligence."

> "Nevertheless, the difficulty of the specialized mathematics involved rendered the indispensable contribution of the theorists – their active and intelligent input of information – opaque even to many other scientists. This made it possible for quantum cos-

mologists to hide behind the mathematical complexity of their models as they made highly dubious, and even absurd, metaphysical claims."

"To the limited extent it succeeds, it attributes causal powers to abstract mathematics and depends upon intelligent inputs of information from theoretical physicists as they model the origin of the universe. Thus, it does not dispense at all with Intelligent Design or with theism as an explanation for the origin of the universe.

Instead, quantum cosmology implies the need for an intelligent agent to breathe, if not "fire into the equations," then certainly specificity and information. Thus, it implies something akin to the biblical idea that "in the beginning was the Word." And that's not nothing – by anyone's definition." (Stephen Meyer, *The Return of the God Hypothesis, Three Scientific Discoveries That Reveal the Mind Behind the Universe*, page 385, 386, 387)

Analogous problems exist with other cosmological models assuming the existence of something such as prior existing laws, but not being upfront about it. They also often rely on the intelligent input of the scientists doing the modelling whilst denying it is occurring. They can thus claim to have developed a purely physical model of the origin of the universe, when in fact they have not. It is hardly an argument against intelligence and Design.

So, scientific models of the universe either assume something came from nothing but can't explain how or assume that laws pre-exist the formation of the universe but can't say on what basis, or undertake selective mathematical modelling which demonstrates the indispensable role of the scientist's minds in crafting the models. Or they invoke an infinite number of universes when one God as creator is the far simpler solution!

Therefore, when we look critically at cosmology, I would suggest that we are coming to the realisation that *information and mind are more fundamental than matter.* Just a few decades ago, who would have thought it?!

In the meantime, we have scientific models of the Universe where it is claimed that it is made up of 25% dark matter and 70% dark energy, but we haven't found them yet! (See John Hartnett, chapter 7, *Evolution's Achilles Heels,* page 22). Not unreasonably, quite a few scientists, and of course many others, are uncomfortable with models of the universe that need so much stuff we cannot see, detect, interact with or even prove exists.

> "Cosmology is in trouble. It has departed from scientific method and its principles... it has raised imaginative invention to an art form... lost and misdirected; trapped in debilitating dogma." (Roy Martin, *Astronomy on trial: A Devastating Critique and Compete Repudiation of the Big Bang Fiasco*, cited in Subodh Pandit *Come Search With Me, Book 1 Does God Really Exist?* page 95)

Yet, what we *do* know of the universe with any degree of certainty causes us serious pause for thought. As David Berlinski observes,

> "The fact that the cosmological constant is tuned to an order of 120 decimal places is vexing because it is arbitrary. The same might be said of Newton's law of gravitational attraction or Schrodinger's equation in quantum mechanics." (David Berlinski, *The Deniable Darwin,* page 527)

This of course has not gone entirely unnoticed by the scientific community.

> ""Scientists", the physicist Paul Davies has observed, "are slowly waking up to an inconvenient truth – the universe looks suspiciously like a fix."" (i.e. it does not look like the result of an accident) (quoted in *The Deniable Darwin*, page 527)

Whatever the inadequacies of our understanding of the universe, we have discovered many examples of exceptional fine tuning, without which life would not be here and we wouldn't be considering any of these issues. Here are a couple of analogies by way of illustration.

> "Imagine covering the entire North American continent in dimes and stacking them until they reached the moon. Now imagine just as many dimes on another billion continents the same size as North America. If you marked one of those dimes and hid it in the billions of piles you'd assembled, the odds of a blindfolded friend picking out the correct dime is approximately 1 in 10^{37} – the same level of precision required in the strong nuclear force and the expansion rate of the universe." (Ross, *Creator And The Cosmos, page 115*, cited in J. Warner Wallace *God's Crime Scene, A Cold-case Detective Examines the Evidence for a Divinely Created Universe*, page 54)

> "Imagine trying to fire a bullet at a one-inch target on the other side of the observable universe. The accuracy required to accomplish such a feat has been calculated at 1 in 10^{60}. Compare this to the precision required in calibrating the mass density of the universe (fine-tuned to within 1 unit in 10^{59}." (John Jefferson Davis, *The Design Argument, Cosmic Fine-*

tuning And The Anthropic Principle, The International Journal of Philosophy of Religion 22 (1987), p 140, cited in J. Warner Wallace *God's Crime Scene, A Cold-case Detective Examines the Evidence for a Divinely Created Universe*, page 54)

You can see why fine-tuning presents such a perplexing enigma; it is so far beyond the bounds of any sense of possible coincidence that it compels us to not just note it but to seek a reasonable explanation as to why it is so.

What can we conclude? The present scientific consensus suggests the universe had a beginning but can't provide an ultimate explanation of how that occurred. Christians also believe the universe had a beginning but believe that God created it!

Scientific models are never the final answer to any question and are always subject to change and development, so we must be cautious if we expect science to ever answer the question of where everything came from with any finality; that is almost certainly beyond what it is possible for science to do.

We should also recognise an even bigger problem. Science has restricted itself to questions around the origin of the *physical* universe and run into serious problems doing so, not the least of which is that models of the physical universe are held in the *minds* of physicists! However, the question of the origin of the physical universe is way too small a question. We need answers to the origin of *the whole of reality* in all of its dimensions. That means every aspect of reality; cause and effect, life itself, human agency, meaning, morality, hope; all these and more need coherent explanation, not just physical matter. That leaves us with much to discuss in upcoming chapters.

We need a coherent explanation of the origin of all aspects of reality, not just the physical universe

"For this is what the LORD says – he who created the heavens, he is God; he who fashioned and made the earth, he founded it; he did not create it to be empty, but formed it to be inhabited – he says: "I am the LORD, and there is no other. I have not spoken in secret, from somewhere in a land of darkness; I have not said to Jacob's descendants, 'Seek me in vain'. I, the LORD speak truth; I declare what is right.""

Isaiah 45 vs 18, 19

"In the beginning was the Word, and the Word was with God, and the Word was God. He was with God in the beginning. Through him all things were made; without him nothing was made that has been made."

John 1 vs 1 -3

12 COSMIC LEGO™

Making the building blocks for life

Many children love Lego building blocks. They bring seemingly endless creative possibilities. For several years I could never get enough Lego to play with and I was obsessed with seeing what I could create, especially model cars and houses. However, how would it have been if instead of giving me Lego blocks as a gift, my parents had given me plastic substrate and said, "Why don't you make your own blocks!" As a child of six, it would have been an impossible task to produce exactly scaled repeating blocks ready to build with, from raw materials alone. What if they said, why don't you build your own oil refinery, drill for some oil to use in it, and then make some plastic blocks of your own? Clearly as a child I had to take the building blocks for granted and I could then let my imagination run wild, conceiving what I wanted to build and assembling it.

If purely for arguments sake we assume that somehow, miraculously, I could produce perfect Lego block replicas, if I then assembled them into a racing car or a spaceship, they would only resemble a race car or a spaceship. If I had enough blocks to make replicas that were actual size, they would be amazing, but the car would not drive, and the spaceship would not leave our atmosphere. Not just any old blocks will do, but exactly the right parts need to exist to be able to then be assembled correctly into a genuine functional racing car or spaceship

Well, evolutionists assign Random Chance with the far greater task of making the building blocks for life from pre-existing constituent chemicals (chemical evolution) and then the task of putting those chemicals together as molecules and then assembling those molecules in the right way to make a living cell. We have seen already that it is not reasonable to just assume the pre-existence of all the right materials to start working with, or to assume that "The Big Bang" has solved that question. However, let's go with the argument for now and see where it leads us.

From non-life to life

To be able to have a cell, any cell, many molecules need to exist in the correct functional forms. Proteins are some of those fundamental building blocks. So, can we get to the right proteins by chance assuming that the necessary chemicals just happen to be hanging around somehow (and not unhelpfully combining in the wrong way and making each other useless for making life)?

Evolutionists claim that chemicals, randomly associated together, produced the right combinations for life to begin. Yet, as John Walton points out, the total number of possible chemical combinations available from the elements we have, what we might call 'Chemical Space' (other authors have called this the Interactome), is so vast that there are simply too many possibilities for random association to be a plausible explanation.

> "The practically boundless extent of Chemical Space, that's the virtual domain containing all possible molecules, is coming to the attention of more and more

scientists. It's found that taking just 30 atoms and coupling them together in all possible ways can produce an enormous number of molecules, somewhere in the region of 10^{24}; that's 10 followed by 24 zeros!

Pharmaceuticals typically contain many more atoms than 30 and "drug-like" chemical space has been estimated to contain over 10^{60} molecules. The vast size of these sets of potential molecules can be gauged by comparison with the number of stars in the visible Universe which is about 10^{24}. Even these enormous molecule spaces pale into insignificance in comparison with protein or nucleic acid spaces. The number of polypeptide chains (proteins) of modest length (250 units) that could be made from the 20 natural amino acids is in excess of 10^{325}. The resources of time and matter available on Earth (or in fact in the whole Universe) are far too small for random, undirected searches of chemical space to find molecules with particular wanted properties." (John Walton *Compact Time, A Short History of Life on Earth*, page 147).

It is easy for such large numbers to feel incomprehensible. We are all familiar with the analogy of the difficulty of finding a needle in a haystack. Locating one small item in such a huge pile of straw would seem a near impossible task. What if the haystack was the size of the world and you were still looking for one needle? That starts to sound more than impossible. But what if the haystack is the size of the known universe and you need to not just find one needle, but then having found it you need to come up lucky again many times over to find other needles and then put them together in a specific order, to build the proteins and enzymes necessary for life for example?

How impossible does something have to be before we can say it can't have happened? Then you face those more than impossible odds again and again as the process is repeated to assemble all the other building blocks for the simplest cell. Then you need to put all those bits of a cell together in the right order as well, all by Random Chance. It cannot have happened!

We can add to John Walton's observation on the size of Chemical space, a bit more detail about the limited size of actual time and space. John Baumgardner sets it out this way. If we take 10^{80} as physicist's own estimate of the total number of atoms in the universe. Then take 10^{12} as the upper limit of the average number of interatomic interactions per second per atom and 13 billion years' worth of seconds which is 10^{18},

> "we get 10^{110} as a very generous upper limit on the number of interatomic interactions which could have ever occurred during the long cosmic history the evolutionist imagines". Even if every interaction always produced a unique molecule, "we can conclude that no more than 10^{110} unique molecules could have existed in the universe in its entire history." (John Baumgardner, in, *In Six Days, Why 50 Scientists Choose to Believe in Creation*, page 207).

Remember that John Walton pointed out that the 20 natural amino acids for life, brought together in polypeptide chains of 250 units could form in 10^{325} combinations and John Baumgardner demonstrated that the Universe has only had enough time for a maximum of 10^{110} unique molecules in its existence. Clearly, we have a problem.

If we move on a step and assume that somehow, by means unknown, lots of amino acids are available, then we must recognise that the problem of generating first life by chance is even greater than just making chemicals. Functional proteins are not randomly linked sequences of amino acids. They exist in left-handed and right-handed symmetry. Only those with left-handed symmetry appear in the proteins that are essential for life. They would also be likely to react in unfavourable ways if mixed together in a supposed primordial chemical soup. Although we must note on route that,

> "There is not a shred of evidence to support the hypothesis that life began in an organic soup." (Fred Hoyle, *The Intelligent Universe,* cited in Subodh Pandit, *Come Search With Me Book 1 Does God Really Exist?* page 97)

In addition, the chemicals must be assembled in the right sequence for a functional protein. John Baumgardner points out that if we assume that at least half the amino acids must be in the correct specific locations and not worrying if they are left-handed or right-handed at this point, then,

> "For a relatively short protein consisting of a chain of 200 amino acids, the number of random trials needed for a reasonable likelihood of hitting a useful sequence is then in the order of 20^{100} (100 amino acid sites with 20 possible candidates at each site), or about 10^{130} trials. This is a hundred billion billion times the upper bound we computed for the total number of molecules ever to exist in the history of the cosmos!!" (John Baumgardner, in, *In Six Days, Why 50 Scientists Choose to Believe in Creation,* page 208).

And remember those are the odds of forming just one protein. Even the "simplest" forms of life have in the order of 1000 proteins or more. (John Baumgardner, *In Six Days, Why 50 Scientists Choose to Believe in Creation*).

In terms of making functional proteins,

"Once the chain of amino acids is formed it must be folded in a very precise manner at the primary, secondary, tertiary and quaternary levels because the manner of folding is one of the factors that decides the function of that protein. The number of options for folding is astronomical. The supercomputer Titan can perform 20 petaflops (20 thousand trillion floating operations a second) and will take about one year to get all the folds correct for a single protein. The cell does this in a split second! How can anyone even pretend to know how such a 'machine' could have been assembled inside the cell!? We must be honest and declare that the assembling of the first cell cannot be explained by any known natural process. To simply say, "It just happened to happen", does not sound like a scientific statement at all." (Subodh Pandit, *Come Search With Me, Book 1 Does God Really Exist?* page 63).

Many other scientists have posed forms of this problem from Fred Hoyle onwards, highlighting the inadequacy of Random Chance explaining life. What has been the response?

"Most scientists just put their hands over their ears and refused to listen." (John Baumgardner, in, *In Six Days, Why 50 Scientists Choose to Believe in Creation*).

The fact that there has not been sufficient time and resources within the claimed life of the universe, for Random Chance to be able to achieve anything necessary for life at a chemical level, provides such a devastating critique of the Darwinian commitment to Random Chance that it deserves much wider recognition.

Unfortunately, most chemists seem to have been so engrossed in their labs to have not noticed the implications of the vast size of Chemical Space. But when we consider the size of the total number of theoretically possible chemicals (Chemical Space) and the improbability of forming even one functional protein by chance alone within the decidedly finite limits of the time and space we have available (the practical limits to Random Chance) (see Axe, *Undeniable, How Biology Confirms Our Intuition That Life is Designed*) we must conclude that life cannot have occurred by chance alone.

This is not something that Darwin could have known. But we do, and we must take account of it.

However, since we are making the claim that evolution by Random Chance from chemical constituents to even the simplest single cell life form could not have happened, it is worth taking in some further work done on this problem.

> "The cell, like individual genes and proteins, faces an extreme combinatorial problem. Tompa and Rose calculate, building on the work of protein scientist Cyrus Levinthal, that there are a whopping $10^{79000000000}$ ways of combining just the proteins in a relatively simple unicellular yeast. That number grows exponentially larger when biologists attempt to calculate the number of possible ways of combining all the proteins and all the other large molecular components necessary for that one-celled organism, including DNA and RNA molecules, ribosomes, lipids and glycolipid molecules and others. The number of possible combinations of these cellular components (called the "Interactome") vastly exceeds the number of elementary particles in the universe (10^{80}) and even the number of events since the Big Bang (10^{139})." (Stephen Meyer, *The Return of the God Hypothesis, Three Scientific Discoveries That Reveal the*

Huge numbers

It can be hard to grasp what such very large numbers mean. Let's go over some of the numbers that have come up in the discussion so far.

There have been various estimates of the number of stars in the visible universe. Where different estimates arise with such immensely large numbers let's not quibble, the argument we are making still stands. For argument's sake we will take one recent estimate which is 10^{22} (BBC, *More or less, Are there more stars than grains of beach sand?* 7 July 2018). That is 1 followed by 22 zeros: 10000000000000000000000. It is self-evidently easier to write that number as 10^{22} than write it out longhand.

Just for comparison, to try to give some form of context, Carl Sagan famously claimed that there are more stars in the universe than there are grains of sand on all the beaches in all the world and calculations bear that claim out. (BBC, *More or less, Are there more stars than grains of beach sand?* 7 July 2018).

Remember that the number 10^{23} adds another zero and is 10 times bigger than 10^{22} then 10^{24} is 100 times bigger than 10^{22} and so on.

10^{80} is the physicist's estimate of the total number of atoms in the universe and looks like this,

10000000000000000000000000000000000000000000000000000000000000000000000000000000 (Stephen Meyer, *The Return of the God Hypothesis, Three Scientific Discoveries That Reveal the Mind Behind the Universe*, page 290)

It is estimated that **no more than 10^{110} unique molecules**

could have existed in the universe *in its entire history*, or if written out in full:

1000000000000000000000000000000000000000000000000 0000000000000000000000000000000000000000000000000 0000

(See John Baumgardner, in, *In six days Why 50 scientists choose to believe in creation,* page 207).

However, when it comes to calculating all the possible combinations of just the proteins making up just a single cell yeast, that could occur by randomly putting them together, we get a number that is so much larger it is exceptionally hard to grasp what it represents: $10^{79000000000}$ (Stephen Meyer, *The Return of the God Hypothesis, Three Scientific Discoveries That Reveal the Mind Behind the Universe*, page 290)

So here goes.

$10^{79000000000}$ written out long-hand as a number looks like this.

10000000000000000000000000000000000000000000000000000000000000000 00000000000000000000000000000

00000000000000000000000000000000000000000000000000000000000000000 00000000000000000000000000000

00000000000000000000000000000000000000000000000000000000000000000 00000000000000000000000000000

00000000000000000000000000000000000000000000000000000000000000000 00000000000000000000000000000

00000000000000000000000000000000000000000000000000000000000000000 00000000000000000000000000000

00000000000000000000000000000000000000000000000000000000000000000 00000000000000000000000000000

00000000000000000000000000000000000000000000000000000000000000000 00000000000000000000000000000

00000000000000000000000000000000000000000000000000000000000000000 00000000000000000000000000000

000000000000000000000000000000000000000000000000000000000000000000
0000000000000000000000000000

000000000000000000000000000000000000000000000000000000000000000000
0000000000000000000000000000

000000000000000000000000000000000000000000000000000000000000000000
0000000000000000000000000000

000000000000000000000000000000000000000000000000000000000000000000
0000000000000000000000000000

000000000000000000000000000000000000000000000000000000000000000000
0000000000000000000000000000

000000000000000000000000000000000000000000000000000000000000000000
0000000000000000000000000000

000000000000000000000000000000000000000000000000000000000000000000
0000000000000000000000000000

000000000000000000000000000000000000000000000000000000000000000000
0000000000000000000000000000

000000000000000000000000000000000000000000000000000000000000000000
0000000000000000000000000000

000000000000000000000000000000000000000000000000000000000000000000
0000000000000000000000000000

000000000000000000000000000000000000000000000000000000000000000000
0000000000000000000000000000

000000000000000000000000000000000000000000000000000000000000000000
0000000000000000000000000000

000000000000000000000000000000000000000000000000000000000000000000
0000000000000000000000000000

000000000000000000000000000000000000000000000000000000000000000000
0000000000000000000000000000

000000000000000000000000000000000000000000000000000000000000000000
0000000000000000000000000000

000000000000000000000000000000000000000000000000000000000000000000
0000000000000000000000000000

000000000000000000000000000000000000000000000000000000000000000000
0000000000000000000000000000

000000000000000000000000000000000000000000000000000000000000000000
0000000000000000000000000000

000000000000000000000000000000000000000000000000000000000000000000

000000000000000000000000000

000000000000000000000000000000000000000000000000000000000000000000
000000000000000000000000000

000000000000000000000000000000000000000000000000000000000000000000
000000000000000000000000000

000000000000000000000000000000000000000000000000000000000000000000
000000000000000000000000000

000000000000000000000000000000000000000000000000000000000000000000
000000000000000000000000000

000000000000000000000000000000000000000000000000000000000000000000
000000000000000000000000000

000000000000000000000000000000000000000000000000000000000000000000
000000000000000000000000000

000000000000000000000000000000000000000000000000000000000000000000
000000000000000000000000000

000000000000000000000000000000000000000000000000000000000000000000
000000000000000000000000000

000000000000000000000000000000000000000000000000000000000000000000
000000000000000000000000000

000000000000000000000000000000000000000000000000000000000000000000
000000000000000000000000000

000000000000000000000000000000000000000000000000000000000000000000
000000000000000000000000000

000000000000000000000000000000000000000000000000000000000000000000
000000000000000000000000000

000000000000000000000000000000000000000000000000000000000000000000
000000000000000000000000000

000000000000000000000000000000000000000000000000000000000000000000
000000000000000000000000000

000000000000000000000000000000000000000000000000000000000000000000
000000000000000000000000000

000000000000000000000000000000000000000000000000000000000000000000
000000000000000000000000000

000000000000000000000000000000000000000000000000000000000000000000
000000000000000000000000000

0000000000000000000000000000000000000000000000000000000000000000000
0000000000000000000000000000

0000000000000000000000000000000000000000000000000000000000000000000000
0000000000000000000000000000

0000000000000000000000000000000000000000000000000000000000000000000000
0000000000000000000000000000

0000000000000000000000000000000000000000000000000000000000000000000000
0000000000000000000000000000

0000000000000000000000000000000000000000000000000000000000000000000000
0000000000000000000000000000

0000000000000000000000000000000000000000000000000000000000000000000000
0000000000000000000000000000

0000000000000000000000000000000000000000000000000000000000000000000000
0000000000000000000000000000

0000000000000000000000000000000000000000000000000000000000000000000000
0000000000000000000000000000

0000000000000000000000000000000000000000000000000000000000000000000000
0000000000000000000000000000

0000000000000000000000000000000000000000000000000000000000000000000000
0000000000000000000000000000

0000000000000000000000000000000000000000000000000000000000000000000000
0000000000000000000000000000

0000000000000000000000000000000000000000000000000000000000000000000000
0000000000000000000000000000

0000000000000000000000000000000000000000000000000000000000000000000000
0000000000000000000000000000

0000000000000000000000000000000000000000000000000000000000000000000000
0000000000000000000000000000

0000000000000000000000000000000000000000000000000000000000000000000000
0000000000000000000000000000

0000000000000000000000000000000000000000000000000000000000000000000000
0000000000000000000000000000

0000000000000000000000000000000000000000000000000000000000000000000000
0000000000000000000000000000

0000000000000000000000000000000000000000000000000000000000000000000000
0000000000000000000000000000

0000000000000000000000000000000000000000000000000000000000000000000000

00000000000000000000000000000

0000000000000000000000000000000000000000000000000000000000000000
00000000000000000000000000000

0000000000000000000000000000000000000000000000000000000000000000
00000000000000000000000000000

0000000000000000000000000000000000000000000000000000000000000000
00000000000000000000000000000

0000000000000000000000000000000000000000000000000000000000000000
00000000000000000000000000000

0000000000000000000000000000000000000000000000000000000000000000
00000000000000000000000000000

0000000000000000000000000000000000000000000000000000000000000000
00000000000000000000000000000

0000000000000000000000000000000000000000000000000000000000000000
00000000000000000000000000000

0000000000000000000000000000000000000000000000000000000000000000
00000000000000000000000000000

0000000000000000000000000000000000000000000000000000000000000000
00000000000000000000000000000

0000000000000000000000000000000000000000000000000000000000000000
00000000000000000000000000000

0000000000000000000000000000000000000000000000000000000000000000
00000000000000000000000000000

0000000000000000000000000000000000000000000000000000000000000000
00000000000000000000000000000

0000000000000000000000000000000000000000000000000000000000000000
00000000000000000000000000000

0000000000000000000000000000000000000000000000000000000000000000
00000000000000000000000000000

0000000000000000000000000000000000000000000000000000000000000000
00000000000000000000000000000

0000000000000000000000000000000000000000000000000000000000000000
00000000000000000000000000000

0000000000000000000000000000000000000000000000000000000000000000
00000000000000000000000000000

0000000000000000000000000000000000000000000000000000000000000000
00000000000000000000000000000

0000000000000000000000000000000000000000000000000000000000000000000
00000000000000000000000000000

0000000000000000000000000000000000000000000000000000000000000000000
00000000000000000000000000000

0000000000000000000000000000000000000000000000000000000000000000
00000000000000000000000000000

0000000000000000000000000000000000000000000000000000000000000000
00000000000000000000000000000

0000000000000000000000000000000000000000000000000000000000000000000
00000000000000000000000000000

0000000000000000000000000000000000000000000000000000000000000000000
00000000000000000000000000000

0000000000000000000000000000000000000000000000000000000000000000
00000000000000000000000000000

0000000000000000000000000000000000000000000000000000000000000000
00000000000000000000000000000

0000000000000000000000000000000000000000000000000000000000000000000
00000000000000000000000000000

0000000000000000000000000000000000000000000000000000000000000000000
00000000000000000000000000000

0000000000000000000000000000000000000000000000000000000000000000000
00000000000000000000000000000

0000000000000000000000000000000000000000000000000000000000000000
00000000000000000000000000000

0000000000000000000000000000000000000000000000000000000000000000
00000000000000000000000000000

0000000000000000000000000000000000000000000000000000000000000000000
00000000000000000000000000000

0000000000000000000000000000000000000000000000000000000000000000000
00000000000000000000000000000

0000000000000000000000000000000000000000000000000000000000000000
00000000000000000000000000000

0000000000000000000000000000000000000000000000000000000000000000
00000000000000000000000000000

Ok, so far there has been only 10,000 zeros written out. We have hardly made a dent in the **79,000,000,000 zeros** needed. I trust you don't want a book that long!

1 followed by 79000000000 zeros

Do you still believe that randomly putting proteins and other chemicals together has any realistic prospect of accidentally, by Random Chance, producing even a single cellular organism such as a yeast?

Really, are you sure?!

We aren't done with very big numbers yet though, because there are about 3 billion letters in the code of the DNA in the human genome. This is perhaps the most extreme combinatorial challenge of all, because as we noted elsewhere, the letters of the code, A,C,G and T, are free to associate in any order. In fact, it is important that they can if they are to operate as a coding system for life. To make a fully functioning healthy person who is able to grow, mature and successfully reproduce, the vast majority of that chemical coding must be in the correct specific order, or you are diseased or dead. The number of potential combinations of those 3 billion letters is staggeringly larger than the number of possible combinations of the proteins in a single cell yeast as just illustrated. The impossibility of that code forming by undirected Random Chance is so great it hurts the brain to try to imagine it. Surely this again shows that evolution driven by Random Chance did not happen, because it could not happen.

If you are not yet convinced by the force of this argument, though it really should be hitting home by now, then you could read more in Douglas Axe, *Undeniable how biology con-*

firms our intuition that life is designed. He examines carefully what Random Chance can actually achieve. In chapter 8 he discusses the impossibility of Random Chance ever resulting in life. In defence of Random Chance, the argument is often made that somehow given enough time and opportunity the right outcome has to result. He explains how whilst this might seem conceptually reasonable, as we have just seen, in practical terms it is not. Some odds are so small that they represent a physical impossibility within the time and matter available within the universe, (*Undeniable how biology confirms our intuition that life is designed,* page 133).

So, summing up, even if we assume that by means unknown, matter and thus the necessary chemicals are available in the first place, and the laws necessary to govern their interactions exist by unexplained means, then randomly associating chemicals together to get the molecules for life is simply not possible. And then randomly associating those molecules together does not get us to even a unicellular life form. **Time plus chance is not the answer.**

When considering scientific attempts to explain the origin of life, David Berlinski puts it starkly,

> "No-one has the faintest idea whether the immense gap between what is living and what is not may be crossed by any conceivable means." (Berlinski, *The devil's delusion,* page 202)

Even if we just assume that life can somehow get off the starting blocks by natural processes alone, which we have just demonstrated it can't, there remain other no less serious problems for the evolutionary explanation of life which we will come to in the next chapters.

How can science have gotten into such a mess?

Donald Rumsfeld is quoted as saying (about US Intelligence operations),

"The message is that there are no "knowns." There are things we know that we know. There are known unknowns. That is to say there are things that we now know we don't know. But there are also unknown unknowns. There are things we do not know we don't know. So when we do the best we can and we pull all this information together, and we then say well that's basically what we see as the situation, that is really only the known knowns and the known unknowns. And each year, we discover a few more of those unknown unknowns. It sounds like a riddle. It isn't a riddle. It is a very serious, important matter." (https://en.wikiquote.org/wiki/Donald_Rumsfeld)

Steve Rayner commenting on Rumsfeld's famous quote says;

"Rumsfeld altogether omitted what is possibly the most intriguing combination: what we don't know we know." (Steve Rayner, *Uncomfortable Knowledge: The Social Construction of Ignorance in Science and Environmental Policy Discourses*, see supporting references)

For a range of reasons, it is hard for individuals and institutions to recognise their implicit assumptions, their shared tacit knowledge, and even their mutual awareness of things they know but are choosing not to integrate into their understanding of a particular problem, such as the origin of life. We see a social process in operation amongst groups of individuals and institutions whereby their "knowledge" is shaped and promulgated to the wider world, whether they be research institutes or bodies representing professionals' views.

Steve Rayner suggests,

> "To make sense of the complexity of the world so that they can act, individuals and institutions need to develop simplified, self-consistent versions of that world. The process of doing so means that much of what is known about the world needs to be excluded from those versions, and in particular that knowledge which is in tension or outright contradiction with those versions must be expunged. This is 'uncomfortable knowledge'." (Steve Rayner, *Uncomfortable Knowledge: The Social Construction of Ignorance in Science and Environmental Policy Discourses*)

In relation to evolution, we have seen a century of uncomfortable knowledge building up to the point where it cannot credibly be ignored any longer even though so many are determined to do so.

Two things are worth noting.

First, even if science and evolution are taken on their own terms it is not hard to find huge problems in their attempt to explain many things that most people think have been settled and are "known". When it comes to evolution and the origin and development of life, we should question whether we "know" what we think we know. Since the 19th Century science has revealed so many more previously unknown unknowns such as DNA and the biochemical complexity of life, that we must reassess what we believe we know and incorporate this knowledge as well. It may indeed be uncomfortable for many people to recognise the implications of such knowledge for evolutionary theory, but it isn't credible to ignore it any longer. An increasing number of authors from a wide variety of backgrounds have been pointing out the gulf between what the science establishment believes it knows and the evidence as we have it. Many are not Christian so if you are inclined to believe everyone is biased, clearly not all have a bias to wanting to prove the existence of God as creator and designer, they are just looking at the evidence. The scientific evidence itself undermines belief in evolution 'from molecules to man'.

Second, it is in fact not reasonable to take science only on its own terms because there is too much that it cannot explain, or ever explain. The way it frames problems and the underlying assumptions embedded in scientific work on origins need challenging, because they are fundamentally flawed. There are also significant limitations as to what the scientific method can ever address. These points are then returned to later, where we look at what is left out of scientific explanations of origins and why that is not acceptable if we want to find robust explanations for the origin of all of reality and life.

There is an immense social pressure to deny that anything like this is going on. Fundamental problems with evolution? What problems? The pressure on scientists, teachers, and others, is to maintain the consensus in public that there aren't any fundamental gaps in our understanding and that evolution from nothing to a single cell, to all life today, is an established "fact".

The illusion is achieved in astronomy and cosmology (the study of where the universe came from) by building immensely complicated mathematical models which intimidate most people whose mathematics is not up to challenging them. However, these models are based on questionable assumptions that can be challenged.

The illusion is maintained in biology by putting forward any evidence of small changes in the animal or plant kingdom as evidence of evolution and claiming that this therefore proves evolution 'from molecules to man'.

The illusion is maintained in geology by falling back on

immense time periods to somehow solve everything and insisting that all the missing links in evolution will be found eventually.

The more you read into any of these areas, the more problems you find, but the illusion is maintained by referring to all the other areas of claimed knowledge that are supposed to support evolution – it must be right because they all agree with it too. Each set of unknowns is used to reinforce belief in other unknowns.[9] It really is a hall of mirrors. Rather than undeniable facts these are beliefs, with a weak basis in evidence.

So, we have considered in this and the previous chapter, two vast gaps that no-one has the faintest idea as to how they may be crossed by naturalistic explanations alone. Yet, we are asked by evolutionists to believe that somehow, by means unknown, these gaps have been crossed with no involvement of the super-natural:

1. Getting from absolute nothing to something

2. Then getting from non-life to self-sustaining, self-replicating life

It really is a lot that evolutionists are asking us to just assume and take for granted.

There is too much about the origin of life that cannot be explained by natural causes alone

"The fool says in his heart, "There is no God.""

David, Psalm 14 vs 1

13 THE BROKEN CHAIN

More gaps, less evidence

We are all familiar with chains of cause and effect. One thing leads to another. Cookery is very much about chains of events: linked causes and effects. Just assembling all the right ingredients is not enough. They have to be washed, prepared, weighed and then mixed in the right order. Even modest recipes, like making bread, go wrong without taking care to get things in the right amounts in the right order and then applying the right amount of resting time, heat and cooling etc.

Starting with same ingredients, flour, water, salt, yeast, butter, oil, then using some or all of them but mixing them in different proportions and orders, and then applying different processes to them we can produce outcomes as diverse as pancakes, bread loaves, bread rolls, doughnuts, wallpaper paste, play dough, salt dough for Christmas decorations, croissants, flat bread and burnt dough bricks. We can even produce an explosion and burn up the ingredients. To get from raw ingredients to the desired outcome requires intentionality, Design and the correct association of parts assembled in the correct sequence. The ingredients don't do the baking, a baker does. But the baker has to get the necessary ingredients from somewhere, and it turns out that they too are the result of many processes and choices. Flour does not blow out of fields into waiting nets, wheat is processed extensively to make good bread flour. The baking then occurs in an oven which also had to be made from many parts. Just mixing the right ingredients at room temperature does not produce an appetising outcome. The baked product is the outcome of multiple converging sequences of events that must all occur in the right order and be undertaken in the right way.

Evolution proposes a chain of events that are causally linked, because they must come in the right order, that is so long that to estimate the number of links would be to come up with a number immensely larger than the number of seconds in the history of the universe. And on the end of that chain, apparently, dangles human life in all its dimensions, or so the story goes.

We are asked to believe in an almost endlessly long chain of living things from the first living cell to us. It's that simple and the whole chain must have been possible at every link, or we would not be here thinking about it.

The story of life when told in evolutionary terms tends to skip fairly rapidly past the questions of where everything came from in the first place and the existence of matter is just assumed. It also then tends to skip over the question of how life got started, except to point to a few not very convincing origin-of-life experiments and progresses rapidly to a story of a single cell being the progenitor of all subsequent life and then how that life has supposedly developed in ever greater complexity to become all life there is today.

This process of getting from one cell to all life, turns out to be no less challenging than getting from non-life to life. It is also just as lacking in credible evidence that it is possible in any way at all, by natural processes alone.

The previous chapter looked at the chances of evolving the chemical building blocks for life (chemical evolution). We will now consider in more detail the probability of putting them together to make cells and living creatures by Random Chance alone (biological evolution).

From a single cell to all life today

Life is inherently interconnected in multiple levels of functional hierarchies, from chemical processes in organelles within cells, to the functioning of cells, to organ systems, to organisms, to ecosystems.

As soon as you examine the implications of how Random Chance can't explain life at one level, you are immediately drawn to the implications at other levels. Indeed, separating them out as though it is possible to meaningfully consider them independent from one another, is yet another example of the simplistic thinking that might just have been excusable with the level of knowledge in the 19th Century, but it isn't credible now.

However, Darwin had more foresight than many people realise. He famously wrote that,

> "If it could be demonstrated that any complex organ existed which could not possibly have been formed by numerous, successive, slight modifications, my theory would absolutely break down." (Quoted in Phillip Johnson, *Darwin on Trial*).

Let me help you out. Darwin's nightmare has come true.

So many people have taken up Darwin's challenge and found exactly the examples he feared that his theory has completely broken down. We have seen Michael Behe's argument in *Darwin's Black Box,* using the bacterial flagellum for example. The beauty of the examples Behe uses are that at multiple levels there are interconnected functional hierarchies of physical and chemical processes occurring to achieve biological functionality. To chip away a bit at any given example of biological irreducible complexity by suggesting that perhaps this part or that part might be able to be taken away, misses the point. That is still only making an analysis at the level of the physical functional interdependence of parts within a cell. It gets nowhere near undermining the force of the argument when we also consider the underlying biochemistry and genetics making those biological structures a reality. Behe's Irreducible Complexity and Axe's Functional Coherence seem to be expressions of aspects of the same conundrum that is observed at multiple scales in the chemistry and biology of life; namely that all the parts need to be together and relating to one another correctly, at the same time, for life to exist and if parts are missing there is no life, just a collection of dead parts.

The problem we have is with the scientific orthodoxy refusing to recognise the state of affairs, not with the refuting evidence itself.

Douglas Axe argues that living things have to have the right parts in the right places all relating to one another in the right way. He calls this Functional Coherence. They are not just random associations of lots of parts together. It is not enough to just evolve the chemical constituents for life, by chance, they must be organised correctly. The invention of every life form by whatever means, must overcome this hurdle.

"Serious invention requires not just a smidgen of functional coherence but extensive amounts arranged over a hierarchy of levels, and this simply can't happen by accident – for any kind of invention." (Douglas Axe, *Undeniable, How Biology Confirms Our Intuition That Life is Designed*, Page 202)

Cells have multiple levels of Functional Coherence, then for more complex life, those cells exist in organs and in systems and in whole bodies and those creatures exist in ecosystems. There are multiple levels of Functional Coherence and interdependent complexity.

Darwin's proposed mechanism was Random Chance working through Natural Selection leading to survival of the fittest. Most people have heard of this, they may think the matter is settled. It isn't.

Douglas Axe has worked for a long time with enzymes and proteins. His experiments with enzymes to see if selection can achieve any functional improvements have shown it can't. He concluded from experimentation,

"Enzyme A can't evolve to work like enzyme B." (Douglas Axe, *Undeniable, Undeniable, How Biology Confirms Our Intuition That Life is Designed*, page 84)

And if you can't evolve enzymes, you can't evolve cells.

Stephen Meyer, in *Darwin's Doubt*, takes this further.

"Darwin's evolutionary mechanism is incapable of generating new animal forms, in part because it's incapable of generating new protein forms." (Quoted in Douglas Axe, *Undeniable, Undeniable, How Biology Confirms Our Intuition That Life is Designed*, page 84)

So, Random Chance can't produce functional proteins in the first place and then Natural Selection can't modify them to new functional forms.

How big a problem is this? When Darwin and others were first proposing evolution as an explanation of all life from natural causes alone, they had a very limited idea of what goes on within each living cell, whether that is a single cellular organism or a cell in a more complex organism. Today science has uncovered a picture beyond anything they could have known.

To give an idea of the scale of the challenge, a typical cell in our bodies may contain 42 million proteins (see for example, Alberts et al, *Molecular Biology of the Cell 6th Edition*). That does not mean each one is different from all the others, but all 42 million must be organised very carefully to undertake specific tasks and be able to do so reliably. For chance to be a convincing explanation, every one of those proteins would have to be selected for out of a soup of chemicals and be able to come together at the same time into a functional whole.

If you look at a cell with a basic 19th Century microscope you might detect a few constituent parts and wonder if they could somehow form separately and then come together in a "simple" form. You would to some extent be a victim of your level of observation/ magnification. But now that it is clear, that many cells require millions of proteins to simply exist, the problem is of a whole different order of magnitude.

This multiplies up for the whole of the human body, which for example, has 30 to 40 trillion cells of 200 different types (Bianconi et al, *An Estimation of the Number of Cells in the Human Body*). Those cells are organised in systems that inter-relate and they too must be co-ordinated. When those systems malfunction, they cause disease or death.

The sheer scale of the chemistry going on within our bodies all the time simply to keep us alive is awe inspiring. There are vast thousands of chemical reactions per cell per second in our bodies. It is reasonable to estimate that the human body overall performs something in the order of approximately 400 billion synchronised chemical reactions per second for us to be alive[10]. Higher and lower estimates can be made but the essential point is still valid that a vast amount of carefully regulated and synchronised chemistry is going on all the time in our bodies. (For further detail have a look at Roche Metabolic Pathways; www.biochemical-pathways.roche.com). These are not random reactions, but carefully controlled, often in complex chains of events, that also interact with one another. And remember, the information to form this complex whole, is contained within the DNA of each cell. Although cells are different from one another in function, they all contain the overall blueprint, as Stephen Meyer describes it, the designer's "Signature in the cell".

Douglas Axe gets to the point about achieving even one tiny part of this complexity by chance through Natural Selection alone; for just <u>one</u> new enzyme,

> "No one has a truer sense of what selection can and can't do than those who've attempted to harness its power, to make it perform before our very eyes. When I say that these people - myself included - have, over the decades, come to a much more modest view of natural selection, I'm saying something worth listening to." (Douglas Axe, *Undeniable, Undeniable, How Biology Confirms Our Intuition That Life is Designed*, page 103)

In that case what can Natural Selection do? Selection seems to be able to tinker with what is already in existence, but not to make it in the first place.

> "So by the time selection begins to favour an invention, something **other than selection** has already in-

vented it. This is one of those common-science gems to be treasured – an obvious realization that gains revolutionary status for no other reason than a long tradition of ignoring it." (Douglas Axe, *Undeniable, Undeniable, How Biology Confirms Our Intuition That Life is Designed,* page 96) (emphasis shown in bold rather than italics as was originally in this quote)

He goes on,

"Dan Tawfik hit the nail on the head: nothing evolves unless it already exists." (Axe, *Undeniable, Undeniable, How Biology Confirms Our Intuition That Life is Designed,* page 97)

And that evolving even then seems to be quite modest, varying within clear boundaries and quite narrow limits.

Clearly this doesn't get us from non-life to life, or then from a presumed first life to all life.

"To attribute the invention of all complex life to a natural mechanism set in motion with the earliest simple life is to ascribe astonishing creative power to that mechanism. Yet when colleagues and I challenge this evolutionary mechanism to invent on a far less impressive scale – by altering an enzyme to perform a new function – we find that it fails." (Douglas Axe, *Undeniable, Undeniable, How Biology Confirms Our Intuition That Life is Designed,* page 225)

Is this news? Well, not exactly; Darwin saw the outline of this problem right from the start, although at a much coarser resolution.

"When we descend to the details, we cannot prove that a single species has changed; nor can we prove that the supposed changes are beneficial, which is the groundwork of the theory." (Charles Darwin, *The life and letters of Charles Darwin*, Vol 1 page 210, cited in Subodh Pandit, *Come Search with Me, Book 1 Does God Really Exist?* Page 90)

The difficulty for evolutionary explanations is that the evidence against Natural Selection being able to originate any new life forms has grown much, much stronger.

What does this mean?

"If nothing can evolve itself into existence, then nothing did." (Douglas Axe, *Undeniable, Undeniable, How Biology Confirms Our Intuition That Life is Designed,* page 226)

If life can't evolve by Random Chance, then it didn't

"Let me understand the teaching of your precepts; then I will meditate on your wonders."

David in Psalm 119 vs 27

14 THE DIY MANUAL FROM HELL

Unworkable instructions for
making living creatures

I once set about putting two broken cars together to make one good one. My Nissan had a blown engine. I bought another Nissan of the same model with a good engine but caved in body work from a crash. I had a brilliant plan; combine the good bits from both and have one good car for much less than the cost of buying a new one! As I got out the Haynes Automotive Repair Manual for my car and started reading, it became clear I had bitten off more than I could chew. There was a whole pile of tools I needed but didn't own. Then I needed an engine hoist and I had to clear out the garage to make a workspace. I started on the job anyway and steadily a large number of parts built up in boxes. Before long I had to admit it wasn't going well. The manual I had was for a slightly different model. It looked the same on the outside, but it had a totally different engine and gearbox and just about everything else under the bonnet was different too. It would be a huge learning task, without a workable instruction manual to guide me, or the right tools to achieve anything, or a sensible work-space. I admitted defeat and thankfully my long-suffering friends at the garage who did have the necessary knowledge and tools, took both cars, a pile of pieces and expertly built me one good car and scrapped the rest.

Evolution's proponents would have you believe that they have discovered the design manual for life and the toolbox by which it made things; that they know the mechanism by which biological evolution happened. Have they really found these things?

Evolution, a theory with no plausible mechanism for the origin of new life

In the previous chapter we looked at Douglas Axe's evidence that getting from one cell to all other life is just as hard to explain in evolutionary terms as the origin of the first cell. Yet, many people seem happy to believe that somehow Natural Selection has solved this problem, so in this chapter we will look in more detail at the mechanism of evolution to see if it does indeed have the creative power necessary to originate life. First of all, however, we will remind ourselves of some of the grand claims of evolution.

What are the great insights of evolution that it relies on to make the claim to be an overall theory of the origins of life, and subsequently its purpose? Well, when boiled down, they are very few indeed. Here are some of the more important of them.

First, <u>living creatures have visible similarities</u>.

This is a problem, because we are discovering that visible similarities or differences are not necessarily connected to the underlying genetic reality. Things can look similar on the outside but quite different on the inside. The proposed mechanism of evolution, Natural Selection driven by random mutations and chance, to develop new species was read from the apparent external evidence based on observing the visible similarities of different creatures.

> "A great deal of variation can be obtained within a biological species (remember those dogs), whereas separate species are often very similar in visible characteristics. Speciation and change in form therefore seem to be different phenomena." (Phillip Johnson, *Darwin on Trial*, page 75) (Note: Speciation is the development of new species)

Second, <u>older rocks have apparently simpler fossils</u> in them.

This is also a problem, because there is also a total lack of the record of small gradual changes between one life form and another that Darwin was so confident that we would find if we looked hard enough.

Niles Eldridge:

> "We palaeontologists have said that the history of life supports (the story of gradual adaptive change), all the while really knowing that it does not." (Quoted in Phillip Johnson, *Darwin on Trial*, page 82)

'The fossil record', for what it is, appears to show the sudden appearance of creatures, which then don't change, and eventually disappear with extinction.

It has also transpired, from the discoveries of genetics, that there are no simple life forms and a vast uncrossable gulf exists between them and inert non-living things.

Third, <u>living creatures can adapt</u> to changes in their environment.

Again, this is a problem, because the immediate evidence of change from observation of the natural world shows that it can go in more than one direction. Birds, for example, may "adapt" with one sub-group being favoured and thus a different beak shape becoming more common for a time, but the process can then go in reverse.

The Galapagos Finches were made famous by Darwin. He claimed they demonstrated evolution visible through varying beak size – focusing on visible similarities and differences. He defined as new 'species' finches which he saw as different enough from other finches. Well, what he saw and the underlying reality it seems are not the same thing. The variation of beaks has in recent years reduced, leading to claims that one "species" of finch that has bred with another "species", through hybridisation, has gone extinct through "reverse evolution". (Elizabeth Mitchell, *Reverse Evolution Causes Darwin's Finches to go Missing?* Answers in Genesis, March 20, 2014)

The problem is much simpler than it might appear. It all depends on what you define as a species, and what change you observe that you then claim is evidence of evolution and how far you then stretch that. Evolutionists claim that finches arrived on the islands about 2 million years ago, thus there would have been about a million generations subject to variation and selection and the result is variations in body length and beaks and that's it,

> "Beginning with something very much like a finch, Darwinian processes laboured long and mightily in the Galapagos and brought forth... a finch. As John Gould informed Darwin a century and a half ago, all of the species remain recognizably finches."
> "Even at such a limited level, Darwinian evolution has been frustrated for the better part of a million

years." (Michael Behe, *Darwin Devolves, The New Science About DNA That Challenges Evolution*, page 147)

The finches are all still finches. All they have done is vary within very firm limits. None of the finches became an ostrich-like bird. None of the reduced variation in beaks has turned a finch back into some presumed ancestor. Perhaps if sufficient environmental pressure were to be exerted on the finch populations some other changes could occur. Let's be clear here. Apart from problems of definition allowing evolutionists to claim they have "evidence" for evolution, all that has happened is that visible differences in finch beaks have occurred and then disappeared. Nothing more, nothing less; not evolution (in the sense of the origin of all life by a naturalistic process alone) just adaptation. (Elizabeth Mitchell, *Reverse Evolution Causes Darwin's Finches to go Missing?* Answers in Genesis, March 20, 2014)

Adapting and evolving are clearly not the same thing and calling all change evolution is just misleading. Michael Behe points out that,

> "The mere fact that species such as Galapagos finches and African cichlids can diversify in different environments understandably impresses many people, who then mistakenly attribute vast constructive powers – rather than merely adaptive ones – to Darwinian processes." (Michael Behe, *Darwin Devolves, The New Science About DNA That Challenges Evolution*, page 222)

He goes further in discussing what was happening with the Galapagos finches,

> "And the fundamental principle seems very likely to be this: minor random variations around a designed blueprint are possible and can be helpful, but are se-

verely limited in scope. For new basic designs such as those at the biological level of family and above, additional information is necessary, information that is beyond the ability of mindless processes to provide." (Michael Behe, *Darwin Devolves, The New Science About DNA That Challenges Evolution,* page 169)

You might of course be wondering how much variation <u>can</u> occur within a family on the biological classification?

"For the dog family, it is the difference between a domestic dog and a wolf and a fox. For the cat family, it's the difference between a lion and a leopard and a lynx. For the seal family, it's the difference between a ringed seal and a hooded seal and a bearded seal. That degree of variation can likely be achieved by random mutation and Natural Selection. What is the difference between members of two separate families? For birds, it's the difference between a swift and a hummingbird, or a woodpecker and a toucan, or a thrush and a starling. For mammals it's the difference between a cat and a dog, or a rat and a muskrat, or a porpoise and a narwhal. If my argument is correct, those differences required explicit design." (Michael Behe, *Darwin Devolves, The New Science About DNA That Challenges Evolution,* page 156)

Taking simple observations like these

- living creatures have visible similarities

- older rocks have apparently simpler fossils in them

- living creatures can change to adapt to changes in their environment

the claim of common descent of organisms from "simpler"

predecessors is then welded to the claim that over time enough change can result from innumerable small changes to get from non-life, to life, to all life that now exists. And there we have it; evolution in its stark and straightforward form; a few simple observations and a lot of wishful thinking.

However, when evolution is tested to see what random mutations can actually achieve under the claimed pressure of Natural Selection – the very mechanism of Darwinian evolution - we find it cannot deliver anything like what has been claimed for it. Michael Behe discusses this at length in his book *Darwin Devolves: The New Science About DNA That Challenges Evolution*, it is hard to do justice to his work in such a short summary and he is well worth reading in more detail. He discusses the work of Richard Lenski over more than 25 years with bacteria cultures in his lab. It is the most detailed evolutionary experiment ever conducted. Changes did occur in the bacteria improving their growth rate, but nearly all resulted from losing genetic information because counter-intuitively, a mutation that damages a gene can be just what an organism needs to survive in the short term.

> "After fifty thousand generations of the most detailed, definitive evolution experiment ever conducted, after so much improvement in the growth rate... it's very likely that all of the identified beneficial mutations worked by degrading or outright breaking the respective ancestor genes. And the havoc wreaked by random mutations had been frozen in place by Natural Selection." (Michael Behe, *Darwin Devolves, The New Science About DNA That Challenges Evolution*, page 179)

What on earth was going on? Well only in the last 20 years or so has it been possible to peer into cells and study their fundamental molecular biology and their DNA in enough detail to get at what is actually going on when organisms change. The result of doing so has shocked very many people, because it has demonstrated a real but much more limited role for random mutations and Natural Selection than anyone previously envisaged. The beauty of this science is that it is not a philosophical or abstract discussion anymore, it is based on real observations of what is actually going on and it is amazing, but absolutely not what is needed if we want mutation and Natural Selection to explain all of life.

> "Random mutation and natural selection both promote evolution on a small scale and hinder it on a larger one. Mutation supplies the variation upon which natural selection acts, but the greatest amount of that variation comes from damaging or outright breaking previously working genes. In the case of an already functioning complex system, natural selection shapes it more and more tightly to its current role, making it less and less adaptable to other complex roles." (Michael Behe, *Darwin Devolves, The New Science About DNA That Challenges Evolution,* page 246)

It is probably fair to question whether Natural Selection is in fact a mechanism at all, or just an *outcome* resulting from Random Chance operating within certain constraints.

What can we conclude? Darwin did discover something amazing; that creatures can adapt to their environment. He also made a pretty good job of identifying how they might do so, but he did not discover the mechanism for generating all the complex structures of life in the first place, from the cellular level upwards and so far, no-one else has either.

The tragedy of Darwin is the tragedy of human imagination

writ large. He found something stunning and utterly amazing and mistakenly believed he had found the answer to everything!

In the face of this, we must ask yet again, why do scientists and indeed western culture, cling so fervidly to evolution as an explanation of anything? A major part of the answer is its cultural significance.

> "The story of human descent from apes is not merely a scientific hypothesis; it is the secular equivalent of the story of Adam and Eve, and a matter of immense cultural importance." (Phillip Johnson, *Darwin on Trial*, page 110)

Those same pieces of evidence we have outlined, can be seen quite differently.

First – <u>living creatures have visible similarities</u> - If everything were intentionally created why should life forms not share common building blocks at different levels, from basic chemistry through the function of cells to the operation of organ systems up to the form of overall organisms? Carbon based life forms will have similarities in chemistry and design. If RNA does the job, why is another carrier needed?

Also, as mentioned previously, creatures that look similar can have very different genetics. Just judging biological similarity on the basis of appearance can be misleading. For example, the marsupial mole and the placental mole look very similar, but this cannot be due to how they are claimed to be related in evolutionary terms. Any ad hoc explanation of this such as "convergent evolution", is not really an explanation at all but simply the secular equivalent of a 'Just So' story and no more convincing. (Don Patten, in *In Six Days, Why 50 Scientists Choose to Believe in Creation*, page 358).

Genetics supports this claim. We must not be seduced by the apparent visible similarities of organisms if the underlying genetic reality does not bear out our assumptions of how they are related. Douglas Axe discusses evidence from just one group of 16 strains of cyanobacteria.

> "Since they're all cyanobacteria, you might think they would carry the same set of genes, with perhaps an extra gene here or a missing gene there. The scientists found that they do share a common set of 660 genes... Much more surprising, though, was their finding that nearly 14,000 genes are unique to individual strains! At an average of 869 unique genes per strain, this makes these bacterial strains more genetically different than alike, despite their overall external similarities. The proportion of species-specific genes varies from one species to the next, but their existence in large numbers seems to be a property of all life, not just cyanobacteria." (Douglas Axe, *Undeniable, How Biology Confirms Our Intuition That Life is Designed,* page 183)

But even where there is similarity genetically, that too may be misleading. Modules of computer code performing useful functions are routinely built into quite diverse applications that achieve totally different purposes overall. Lego blocks can be used to build endless different shapes of houses, but it is not the blocks themselves that have created the house.

Second - <u>older rocks have apparently simpler fossils in them</u> - 'Simpler' creatures have turned out to be incredibly complex, from the level of their cellular chemistry upwards. With the insights of genetics, biochemistry and micro-biology there are no 'simple' organisms after all. As we have noted before, what looked simple to 19th Century eyes is far from simple now.

Third – <u>living creatures can adapt to changes in their environment</u> - Why wouldn't a designer make robust adaptable creatures and systems? It is just good Design, which we see at every level from the self-repair mechanisms of DNA to the adaptability of ecosystems. Without that forethought one critical failure in one part of the system could result in a cascade of failures taking out the whole of the rest. Engineers readily understand this principle. Adaptability is simply an essential Design requirement.

The missing parts of an explanation that prevent evolution from providing a convincing over-arching theory of the origins of life are many and include:

No convincing idea where everything ultimately came from

No idea how external influences can result in new genetic information or indeed in any genetic information existing at all

No idea how a single cell can arise by random undirected processes alone

No idea how all other more complex creatures can arise from a single cell by random undirected processes

and thus

No idea how Random Chance can result in <u>directed</u> outcomes from the cellular level to organisms, to ecosystems and up to the whole planet ecosystem

In short, no plausible means for how undirected small random changes starting from nothing, can result in anything functional at all.

Let's return to the arguments of Richard Dawkins, possibly the most influential recent populariser of the idea that evolution explains the origin of life. Timothy Standish suggests that Richard Dawkins, in defending evolution in his best-seller, *The Blind Watchmaker*, has basically just two main arguments. (Timothy Standish, in, *In Six Days, Why 50 Scientists Choose to Believe in Creation*). This is, in effect, Dawkins' evolutionary Design manual for life.

Standish suggests that Dawkin's first argument is essentially that given enough time the impossible becomes possible. We have seen that he is absolutely and categorically wrong on that point. Dawkins does equivocate somewhat on what Random Chance can achieve, but to claim that Natural Selection somehow overcomes the obvious shortcomings of Random Chance immediately brings other problems as we have seen from Michael Behe's work.

Standish then suggests that Dawkins' second argument, is an argument by analogy whereby he claims it is possible for monkeys to type out the phrase *"Me thinks it is a weasel"* in an afternoon by randomly typing on typewriters and that this analogy proves the power of Random Chance. Now he knew that even this tiny phrase was highly improbable so the odds have to be rigged in evolution's favour by claiming that Natural Selection could 'fix' the right characters in place, once one is typed in the right location, thus reducing the size of the problem for the next round of Random Chance. But on what basis can evolution "know" to do this? (Timothy Standish, in, *In Six Days, Why 50 Scientists Choose to Believe in Creation*, pages 98- 102). Also, remember how short Dawkin's phrase is compared to the length of the genetic code in every cell of our bodies containing about 3 billion letters. (Robert Carter, chapter 2 in *Evolution's Achilles Heels*, page 53). As we have discussed at length, Random Chance has no overall plan to work to and if it does then it is not random anymore and is Design.

Therefore, Dawkins has produced an argument, by analogy, for the need for a designer with an overall plan, not an argument for Random Chance being able to achieve anything like life!

The attribute of agency is ascribed to what is claimed to be a random process, Natural Selection. Only beings (or persons) have agency, thus the analogy is inconsistent with seeking an explanation from natural causes alone.

In fact, in all naturalistic origin of life experiments, the researchers presuppose pre-existing matter and information, which is then sequenced by the intelligent investigator. It is hardly an argument for the absence of a designer! It clearly demonstrates the indispensable role of intelligence and a mind in steering the chemistry towards a goal, an end-directed outcome.

So, the only way for Random Chance to be made to look like a plausible explanation of the origin anything, is for it to be made into not being random at all, but directed to some form of plan, intervention or in fact Design. That shows its proponents to be so confused as to what they are arguing for that it would be comic if it were not so tragic; the answer has been staring them in the face all along.

If evolution by Random Chance can't make the chemicals for life, then can't organise them in the right way to result in functionally coherent cells and then creatures, and if Natural Selection is only capable of much more modest change within limits, <u>operating on life that</u> <u>already exists</u>, then we can conclude that evolution from nothing to a single cell, to all life today, by Random Chance alone, cannot have happened.

> "Random mutation and natural selection can't accomplish anything remotely like what has been ascribed to them. Consequently, the actual "illusion" is a thoroughly modern one – the illusion that Darwin's or any other proposed evolutionary mechanism can account for the elegance of life. Their supposed power was all in our heads." (Michael Behe, *Darwin Devolves, The New Science About DNA That Challenges Evolution,* page 266)

Therefore, Darwin's mechanism for evolution, Natural Selection, can longer be considered a plausible explanation of the origin and development of all life. And the more recent versions of Darwinism are no more able to explain the origin of life because they ultimately still rely on Random Chance and Natural Selection to achieve survival of the fittest. (For a fuller discussion see Michael Behe chapter 5 *"Overextended"* in *Darwin Devolves, The New Science About DNA That Challenges Evolution*).

Now we have demonstrated that an explanation of the origins of life cannot be achieved through an appeal to Random Chance, it has to be off the table and other potential explanations have to be very firmly back on.

If you read popular science journals, listen to science programmes on TV, or read heavy weight scientific journals, people talk about how evolution "made" this or that happen. Or that something has an evolutionary "purpose". Let's be ultra-clear. The only mechanism proposed for evolution is Random Chance, operating through "Natural selection" to achieve survival of the fittest.

Random Chance is not directed. It has no consciousness or purpose. It does not plan or have any goals. When those things are attributed to it, the persons doing so are simply involved in a great conjuring trick, maintaining the illusion of evolution; sustaining the pretence that it is an adequate explanation of who we are and the whole of reality around us. It may comfort them. It may help them get research grants or sell books, but it is still total utter nonsense. What Phillip Johnson wrote in the 1990s still holds true,

> "Natural selection is a force for building adaptive complexity only when it is defined as a tautology or as a logical deduction unconnected to any empirically verifiable reality. Whenever natural selection is actually observed in operation, it permits variation only within boundaries and operates as effectively to preserve those constraining boundaries as it does to permit the limited variation. The hypothesis that natural selection has the degree of creative power required by Darwinist theory remains unsupported by empirical evidence." (Phillip Johnson, *Darwin on Trial*, page 124).

Species can be seen to vary only within clear limits. Dogs can be bred to look as different as a Chihuahua does from a Mastiff, but they can't be bred into cats, or horses, or jellyfish, or ostriches. And when there is no human input forcing the selection as with dog breeding, we see the same thing in nature, lots of variation and adaption to environments, but within clear limits.

> "In the Origin of Species Darwin argued that artificial selection – such as has produced various dog breeds – was an analogy for natural selection. He was more right than he knew: they both work predominantly by degrading genes." Michael Behe *Darwin Devolves, The New Science About DNA That Challenges Evolution,*

page 196)

Random Chance is not an adequate explanation of how these multiple genetic forms can arise in the first place and be functionally coherent (i.e. work together effectively as functional wholes). Natural Selection simply works with what is already there and largely it seems to do so by losing information, degrading genes in adapting creatures to fit their environment.

> "Darwinian evolution is self-limiting." "New life hasn't evolved. Overwhelmingly it has devolved." (See chapter 7 of Michael Behe *Darwin Devolves, The New Science About DNA That Challenges Evolution,* page 172 and 197)

In a previous chapter we looked at Douglas Axe's work and concluded that it is not possible to get to a single living cell by Random Chance. We can now conclude that there is no way to go from one cell to other cells to all creatures by random undirected processes either.

If there is no way for chance to drive a process of getting from one life form to another (in biologists' terms, to new levels above the level of species and family) then we have to conclude with Douglas Axe that,

> "Each and every new form of life must therefore be a masterful invention in its own right, embodying its own distinctive version of functional coherence at the very highest level." (Douglas Axe, *Undeniable, How Biology Confirms Our Intuition That Life is Designed,* page 184)

The multiple layers of chance outcomes that must coincide perfectly for the necessary proteins to exist and the right enzymes to exist and then the correct assemblage of those building blocks and the immense number of interactions between the chemical systems in each cell and the further coincidences that must occur for all those cells to be assembled into a functional living creature defy calculation and beggar belief.

Therefore,

> "Because each new form of life amounts to a new high-level invention, the origin of the thousandth new life form is no more explicable in Darwinian terms than the origin of the first." (Douglas Axe, *Undeniable, How Biology Confirms Our Intuition That Life is Designed,* page 194)

Michael Behe and Douglas Axe lead us to the same conclusion; random mutations plus Natural Selection have not originated life. The grand theory of evolution turns out to not have a working Design manual.

Recognizing Design in nature – the Intelligent Design argument – does not get you to who the designer was, it is simply looking at the evidence and admitting what it shows. However, many people are unwilling to admit even that much, not because the evidence isn't compelling, but because they can see where that evidence is inexorably leading them.

We have seen convincing evidence that there is a God. We have seen his 'signature' in every cell. We have seen the total inadequacy of evolutionary explanations of the origin of life when examined on their own terms. It is therefore completely reasonable to consider the claims of the one and only God whom Christians acknowledge to be the Creator of all things.

However, we are not done with evolution quite yet because when one area of supposed evidence for evolution is shown to be no such thing, its proponents always point to another and say that it proves evolution anyway. So, just to be sure, we must look at some other claims and the evidence put forward to support them.

The existence of God as Designer and Creator is the cornerstone of a coherent framework to understand all dimensions of reality

> "In the beginning was the Word, and the Word was with God, and the Word was God. He was with God in the beginning. Through him all things were made; without him nothing was made that has been made."
>
> John 1 vs 1, 2

The Gaps in Evolutionary Explanations

Evolution has attempted an explanation of where life came from by purely naturalistic means without any involvement of God.

It has failed to provide a convincing explanation of how by natural means alone, the following gaps can be crossed.

- From nothing to something

- From chaos to an ordered Universe

- From chemicals to proteins and enzymes

- From proteins and enzymes to a single cell

- From a single cell to all life

- From physical life to consciousness and mind

- From consciousness and mind to morality, hope and meaning

Evolution cannot explain how these things are possible without any original cause and without them being guided or planned or designed in anyway, but achieved by undirected Random Chance alone, even after a century and a half of trying.

15 SET IN STONE

What do the fossils tell us?

W hen we talk of something set in stone, we mean to convey that it cannot be changed. The Ten Commandments given to Moses were written on tablets of stone to emphasize their permanence. Tomb stones and memorials to famous figures are typically in stone to make sure they endure. The Egyptians built pyramids and temples to eternity. Their hubris is now on display in museums, their immortalisation by mummification producing nothing but historical and archaeological curiosities. Percy Bysshe Shelley caught it well in the poem Ozymandias.

> "And on the pedestal, these words appear:
> My name is Ozymandias, King of Kings;
> Look on my Works, ye Mighty, and despair!
> Nothing beside remains. Round the decay
> Of that colossal Wreck, boundless and bare
> The lone and level sands stretch far away."

For a long time now, fossils preserved in rocks have testified to the existence of many extinct creatures. From the time of Wallace and Darwin, scientists have eagerly expected those fossils, if collected and studied in sufficient numbers, to corroborate the story of evolution, the claim of common descent from a single cell organism to all life today. In fact, the impression that they do has been cultivated in school textbooks and classrooms and television nature documentaries. So, is that what we have found?

When all other arguments have failed, those who wish to promote evolution fall back on the assertion that the world is very old so there must have been enough time for evolution from non-life to the first cell, to all life today to have happened. They then point to fossils and believe the argument is closed.

We have seen that the difficulty of Random Chance achieving anything is typically "solved" by saying that there has been so much time it has to be possible, and we are here so it "must" have happened. That is circular reasoning par excellence. We could go around that loop for a very long time.

So, we must ask two very simple questions:

Do the fossils prove evolution?

Can an appeal to long time periods rescue evolution as an explanation of life?

We will look at the fossil record as the last line of evidence that evolution can lean on. We will also see whether simply adding enough time solves any of the problems we have been exploring, even though we have already seen compelling evidence that time plus chance can't even produce the building blocks for life to be assembled from.

Don't the fossils prove that evolution has happened?

Darwin held that random changes coupled with Natural Selection could accumulate over time to make all the diversity of life we see today. Geologists insist the earth is over 4 billion years old. Most people then say, well that is a very, very, long time, so presumably it must have been possible. In fact, people in western countries over the last century and a half have been so conditioned to this claim that it is hard for them to examine it critically.

Two problems emerge when we dig deeper. First, when we look at the geological evidence, the "fossil record" doesn't support the evolutionary model. Second, in various ways we can show that there hasn't been enough time anyway even within the very long timescales that scientists claim have happened.

The fossil record does not bear out the claim of endless small changes from a single cell to all life today through endless intermediate forms. When we look at the fossil record, we see that pretty much nothing is supposed to have happened until the Cambrian explosion when fossils suddenly appear in abundance, conventionally dated about 541-530 million years ago. Those fossils then present very real problems for evolution.

Stephen Meyer points out that the fossil evidence emerging from the Cambrian Explosion, however those fossils are classified and categorised, presents significant problems. (I am deliberately avoiding getting into the Taxa, Phyla and other classification terms, because they make the discussion much less readable for the non-expert and add nothing to the basic point that classification into similar groupings is what is being done). Meyer's point is that life forms are not shown to be connected by endless intermediate forms preceding them, but instead stubbornly appear in distinct groupings without evidence of predecessors. Instead of a branching tree of life starting with one single cell and widening out to all life today, what is found is a series of distinct columns in effect, which start suddenly and often end abruptly. Groups of organisms in any given distinct column appear suddenly, may vary, then often disappear just as suddenly from the fossil record. (See Stephen Meyer, *Darwin's Doubt*).

In fact, wherever we look at the fossil record, it does not show endless intermediate forms. They simply aren't there. Palaeontologists been looking for 150 plus years and the problem just keeps getting worse. The fossil record is fundamentally discontinuous, that is, it shows discreet life forms without intermediate forms, just as is all life today. There simply is no record of a huge number of small steps of change, with for example, a horse like creature gaining a progressively longer neck to become a giraffe. Yet it is that imagined chain of endless intermediate forms that is needed to sustain the theory of evolution, in fact in a real sense it *is* the theory.

John Morris sums up what the fossil record shows:

(1) "that life forms manifest little or no change during their history

(2) that most fossil types are virtually identical to their living descendants

(3) that fossil types appear in the fossil record without ancestral lineages

(4) that fossil organisms either become extinct of have survived into the present."

(John Morris, *In Six Days, Why 50 Scientists Choose to Believe in Creation*, page 289)

Many geologists and others have recognised this problem. Phillip Johnson sums up the picture,

"In short, if evolution means gradual change of one kind of organism into another kind, the outstanding characteristic of the fossil record is the absence of evidence for evolution." (Phillip Johnson, *Darwin on*

Trial, page 73)

What do evolutionists typically do in response to this absence of evidence? Well often they hold faith that somehow, suddenly, evidence will start appearing that does show endless intermediate forms. Or, they try to force the evidence to appear to support their position.

> "A circular argument arises: interpret the fossil record in the terms of a particular theory of evolution, inspect the interpretation and note that it confirms the theory. Well, it would, wouldn't it?" (Thomas Kemp, *A fresh look at the fossil record*, cited in Subodh Pandit, *Come Search With Me, Book 1 Does God Really Exist?* page 92)

Has there been enough time from other perspectives?

There hasn't been enough time for evolution from the perspective of genetic change either. Given the rate of change needed, there isn't enough time to have evolved all life today even if evolution upwards from single cells were possible. The rate of accumulation of genetic changes across populations is too slow to allow this, even if somehow, they are beneficial, can be captured and passed on. (See Donald Batten chapter 1, *Evolution's Achilles Heels*).

For Natural Selection to work new genes would have to become fixed in populations by "less fit" genes dying off. That is clearly dependent on the reproductive rate of species (i.e. the time to mature and produce the next generation). There has not been anywhere near enough time for all the necessary changes to accumulate given the life spans of organisms involved and therefore the number of generations that are possible.

The same problem repeats itself with the idea of evolution

from a supposed common ancestor with apes, all the way up to man, in a short enough time. Genetics doesn't support the necessary speed of change from an assumed common ancestor to us. Not enough beneficial mutations could have occurred in the maximum number of generations available, even if they could be captured somehow and passed on, (for which we must remember, there is no known mechanism to accumulate information, only to lose it or degrade it.) (See, Robert Carter chapter 2, *Evolution's Achilles Heels*).

So, if the fossils do not show what we need to sustain the theory of evolution and from a range of perspectives there hasn't been enough time anyway, then by its own evidence and on its own terms, evolution again fails to explain life.

> "The important claim of Darwinism is not that relationships exist, but that those relationships were produced by a naturalistic process in which parent species were gradually transformed into quite different descendant forms through long branches (or even thick bushes) of transitional intermediates, without any intervention by any Creator or other non-naturalistic mechanism. If Darwinism so defined is false then we do not have any important scientific information about how life arrived at its present complexity and diversity, and we cannot turn ignorance into information by calling it evolution." (Phillip Johnson, *Darwin on Trial,* page 117)

Truly, *"We don't know"*, are some of the hardest words for many scientists.

The rocks cry out to us that time alone is not the answer

If this lack of evidence for evolution causes any one to stumble it is worth remembering another "rock" who challenges our worldview.

"A stone that causes men to stumble and a rock that makes men fall."

The Apostle Peter writing about the Messiah in the first letter of Peter.

1 Peter 2 vs 8

16 MIND THE GAP

More un-crossable gaps

When you get off a Tube train on the London underground a recorded voice gives the iconic message,

"Mind the gap, mind the gap".

Therein lies the problem for evolution.[11]

Travellers from South America to the Central Americas must cross the Darian gap that is not bridged by a highway. It is full of danger to cross the dense jungle on foot, with bandits, poisonous creatures and disease to contend with. It is extremely hazardous, and it is quite likely you will die trying. An alternative is to go around the problem by boat, or to fly past it if you can afford to do so.

It is one thing to know a gap exists, it is quite another to work out how to cross it. Some gaps you can step across easily, some you can't.

From basic life to consciousness and a mind

Our search for an explanation of life in all its dimensions, must not be cut short at the level of physics and astronomy, of biology and biochemistry even though the evidence in those fields presents insurmountable obstacles to an evolutionary explanation.

We know there is much more to life and that needs explaining too.

"If we want to try to understand the world as a whole, we must start with an adequate range of data, and those data must include the evident facts about ourselves." (Thomas Nagel, *Mind and Cosmos, Why the Materialist Neo-Darwinian Conception of Nature is Almost Certainly False*, page 20).

And we must see our part in what we are trying to explain as Nagel puts it;

"The intelligibility of the world is no accident. Mind, in this view, is doubly related to the natural order. Nature is such as to give rise to conscious beings with minds; and it is such as to be comprehensible to such beings. Ultimately, therefore such beings should be comprehensible to themselves." (Thomas Nagel, *Mind and Cosmos, Why the Materialist Neo-Darwinian Conception of Nature is Almost Certainly False*, page 17)

Any explanation at higher levels such as consciousness and the mind cannot be built on explanations that have failed at more modest (though still immense) tasks, such as explaining the origin of life itself, cells, creatures and ecosystems. If the materialist and reductionist explanation of Random Chance acting through Natural Selection has failed as an explanation of the origin of those physical elements of life, there is no logical reason to believe it has any explanatory power for more intangible phenomena such as the mind. In fact, a reductionist explanation that seeks to reduce the mind to being merely the sum of the physical and chemical transactions within it ends up undermining the very idea of conceptual thought. Nagel's attempt at a solution to this is to seek a naturalistic explanation of the phenomena of the mind as something inherent within nature, but it is not clear in any way how that can be possible.

> "A genuine alternative to the reductionist program would require an account of how mind and everything that goes with it is inherent to the universe." (Thomas Nagel, *Mind and Cosmos, Why the Materialist Neo-Darwinian Conception of Nature is Almost Certainly False,* page 15).

Many strategies are employed to deal with the increasing disconnect between the evidence science itself keeps producing and the evolutionary framework. This is true of the mind as well as other phenomena that evolution has failed to offer a satisfactory explanation of. Steve Rayner's typology, although developed in relation to other debates can, I think, be applied here too. He identifies,

> "four implicit strategies which institutions use to keep uncomfortable knowledge at bay: denial, dismissal, diversion, and displacement." (Steve Rayner, *Uncomfortable Knowledge: The Social Construction of Ignorance in Science and Environmental Policy Discourses*)

All four strategies are relevant to our discussion here and we have seen some of these in operation already, although it isn't the purpose of this book to explore all of these in great detail.

When scientists attempt to explain the mind and consciousness, in evolutionary terms, a fairly limited range of options are typically used, for example:

1 Insist on reducing everything to the physical and

material, by claiming that the mind is just a physical phenomenon of neurons firing in our brains, the
sum of the chemical transactions that occur there – a
commitment to methodological naturalism no matter how absurd the outcome. (Denial)

2   Put the problem aside to solve later by unknown
means – insist on the priority of the existing paradigm and wait while using ad hoc explanations in the
interim. (Displacement)

3   Pretend the problem doesn't exist – a total commitment to the evolutionary paradigm to the point of
blindness. (Denial)

4 Resort to mysticism and make implausible explanations using circular reasoning, complicated terminology and other means of popular mystification – e.g.
we are here so it must have happened or attributing
to Random Chance a plan and intentions that it can't
have. (Diversion)

5   Pretend that science fiction is really science – e.g.
multi-verses and life being seeded on earth by aliens
(so called Panspermia). Neither explains anything, it
just displaces the explanation e.g. where did that life
originate? (Displacement)

Or more reasonably,

6 Accept that science needs other explanations that are
not just about natural causes if it is to be part of a coherent, credible explanation of the origin of life and
all dimensions of reality as we experience it.

Evolutionary science seeks only naturalistic, materialistic explanations of everything (i.e. reductionism) and if those ex-

planations are to be believed and credible, they must be able to explain phenomena such our consciousness and our minds; but they can't.

Up until about the 1870s the vast majority of scientists, including the great names of science, Isaac Newton, Michael Faraday, James Joule, Lord Kelvin and James Clerk Maxwell, accepted that beyond what science could explain there is a God. They saw no conflict because they did not try to seek only naturalistic explanations to questions, such as the origin of the universe and the origin of life, that excluded the possibility of God purely in principle. That did not make them naive, but entirely rational. (Many authors have noted this, see for example, Stephen Meyer, *Darwin's Doubt*).

Life is not just physics and chemistry. You know that because you are reading this and forming a view as to whether you agree with me. My communication to you through the words on this page is meaningful whether you agree with what I write or not. If this is translated into another language or read aloud the information can still get across to you. If you are blind, you could read it in Braille. So, the information is not the same as the code by which it is recorded and shared, or the carrier used to convey it, whether that code is English, French or Chinese and the carrier is the printed page, Braille, a computer screen or an audio recording. The information is still communicated. So, information exists as a distinct category of reality, independent of physical reality. It is a powerful example of non-material reality (or the supra-physical or metaphysical). Evolution can't explain this because it assumes strict materialism; only naturalistic explanations are allowed. The assumption of strict materialism is central to evolution, but easily falsified. It is surprising that its falsification is so simple. Various scientists have made this point, John Baumgardner made it well in the edited collection of essays, *In Six Days, Why*

Non-material reality exists, and we all experience it. So how did it come about? The mind is a powerful example of this. We are a very long way from understanding what the mind is, as opposed to just the biology and chemistry of the brain (which we also know little about), yet it is a defining characteristic of what it means to be human. Even critics of this claim disprove themselves by arguing against it; they have a mind and are willing to use it to argue with those who disagree with them. Clearly our minds are not directly controlled by our brain chemistry. Those who insist, despite the evidence, that the mind is only the result of the chemistry in our brains, are not many steps from then identifying those who disagree with them as "malfunctioning" and in need of "correction". We have seen where that leads in Stalin's Russia and communist China.

If strict materialism is true and if evolution is true, then our very thoughts can only be the result of chemical transactions in the brain and nothing else. They are then not in any meaningful sense thoughts at all, but some form of irrational random phenomena, because randomness is the only mechanism available to evolution in explaining anything. We then know nothing, have explained nothing, and can communicate nothing, because abstract conceptual thought has no means for existing. This book becomes just dots on a screen or lines on a page, or even less than that. Meaning, argument, discussion; all cease to exist.

If you remember back to the discussion of what Natural Selection and random mutation can or can't actually achieve at the level of the cell, as explored by the work of Michael Behe, Douglas Axe and others, it was shown to allow adaptation (mostly involving the loss of genetic information) but not the development of complex structures at the biochemical and cellular level. The brain is surely the most complex structure. Behe concludes,

> "Darwin's mechanism can't begin to make a comparatively simple bacterial flagellum, let alone the human brain. Thus all of the intellectual work built on that vaporous foundation falls with it." (Michael Behe, *Darwin Devolves, The New Science About DNA That Challenges Evolution*, page 274)

The evolutionists' great mission to share this discovery of strict materialism (actually just an unwarranted assumption) as the basis for an explanation of all of life is then self-contradictory and self-refuting. They assume that thought, meaning, reason, communication, are rational, reasonable and achievable but have no basis for doing so. For the adherent of strict materialism, even the tools with which they have sought to explain their own reason cease to exist, and with their passing, all possibility of knowing anything.

As C.S. Lewis put it,

> "I grew up believing in this (Evolution) Myth and I have felt – I still feel – it's almost perfect grandeur. Let no-one say we are an unimaginative age: neither Greeks nor the Norsemen ever invented a better story. But the Myth asks me to believe that reason is simply the unforeseen and unintended by-product of a mindless process at one stage of its endless and aimless becoming. The content of the Myth thus knocks from under me the only ground on which I could possibly believe the Myth to be true. If my own mind is a product of the irrational, how shall I trust my mind when it tells me about Evolution?" (C.S. Lewis, *Christian Reflections,* page 89)

Thomas Nagel argues the same point,

"Evolutionary naturalism provides an account of our capacities that undermines their reliability, and in doing so undermines itself." (Thomas Nagel, *Mind and Cosmos, Why the Materialist Neo-Darwinian Conception of Nature is Almost Certainly False,* page 27). In fact, "Evolutionary naturalism implies that we shouldn't take any of our convictions seriously, including the scientific world picture on which evolutionary naturalism itself depends.", (Thomas Nagel, *Mind and Cosmos, Why the Materialist Neo-Darwinian Conception of Nature is Almost Certainly False,* page 28)

Michael Behe takes it further to its logical conclusion,

"As the history and philosophy of science has shown in the last 150 years, when we lose the ability to recognize the work of another mind in the powerfully purposeful arrangements of nature, we lose the ability to recognize even our own minds." (Michael Behe, *Darwin Devolves, The New Science About DNA That Challenges Evolution,* page 275)

It might shock you even more to note that Darwin also saw something of this problem,

"But then with me the horrid doubt always arises whether the convictions of man's mind, which has been developed from the mind of lower animals, are of any value or at all trustworthy. Would anyone trust in the convictions of a monkey's mind, if there are any convictions in such a mind?" (Charles Darwin letter to William Graham, July 3, 1881, *Darwin correspondence project,* www.darwinproject.ac.uk/letter/ DCP-LETT-13230.xml quoted in Michael Behe, *Darwin Devolves, The New Science About DNA That Chal-*

lenges Evolution, page 269)

'How could it have come to this?' we ask over and over again.

> "Failure to recognize the conspicuous explanation for life is due wholly to the explicit denial by evolutionary biology and other contemporary scholarly disciplines of the necessary foundation for any kind of knowledge – that mind is real." (Michael Behe, *Darwin Devolves, The New Science About DNA That Challenges Evolution,* page 257)

You could sum up the situation as losing your mind!

This chapter is called 'Mind the Gap'; we must remember that Mind is one of the greatest gaps in evolutionary explanations.

The fact that a narrow strict materialism cannot explain the mind leads rapidly into a wider critique of scientific materialism, that inevitably undermines Darwin's ideas and the Neo-Darwinian worldview. This has been argued by an increasing number of scholars in the last 20 years. The philosopher Thomas Nagel is just one example. Starting from the phenomena of the mind he argues the inadequacy of Darwinian ideas that are based on strict materialism, not because he is trying to argue for the existence of God, but simply because the ideas in themselves do not make sense. Thus, he concludes that the Darwinian explanation of life and the mind is too unbelievable and is;

> "a heroic triumph of ideological theory over common sense. The empirical evidence can be interpreted to accommodate different comprehensive theories, but in this case the cost in conceptual and probabilistic contortions is prohibitive. I would be willing to bet that the present right-thinking consensus will come to seem laughable in a generation or two – though of

course it may be replaced by a new consensus that is just as invalid. The human will to believe is inexhaustible." (Thomas Nagel, *Mind and Cosmos: why the materialist and Neo-Darwinian conception of nature is almost certainly false,* page 128)

Or to put it in as plain language as possible, evolutionary explanations of life that claim that the physical world is all there is, are so weak that he believes we will look back at some point and simply laugh at such naïve and inadequate ideas.

From merely existing to morality

There are more dimensions to reality than just the physical. It is dangerous to pretend otherwise. We considered in a previous chapter that we all know that there is a sense of right and wrong within us. We know it is true. We also appreciate beauty. A process of evolution built on survival of the fittest does not lead to a complex moral sense within us, just to the triumph of the strong. It leads to brute force not great artistic achievement. It does not lead to an appreciation of the moral dimension of the universe. Indeed, it cannot explain a moral dimension, or the origin of moral law within us. It cannot explain our moral judgement that genocide is utterly evil and totally wrong, to take one extremely serious example.

The full title of Darwin's book foreshadowed how it would be received; *On the origin of species by means of natural selection, or the preservation of favoured races in the struggle for life.*

Taken at face value, Darwin's concept of the 'survival of the fittest' lead directly to Social Darwinism. The military leaders of Germany in the First World War believed in the "benefit" of war for "improving" humanity.

Darwin himself gave them plenty of reason to think that way.

His thoughts on protecting the weak rather than simply allowing the triumph of the strong, that is survival of the fittest, was not encouraging.

> "We build asylums for the imbecile, the maimed and the sick; we institute poor laws; and our medical men exert their utmost skill to save the life of every one to the last moment.... No one who has attended to the breeding of domestic animals will doubt that this must be highly injurious to the race of man." (Charles Darwin *The Descent of Man*, Part 1 page 134, cited in Tom Holland *Dominion, The Making of the Western Mind,* page 426)

He saw rather than one human race, many races with different levels of evolution.

> "The grade of their civilisation seems to be a most important element in the success of competing nations." (Charles Darwin *The Descent of Man*, Part 1 page 183, cited in Tom Holland *Dominion, The Making of the Western Mind,* page 427)

The Nazis later took the idea on to its logical conclusion attempting to remove those they described as 'lesser races'. 6.5 million victims of the gas ovens later, it is truly incredible that Darwin has any followers left. Yet the appalling legacy of Darwin's ideas is ignored, and evolution is popularly promoted as an explanation for almost everything.

> "One man - Charles Darwin - says: "In the struggle for survival, the fittest win out at the expense of their rivals..." Another man Adolf Hitler – says: Let us kill all the Jews of Europe.

> Is there a connection?

> Yes obviously is the answer of the historical record

and common sense.

> Published in 1859, Darwin's On the Origin of Species said nothing of substance about the origin of species. Or anything else, for that matter. It nonetheless persuaded scientists in England, Germany and the United States that human beings were accidents of creation. Where Darwin had seen species struggling for survival, German physicians, biologists, and professors saw races. They drew the obvious conclusion, the one that Darwin had already drawn. In the struggle for survival, the fittest win out at the expense of their rivals. German scientists took the word "expense" to mean what it meant: The annihilation of less fit races." (David Berlinski, *Connecting Hitler and Darwin* in *The Deniable Darwin*, page 503)

This same mentality built on Darwin's ideas fed racism across the world. From a Darwinian perspective people found it easy to see non-white people as "less developed races", and then treat them as inferior or even less than human with terrible consequences from hunting Hottentots as though they were wildlife to denying the Sami full participation in the modern economy. The mind set was pervasive and corrosive. Even in the early Twentieth Century a young Pygmy man Ota Benga was kept in the ape cages at New York Zoo as a visitor attraction. (Pamela Newkirk, *Spectacle, The astonishing life of Ota Benga*).

You may think it harsh to make such criticism of Darwin's ideas, but there is no coherent evolutionary basis for an explanation of important aspects of our existence such as morality, and the whole-hearted adoption of evolutionary thinking has opened the door to almost unimaginable evil. Truly it is not an adequate basis for a civilised worldview.

Evolution is promoted as the foundational paradigm of biology, geology, astronomy, in fact the whole secular world view and it has been defended aggressively. Yet, if evolution is not founded on indisputable evidence, and there is good evidence that it is not possible, why is it still believed?

We have considered this question from various angles. At this point it is worth noting that it seems belief in evolution is held in place by enough people reinforcing their mutual support for one another's belief in it. That makes belief in evolution a social and cultural phenomenon sustained by peer pressure. It would seem that if "everyone" else thinks that science through evolution explains everything, then "it must be true". Plus, many people have too much invested in it; emotionally, psychologically, and for its key promoters, reputations and careers too.

This makes evolution the great origins myth of modernity, not undeniable "scientific fact."

When we look at the immense unknowns or gaps in knowledge in the evolutionary paradigm, when we line them up starkly one after another, it becomes clear that what is labelled "science" is in reality, weak philosophy or even religion. Why pretend that science can answer all our questions including about origins? The over-reach of science is breath taking.

The table *Origins unexplained by evolution*, at the end of this chapter sums up some of the major problems for evolutionary explanations of the origin of life and the world around us that we are examining. It highlights what is left unexplained by evolution or just simply assumed without explanation and thus taken for granted. It also offers some refuting evidence that shows the evolutionary explanation or claims to be inadequate or incorrect.

In the suggested further reading section, a good place to start would be, *'Can Science Explain Everything?'* by John Lennox. Other sources are also suggested, to read into these questions in much more depth.

However, don't forget this crucial point; science has a massive over-reach from what it can meaningfully address into other areas including morality and philosophy, where its methods tell us near to nothing.

If evolution is not a proven fact, but a troublingly undermined theory, then that has consequences many do not want to face. The most obvious of which is that we must look elsewhere for answers to many of our most fundamental questions such as:

Where did we come from? Who are we? And how should we live?

An evolutionary framework cannot explain all the dimensions of reality as we experience it

> "Where were you when I laid the earth's foundation? Tell me if you understand. Who marked off its dimensions? Surely you know!"

> Job being questioned by God in the book of Job 38 vs 4

Origins unexplained by evolution

Evolution's claims	Unexplained	Refuting evidence
		Some examples
Material reality _The sphere of evolutionary explanations –_ _natural causes alone_ Origin of the Universe **The Big Bang** The Universe made itself Order arose from an explosion	What came before the origin of the Universe? Something from nothing? Laws, limits, structure	All causes must have an initial cause Laws precede what they control Nothing is not some kind of something Fine-tuning of Cosmos We see design everywhere not random chaos
The First cell Chemicals randomly associated together to make proteins and enzymes necessary for life (Chemical evolution) The chemicals for life randomly came together to make the first cell	Origin of the chemicals for life Origin and capture of information in DNA Interdependent organisation of the parts of the cell	Random chance cannot create enzymes and proteins Chemical space too large, not enough time for chance to work DNA information sequence not determined by its chemistry Irreducible Complexity at many levels
All life Beneficial mutations accumulated by chance alone making a tree of life (Biological evolution)	Survival of incomplete cells and incomplete organisms Capture and accumulation and passing on of genetic information	Functional coherence across a hierarchy of levels: cells – organs – creatures Natural Selection has no plan or agency Absence of intermediate fossils Rate of genetic change too slow, insufficient generations
Non-material reality _Beyond evolutionary explanations_	Consciousness and the mind The world of concepts, including morality	We know and experience non-material reality: love, free will, beauty, hope and despair

17 THE IMPOSSIBLE PUZZLE

The pieces that just don't fit

We have all no doubt tried solving jigsaw puzzles. Children often go through a phase when they are fascinated by them. The simplest puzzles take minutes, the toughest days. However, one rule of thumb applies to all puzzles no matter how good you are at solving them; they become much harder to solve if there are pieces missing. It becomes much harder again if you don't have the picture of what the final result should look like. In that scenario, to solve the puzzle, you will have to imagine what the whole picture might be from what you can see in the pieces, then refine that mental picture as more pieces fit together. It might be a rose covered cottage and flower filled garden, or a mountain landscape. As you progress, the pieces that don't fit the picture are examined and put to one side, with the assumption that they will fit later.

Now imagine if you have only some of the pieces and they are in the wrong box, with the wrong picture on it. Since they have recurring shapes, they will seem to fit together and every time a piece fits there is a great cheer that goes up from fellow puzzlers as they keep faith that eventually all the pieces will be made to fit into reproducing the picture on the box. Meantime the pile of pieces that don't fit keeps getting larger and larger. Even worse, many of those pieces are of a shape and pattern that has no chance of ever connecting with the partial picture in front of you on the table, as you puzzle on.

Most rational people would at some point stop working on the picture they had been thinking they would make and start looking more closely at the pieces that were put aside to see if there is any possibility that they might form into a different picture. Then with time, even the pieces from their first attempt might turn out to fit much better in the new picture. Many scientists have done this and stopped seeing evolution as the undisputed explanation of the origin of life and all of reality as we experience it.

After a century and a half of insisting that evolution is the overall picture and cheering every time a small piece of evidence appears as though it may fit that picture, the mountain of evidence that can't fit has grown much larger than Darwin and others could have predicted, or perhaps feared.

In previous chapters we have looked at how the evidence from science, taken purely on its own terms, has undermined any evolutionary explanation of life. In this chapter we return to considering whether we should in fact let science set the terms for how such questions should be addressed. The whole enterprise of seeking only naturalistic explanations for all of reality must be questioned. This debate can only be ignored if we maintain a commitment to the basic pre-suppositions of evolutionary science, regardless of the consequences for what we can know and explain.

So often, arguments stand or fall on their pre-suppositions.

Evolutionary explanations of the origin and development of all life are couched in the firm assumption that there can only be naturalistic explanations, with no input by God in anyway. This has been labelled, strict materialism or methodological naturalism, but the terminology can obscure the simple point; evolution seeks to explain the existence of all life by only natural means. We considered some of the problems with that approach when discussing what led Anthony Flew from atheism to accept the existence of God and we discussed the problems it causes science in its own terms when it tries to explain the origin of life.

We will now look again at some of these problems with evolutionary explanations in a broader critique that does not just take evolutionary science on its own terms, because there are good reasons why we shouldn't.

This jigsaw making analogy has more relevance than you might imagine at first sight. We will look at what has been left out, how what is included is looked at very selectively and how framing a strictly materialistic picture (with no place for God or any other non-material reality) leaves so much outside of the frame of explanation that it undermines itself, because even the enterprise of doing science can't happen in any form without recourse to things which an evolutionary framework can't explain.

Scientists approach the process of collecting evidence (like the puzzle pieces) with an idea in mind of what the overall picture should look like, for example, 'evolution from molecules to man'. This is what may be called theory-laden observation. As a consequence, they focus on the pieces they think will fit and set the others aside. Or, worse still they define as "pieces" those they think will fit and define as "not pieces", those they are sure won't; those pieces of evidence they insist should never be considered as pieces of the puzzle at all. In the most extreme cases they simply deny their existence.

Here is a real beauty. Dinosaurs are claimed to have been fossilised millions of years ago. Therefore, no organic material should exist in dinosaur fossils, it would degrade too quickly. There is no prospect of it surviving for millions of years. However, multiple reports have been made of finding soft tissue in fossils.

John Walton discusses some of the discoveries,

> "Some of the most remarkable finds were made at a site in Christian Malford, Wiltshire (UK) by Dr Philip Wilby and his team. These excavations in Jurassic Oxford clay (145-201 Ma BP) yielded "thousands of exquisitely preserved ammonites, fish and crustaceans." The team reported collecting two crustaceans, three fish and eight coleoids (squid-like creatures) with soft parts. A cephalopod ink sac and duct with impressions of blood vessels was also obtained. "In all cases the soft parts are preserved with exquisite precision, providing tantalizing glimpses of how they functioned." A section through the wall of one coleoid revealed a complex arrangement of muscle fibres. The Times of August 19, 2009 published a remarkable picture of the tiny fossil squid alongside a sketch of the squid drawn by an artist with the squid's own fossil ink!" (John Walton, *Compact Time, A Short History of Life on Earth,* page 113)

> "Know how from laboratory work with tissues, proteins and DNA is emphatic that these fragile materials can't survive natural degradative processes for millions of years. The findings of well preserved and bona fida soft tissues and biopolymers in dinosaur

fossils are therefore ground-breaking. They are formidable evidence that these fossils can't be millions of years old." (John Walton, *Compact Time, A Short History of Life on Earth*, page 121)

What do evolutionists do with this evidence?

The response of those committed to the evolutionary view of extremely long timescales is to,

"either ignore the fossil soft tissue evidence, or claim that it's proof that tissues, proteins and DNA actually degrade orders of magnitude more slowly than the chemistry permits." (John Walton, *Compact Time, A Short History of Life on Earth*, page 110.

This is known as framing of the problem. The theory is conceived and the evidence to support it is collected in such a way as to maximize the support for the theory. Evidence that won't fit is ignored, or explained away with ad hoc explanations, or shelved until it can be made to fit the theory; the denial, displacement and diversion we saw previously. Yet science is sold as "objective"!

Here is another powerful example. Helium is produced from the radioactive decay of Uranium. Helium is a noble gas and not very reactive chemically. Helium is also a very small atom and readily migrates through a crystal lattice. In solidifying magma, uranium concentrates in Zircon crystals in granite. The radiometric age for the rocks can be more than a billion years based on measuring present radiometric decay rates of uranium and projecting backwards. Yet,

"Amazingly, most of the radiogenic helium from this decay process is also present within these crystals, that are typically only a few millimetres across. However, based on experimentally measured helium diffusion rates, the zircon helium content implies a time span of only a few thousand years since the majority of the nuclear decay occurred." (John Baumgardner, *In Six Days, Why 50 Scientists Choose to Believe in Creation*, page 217)

Given the age of the rock, assigned to it by radiometric dating, the helium should have diffused away, but it hasn't. Those committed to radio-metric dating as "proof" of long ages for rocks basically ignore or try to explain away the difference. But we have a problem.

"So, which physical process is more trustworthy – the diffusion of a noble gas in a crystalline lattice or the radioactive decay of an unstable isotope? Both processes can be investigated today in great detail in the laboratory. Both the rate of helium diffusion and the rate of decay of uranium to lead can be determined with high degrees of precision. But these two physical processes yield wildly disparate estimates for the age of the same granite rock." (John Baumgardner, *In Six Days, Why 50 Scientists Choose to Believe in Creation*, page 219)

John Baumgardner suggests that the problem probably lies in,

"extrapolating as constant presently measured rates of nuclear decay into the remote past. If this is the error, then radiometric methods based on presently measured rates simply do not and cannot provide correct estimates for geologic age." (John Baumgardner, *In Six Days, Why 50 Scientists Choose to Believe in Creation*, page 219)

We can reasonably ask, which is potentially subject to the greater error, an extrapolation over a few thousand years or one over more than a billion?

The obvious conclusion is that knowledge produced by science as "certain", such as the age of rocks, is always tentative and contingent. However, evolutionists set aside the ages produced by dating methods that give shorter time spans and favour those that give longer ones.

So, evolutionists are picky as to what evidence they admit because it has to fit the pre-existing theory in their minds.

Phillip Johnson puts it this way,

> "There is an important difference between going to the empirical evidence to test a doubtful theory against some plausible alternative, and going to the evidence to look for confirmation of the only theory that one is willing to tolerate." (*Darwin on Trial*, Page 49)

Let's run through what we are claiming in a little more detail. This book has been written with a range of audiences in mind, so don't worry if this slightly fuller discussion sounds a bit more technical, it is included because it will help some readers.

We must repeat that there is no naive pure scientific observation, it is always done within a framework of understanding. There is no "truth in nature" to discover. All scientific observations are theoretical, not raw brute facts. For example, when you pick up a rock it does not have an age of manufacture stamped on it, its age is inferred from properties of it that we measure, or by its relationship to other rocks we believe we have a date for.

Scientists deriving long ages dates are not upfront about their presuppositions and how those affect what they look for, how they do so, and what they then see. They do their science within a shared worldview along with all its assumptions and presuppositions. Their assumptions include:

- That the physical is all there is
- That there is a continuity of cause and effect unbroken from the beginning of the Big Bang until now
- That present processes can be extrapolated into the past

The outcome is that dating the age of the earth and rocks is treated as a matter merely of which methods to use (methodology). Dating methods are then applied selectively, because they "know" (or in reality assume or have decided in advance) that methods giving a short timespan are wrong because they do not fit their presupposition of very long ages.

Yet, if questions of dating were approached with no presuppositions about cosmology or any long ages worldview, we would find that different methods give wildly differing ages from thousands to millions to billions of years. Without a basis to discount the "wrong" answers giving short time spans we would be left simply knowing that the enterprise of dating the age of rocks is highly problematic and that it may not be possible to definitively resolve the question from scientific observation and modelling alone.

When applying methods to dating, deeper questions around the nature of reality (ontology) and the basis of meaning (epistemology) are ignored as irrelevant. Yet this is not the case. For example, as we have noted elsewhere, models of the origin of the universe and thus its age, are held in the *minds* of physicists, those minds being more than a merely physical phenomenon, undermining their assumption of strict materialism or methodological naturalism. So, as they do the science, scientists are demonstrating their selective view of and understanding of reality, by insisting that dating is only a matter of which method to choose, whilst remaining unable to explain their own independent non-material minds that are enabling them to do the research in the first place and make those choices.

They then use the results of their dating method to justify their worldview (cosmology) whereas in fact they have addressed only parts of the complete picture of our knowledge of the natural world and how it is derived. It is a slight of hand that most involved in doing the science do not themselves notice. However, when it is questioned, they typically insist on the pre-eminence of their prior assumptions and methodology and refuse to engage with the objection, they just repeat their methods as if those methods justify all their other beliefs and claims, but no method can. Methods arise from a worldview they cannot prove it.

Thus, the enterprise of dating rocks is framed by a secular evolutionary worldview with its many embedded assumptions, that does not address essential questions of the basis of knowing and the nature of reality, (epistemology and ontology). That worldview then supports selectively chosen methods (methodology) that give the "right" answer that are then used to justify the complete metaphysical framework from cosmology downwards i.e. their complete worldview. It is an elegant exercise in selective and then circular reasoning. But methods do not in fact justify all those other presuppositions and claims, they flow from them.

I am convinced that if looked at dispassionately without a prior commitment to a long-ages view, most people would give up on dating as a hopeless cause because the range of methods available yield such wildly disparate ages, and it becomes clear that we don't have an ultimate basis for knowing which is the right answer in purely scientific terms.

Those committed to a long-ages view do their science within

that framework then announce that their science has validated their assumptions; well, what a surprise! If any doubts creep in, they then rely on force of numbers – everyone else agrees with us. The science of dating is thus revealed to be a social phenomenon not a scientific one. Its final knowledge claim is therefore,

> "We have decided to agree that the earth and the universe are extremely old,"

but it is sold to the public as,

> "The science objectively tells us that the earth and the universe are extremely old,"

as though scientists had no hand in the answer.

Clearly people involved in such a process are unlikely to face up to what is really going on when the consensus they contribute to is so loud all around them; echo chambers don't contradict the ones doing the shouting!

They also assess the implications of the answers they derive as too important to be cast into any doubt and shut down any differing view. The consensus for long-ages matters because it is considered to be essential for the evolutionary story to be able to be true. The final irony is that even with the long ages they believe they have proven, there hasn't been enough time for evolution to have happened anyway as we have discussed elsewhere. Such bittersweet irony.

Why should science operate in this apparently un-objective way? Well, it often takes outsiders to see the situation with clarity. Phillip Johnson's book is referred to extensively in this discussion because it is accessible for non-scientists. He also brings a valuable perspective as a lawyer used to testing evidence and spotting when things don't add up. His comments on the operation of science in this apparently odd way that we have noted, is built on substantial work by Thomas Kuhn in *The Structure of Scientific Revolutions* and other sociologists looking at the nature of scientific knowledge and how it comes about. Kuhn labelled the set of ideas that become the great organising ideas of a scientific community its "Paradigm".

Michael Denton in his book *'Evolution a Theory in Crisis'* also discusses why scientists cling to Darwinian evolution and calls it *"the priority of paradigm"*, using Kuhn's terminology. Science operates within a set of shared ideas and assumptions; the paradigm, within which it builds theories and models. New evidence is interpreted within the understanding of that paradigm. When evidence stubbornly doesn't fit the paradigm, it tends to be ignored, overlooked, put aside or in some way marginalised until there is such a weight of evidence that the theories and ideas are re-evaluated and the paradigm is adjusted to account for that evidence (or so the story goes). Interestingly, the switch to a new paradigm, a new shared way of thinking, does not typically come from people who are within and defending the existing one. In the meantime, the paradigm is defended vigorously or even aggressively as the nearest thing to "truth" that scientists have in that field of study.

Kuhn was fascinated by how new ideas arose and how scientists behaved and responded to new and challenging ideas and theories, because it is so clearly a social process not merely a technical one. Once the paradigm is well established science operates within it. That is how you get your PhD degree, that is how you get research grants and get published and achieve career progress, in short once you are co-opted into "doing science" you had better do it within the paradigm because that is what puts bread on the table.

"A paradigm is not merely a hypothesis, which can

be discarded if it fails a single experimental test; it is a way of looking at the world, or some part of it, and scientists understand even the anomalies in its terms. According to Kuhn, anomalies by themselves never falsify a paradigm, because its defenders can resort to ad hoc hypotheses to accommodate any potentially disconfirming evidence. A paradigm rules until it is replaced with another paradigm, because "to reject one paradigm is to reject science itself."" (Phillip Johnson, *Darwin on Trial*, page 151)

This would suggest that merely pointing out all the evidence that doesn't fit will have no effect on convincing many scientists to change their minds, because it would be a rejection of their whole worldview with potentially devastating psychological implications. It really is that big a thing. Johnson, captures the situation well,

"It is therefore not as exceptional as it may have appeared that distinguished scientists have praised Darwin's theory as a profound tautology, or declared it to be a logically self-evident proposition requiring no empirical confirmation. A tautology of logical inevitability is precisely what it appears to be: it describes a situation that could not conceivably have been otherwise. From this perspective, "disconfirming" evidence is profoundly uninteresting." (Phillip Johnson, *Darwin on Trial*, page 151)

The less polite way of putting it would be to say that many scientists have closed minds on the matter of evolution and origins and have no intention whatsoever of letting the evidence from the world around them persuade them to hold any different point of view, their pre-suppositions take precedence over evidence.

I must assume that you dear reader are however interested in the evidence that is "disconfirming" or doesn't fit, which is why we have looked at what constitutes such "uncomfortable knowledge".

Science is about theories and models. We must say yet again, observations made by scientists are informed by the theories and models they are working with. There is no naive pure observation in science, it always happens in a context.

> "In scientific practice, the theory normally precedes the experiment or fact-gathering process rather than the other way around. In Popper's words, "Observation is always selective. It needs a chosen object, a definite task, an interest, a point of view, a problem." Without a theory, scientists would not know how to design experiments, or where to look for important data." (Phillip Johnson, *Darwin on Trial,* page 181)

Yet, for a theory to be convincing it needs to account for all the evidence, not just some of it. That does not mean that it needs to explain everything, that is a false hope, but it must not wilfully ignore great bodies of evidence that clearly ought to be able to fit it, as though they don't exist.

What does this mean in practice as to how evolutionary science is conducted?

> ""Evolution" in Darwinist usage implies a completely naturalistic metaphysical system, in which matter evolved to its present state of organised complexity without any participation by a Creator. But "evolution" also refers to much more modest concepts, such as microevolution and biological relationship."

The outcome is that,

> "Because "evolution" means so many different things,

almost any example will do. The trick is to prove one of the modest meanings of the term and treat it as proof of the complete metaphysical system." (Phillip Johnson, *Darwin on Trial,* page 186)

The problem we have is that all the pieces need to be recognised and be able to fit in some form of coherent whole if the theory is correct. So, we must take account of the significant pieces that simply won't ever fit an evolutionary puzzle. Similarly, we must look at the large holes in the evolutionary picture and see if there is any prospect of them ever being filled.

Christian belief has been criticised as using God to fill the gaps in our understanding, the so called 'god of the gaps'. However, the evolutionary picture has immense gaps and the overall picture on the puzzle box, so to speak, is appealed to, to fill those gaps; don't look at the gaps, look at the pretty picture on the box. The theory is pre-eminent regardless of any evidence to the contrary and has become a vague notion to appeal to, to fill any gaps in the evidence. Thus, evolution has truly become 'the theory of the gaps'. (See Robert Carter (Ed), *Evolution's Achilles heels'*).

In fact, it gets worse than this; the absence of evidence has been held up as evidence, which is patently absurd.

"Improbability is to be expected as a result of natural selection; and we have the paradox that an exceedingly high apparent improbability in its products can be taken as evidence for the high degree of its efficacy." (Julian Huxley quoted by Phillip Johnson, *Darwin on Trial,* page 52). As Johnson puts it,

"On that basis the theory has nothing to fear from the evidence". (Phillip Johnson, *Darwin on Trial*)

If the universe is the result of an uncaused explosion and life developed by Random Chance alone, then the fact that we can talk about an overall picture and coherence to the whole runs directly against such assumptions of fundamental randomness. At a profound level, even the search for an over-arching evolutionary picture of life is inconsistent and incoherent in its own terms.

What logic or rationality is there in randomness?

What coherence in chance?

What picture is there to discover if there is no initial cause or overall intention?

At this point many people will still be pointing adamantly at the rather sketchy picture on the lid of a Victorian puzzle box signed by one C. Darwin, insisting that it must be right. Others will be prepared to put the battered old box down and consider what picture might be formed if we take all the pieces, not just a small selection and see how they might fit together and make sense.

It takes a while to think this through, however, once its implications are clear we can see that not only has science failed to find a purely naturalistic explanation of the origin and development of all life, it is doomed to fail. In fact, science alone can never achieve an explanation of the whole of reality as we experience it.

On the one hand we can note gaps in the evolutionary picture. On the other hand, we can see if we can form an alternative picture of the origins of life that is true to the evidence. It must include all the pieces and make a coherent picture; one of Design and an intentional outcome, rather than being the result of many random accidents of chance. It must offer a meaningful explanation of <u>all of reality</u> as we experience it.

If science is constrained to only materialistic explanations (e.g. natural causes alone), then it can't even explain itself, because to do so requires recourse to things it either denies exist or simply assumes without any basis for doing so

> "When I consider your heavens, the work of your fingers, the moon and the stars which you have set in place, what is man that you are mindful of him, the son of man that you care for him?"

David in Psalm 8 vs 3,4

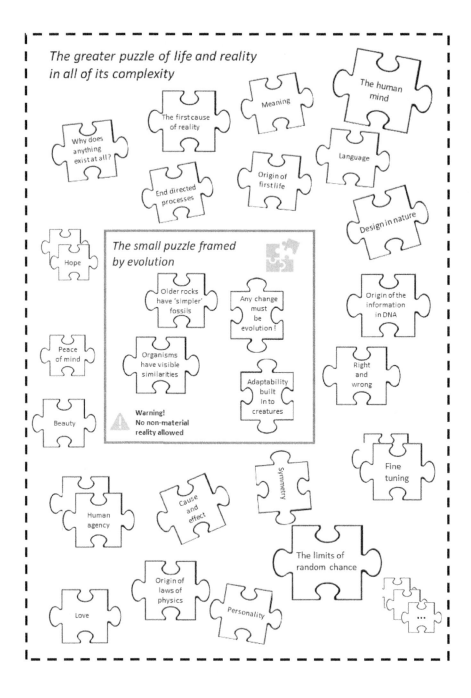

18 "WHO DONE IT?"

*Be careful you are solving
the right puzzle*

Detective work involves piecing together what evidence can be found to try to recreate events in the past. It proceeds according to rules of evidence. The claims it then makes are subject to testing in court and only when they have stood up to scrutiny does the version of events put forward by the prosecution get accepted. If a detective believes they are investigating an unfortunate death at sea and carefully traces the lost person's last movements and contacts and slowly builds as full a picture of events as possible but simply can't find conclusive evidence as to what has happened, they must always retain an open mind as to whether they are following the right line and not close the case. Further evidence may emerge that can change everything. It has transpired in several high-profile cases that the person who is claimed to have died has not in fact died but is living in another country and the family have colluded to claim the life insurance. When they suddenly move to that country and appear to be living a life beyond their means suspicion is aroused. Then tracing their movements, the "dead" person is suddenly found again, and it becomes clear that the detective was solving the wrong case originally.

Using the jigsaw puzzle making analogy we can draw together the threads we have been looking at in several chapters. Those promoting evolution are engaged in building a limited little jigsaw where they have framed the problem in front of them so as to exclude many relevant pieces, to try to maximise the chances of the pieces they do accept as valid, fitting together. If we analyse their enterprise on its own terms, it breaks down. We have looked at several lines of evidence that demonstrate that. They are solving the wrong puzzle.

We must take the critique a crucial stage further. Ironically, outside the puzzle that they are crowded around working on, are pieces that are essential to their whole enterprise of making any kind of puzzle, and without which they could do nothing. Their limited (and incomplete and failing) puzzle cannot even be conceived without beings (as opposed to non-being), mind, language, human agency, symmetry, an acceptance of the existence of Design at some level and cause and effect, to name some of the main phenomena of relevance. We looked at some of these.

And these are not trivial. Each could be a very lengthy and interesting discussion in its own right.

Without all of these things there is no science, no scientists, and no possibility of attempting an evolutionary explanation of anything. These are not irrelevant pieces of the picture that can be explained later. They are part of the very fabric of existence, and they demand coherent explanation in their own right. They cannot be just taken for granted whilst a very modest, tightly constrained picture is constructed, they must be within the frame too, so to speak. The diagram at the end of the previous chapter, "The small puzzle framed by evolution" sums up this problem. The small puzzle evolutionists have framed and are trying to solve is contrasted with the greater puzzle of the whole of reality.

It is vital that we note that an explanation of the world of things has to be undertaken in the world of concepts. Science has enough problems explaining the world of things in its totality. **However, when it comes to origins, an explanation of the world of things that cannot also explain the world of concepts, has, in fact, explained nothing at all**.

What can we say then? Evolution with its commitment to purely naturalistic explanations, tries to constrain the discussion of origins to only the physical and material, but even the enterprise of making those claims exists in the realm of concepts and ideas which lie outside the physical and material.

Therefore, the discussion of origins will inevitably stray elsewhere to philosophy and religious explanations, as it always has since time immemorial, because it must. No matter how much that may not be to anyone's liking it, is inevitable.

The evolutionary picture of origins and thus of all of reality, (for consideration of the one inevitably leads to the other), is like giving a small child paper, crayons and a picture to copy for them to turn around excited and say, *"Look at the picture I have made!"* Yes, they have, but it hasn't even entered their mind that they have a thing called a mind with which they have done this feat, or that the paper has to come from somewhere, or that crayons don't just spontaneously arise when needed. At some point a beautiful moment of profound realisation occurs when they ask, *"Daddy, where does paper come from?"* We hope that much later in their development they will ponder deeper questions as to what creativity is, and how they happen to have an independent mind.

Frankly, too many proponents of evolution are stuck at the

stage of not wondering very deeply where the paper has come from, so to speak, and they rarely seem to have the critical self-awareness to reflect on the questions of what constitutes a mind and how they happen to have one, and how they exercise genuine human agency and are able to communicate anything of their enterprise at all, or why the world around them is rationally organised and comprehensible. One can imagine the Designer and Creator of the universe looking on with deep sadness and incredible pity.

Where have we got to? Evolution's proponents frame too limited a problem, are selective about what evidence is included as relevant or valid and yet do so with recourse to using many of the things that are "outside the box". Clearly that is totally unsatisfactory.

If evolution by Random Chance 'directed' by Natural Selection as the means of agency to achieve Design, is the best explanation science can offer for the origin of life and reality as we experience it, then I would suggest that we should consider whether science is the right way to find answers to such questions at all.

It turns out that the problem we are facing is surprisingly straight forward after all. If we take the question of where everything originates from, then the problem in insisting that science, invoking evolution, is able to provide the answer, is easily exposed as a hopeless cause. To do so is to seek an answer in the wrong category. A strictly materialistic explanation based on scientific observation, will never be able to explain the origins of life and subsequently all of reality, because it must ignore so many dimensions of the reality that it operates within. It is a category error.

If you want to know whether someone really loves you, a forensic examination of their first days of life in a neo-natal ward will tell you nothing. A compilation of their lifetime dietary records will yield no further information of value. Empirical, material data may give hints, but will not get to the question, *'Do they actually love me?'* We all know that other categories of reality exist, it is absurd to argue otherwise. (See Lennox, *Can Science Explain Everything?* and *Gunning for God; Why The New Atheists are Missing the Mark*).

The question of where everything came from (including physical things and concepts; mind and matter) is not primarily a scientific one and science's methods turn out to be impotent on the matter. The fact that it has been wrongly framed as if it were a purely scientific problem should not prevent us from seeing the situation for what it is.

No scientist can go back in time to before the origin of the universe to observe it coming into being, so it is inevitably a philosophical and religious question to consider where it came from, not merely a scientific one. Scientific observation within the existing universe will be constrained to that which is within it. It literally can't see what came before.

When the problem is addressed in those terms, then the answers that Christian belief offers can be seen to make sense. It's not that they should be seen as non-scientific answers and thus somehow inferior. Rather the question of origins should be recognised as not primarily a scientific question after all.

So, we must be very careful of the terms on which we might be tempted to reject out of hand the answers that inform the Christian world view.

When it comes to explaining the existence and phenomena of our minds, we have seen that an evolutionary explanation simply doesn't make sense. The promise of a reasonable evolutionary explanation has been held out in front of us for so long, but it never comes, because it can't. Random Chance will never explain the phenomena of the mind, no matter how long we are told to wait. The mind is inherently a meta-physical phenomenon, and therefore requires at least in part, a meta-physical explanation, which is off-limits to evolution.

So, a Christian explanation that is inherently meta-physical (i.e. we have a mind because God who is the ultimate mind made us that way) is not an inferior or invalid explanation. It is in fact exactly the category of explanation that the phenomenon of the mind itself deserves. It is exactly the type of answer that inherently has a chance of being right.

We have considered evolution from a range of perspectives. The discussion could be much longer, but the critical thing to remember is that once we have shown that evolution from nothing to all life today by random undirected chance could not have happened, the theory has lost its power. I hope it will lose its grip on your mind as it has on so many others before you.

It is perhaps worth taking away with you the images discussed in these few chapters on evolution and origins:

> An atheist who ceased to exist (so to speak), because he followed the evidence that science itself has provided and came to a belief in God.

> An ancient time keeping device found on the seabed and an ancient city emerging from the jungle, because we recognise Design when we see it.

> Scientists leaping across vast gaps in their imagination, that no-one has the faintest idea if, or how, they may have been crossed in reality, by purely natural means.

> A make-belief game of Cosmic Lego, because there is

no known means to make the building blocks of life in the first place, from which everything else is then made.

A Design manual (called Natural Selection) with no mechanism for making any new life at all.

A long chain broken at every link, because every uncrossable gap is a gap that wasn't crossed in the evolutionary story of life.

A record of life literally set in stone, because the rocks with fossils do not show the record of endless small changes that evolution needs - anywhere that we have looked.

"Mind the gap, Mind the gap", because there are multiple gaps that evolutionary explanations cannot cross, not the least of which is the existence of our minds and the moral dimension of existence we all experience.

A group of people crowded round a Victorian jigsaw puzzle trying to make a very tightly constrained picture, while setting to one side a huge pile of pieces that will never fit the picture that they are trying to make. Which is tragic because they can't even set about making any kind of puzzle without recourse to things they refuse to include in their puzzle.

And finally,

A puzzle that turns out to be a search for 'Who done it?' rather than just a physical jigsaw puzzle, because the real question is; 'Who made everything?', not, 'How did everything make itself?'

Secularism and evolution are inextricably linked. Evolution has offered to answer the question; Where did we all come from? and secularism has grasped it with enthusiasm. It appears to fit so well with at least broad agnosticism, or otherwise outright atheism.

Yet now that we see that science through evolution has not been capable of answering that question, where does that leave secularism? Well, as a minimum, knowing much less than it thought and able to explain very little of life at all. Given that such a position is so unsatisfactory, isn't it worth considering other answers?

The more you read into the critiques of evolution the weaker it appears. The fact that the prevailing secular consensus presently believes evolution to be unassailable "truth" should not deter anyone from rejecting its claim that all of reality including us arose by chance alone. Evolution is not a convincing reason to set aside belief in God nor a reason to avoid exploring the basis for belief in God. In fact, when you see the weaknesses in evolutionary ideas, they compel us to seek out the truth about God and His actions.

This brings us back full circle to where we were at the beginning of this discussion some chapters ago. We have extremely limited scientific knowledge on the origins of life and indeed of the origins of all that exists, but exactly how it all came into being remains a significantly less important question than who caused it to be.

Once we see that evolution can't explain life, no matter how long it is given, there is no reason not to consider the possibility that God made everything from nothing, and quite frankly, that He might do so in six days if He so chose. Limiting omnipotence becomes logically incoherent. (See Genesis chapter

1)

We have spent quite a bit of time showing the weaknesses of evolutionary explanations, because in my experience evolution is one of the main reasons secular people dismiss the claims of Christianity and one of the main reasons people cite for a loss of faith. It turns out it provides no such basis for ignoring or supplanting Christian belief after all. In fact, if evolution has previously shaken your faith, take heart, it has no basis for doing so.

We have spent less time on some other barriers to belief because I have found them typically much less of a stumbling block to most people. For example, we simply noted that there is a moral dimension to our existence and have then moved on to what might be the cause of that, and thus we are seeking an adequate explanation for all aspects of reality as we experience them, the physical material world and the non-material reality we all know and participate in.

An explanation of the world of things, that cannot explain the world of concepts, has in fact explained nothing at all

In conclusion, all that we have considered so far comes back to this first and most fundamental point from which everything else flows:

> "In the beginning God created the heavens and the earth."
>
> Genesis 1 vs 1

PART 3 WHERE CAN WE FIND ANSWERS?

The way back to hope

19 WHAT DID THE VICTORIANS EVER DO FOR US?

*The big ideas that led
the world astray*

The Victorian era in Britain was one of profound social and cultural change that also went out from Britain affecting much of the world. The industrial revolution that had started not long before, turbo-charged the UK economy and the British Empire reached its height. Queen Victoria reigned as Queen of the United Kingdom of Great Britain, and a vast empire, from 1837 when she was 18 to 1901 when she died aged 81.

When a country has such economic success, it is too easy for people to assume its ideas must be right, for surely, they are successful aren't they? Colonialism, the empire, trade controlled by Britain for its own benefit and many other things were "right" because that's how they were; an unassailable logic for those on the convenient side of the argument.

When Victoria came to the throne Britain had only just passed the Abolition of Slavery Act in 1833 and it took a long time to fully implement. In the United States, President Lincoln issued the Emancipation Proclamation in 1863 and the Thirteenth Amendment to the Constitution was ratified in 1865. Great positive social change was happening.

However, when we look back, the Victorians believed a range of things that we now consider rather odd, or downright wrong. Queen Victoria was herself famous for taking a bath every month "whether she needed it or not"! It was then a commonly held view as the poet Robert Service expressed it much later, that "Too much washing weakens you". Poorer ordinary people may have bathed as infrequently as once a year. It was common to rub the skin with pig's fat before winter and then not take under clothes off, if possible, all winter and only wash face and hands.

There was a fashion for tight corsets for wealthier women, mostly made with whale bone reinforcements, to make women's waists as thin as possible. This had several nasty side effects. It squeezed women's internal organs and restricted blood supply making them susceptible to fainting. It also helped fuel the whaling industry that drove some species extinct and nearly wiped-out others.

There was a darker side to Victorian society too. Children were made to work in coal mines and sent up chimneys to clean them. Needless to say, these cruel practices killed a lot of children. Even when some people tried to do something "good" to help street children and orphans, it was not always exactly helpful. One of the less savoury schemes that arose was sending thousands of unaccompanied orphans abroad to the colonies, to residential schools or adoption, including to Canada and Australia, with little follow up or care for what happened to them.

It was also a period of development, or at least the popularisation of a range of ideas that have shaped the world since. It is no exaggeration to say that we still live within a world powerfully shaped by those Victorian ideas, they have entered the zeitgeist, or spirit of the times.

In 1859 Charles Darwin published his book, *'On the origin of species by means of Natural Selection, or the preservation of favoured races in the struggle for life',* to give it its full title as published.

Plenty of people were happy to take his title literally and found in Darwinism all they needed to view non-white, non-Europeans as inferior races. As mentioned in an earlier chapter, Darwin's ideas helped fuel the First World War with what has been called "Social Darwinism" and helped open the way for the holocaust, after all who were the *"favoured races"* if not those with the power to prove it in armed struggle? Whilst there have been efforts to protect or rescue Darwin's reputation, his work, simply read at face value did contribute to these horrors. It may not have been what he intended, but then again, can we absolve him and his ideas from all responsibility?

Evolutionary theory has become a cornerstone of the modern secular worldview, yet as we have seen at length in earlier chapters, there is very little evidence to sustain it, immense problems with what it cannot explain and many of the claims made about it are barely coherent.

Darwin's ideas also fuelled the rise of popular atheism. We have discussed that earlier, I will only repeat the quote from Roy Abraham Varghese,

"We have all the evidence we need in our immediate experience and only a deliberate refusal to look is responsible for atheism of any variety." (Cited in Anthony Flew, *'There is a God; How the World's Most Notorious Atheist Changed His Mind'*)

In 1867, Karl Marx published *'Das Kapital'*. He had formed his ideas living in Britain. The book laid the foundation for revolution and a new economic order in Russia, China and other countries. Many ideas of Communism/ Marxism ran directly counter to Christian beliefs, most obviously that the party is the highest authority, and that society and the party are what matters not individuals. So, it is no surprise that Communism was, and still is, a vicious persecutor of Christians. The Communists did not stop there however, hammering anyone who held to any belief that was not fully compliant with Communism, persecuting Muslims, Jews, Buddhists and others. Even today, in China, the government is determined to try to compel people to think in the way it approves with vast re-education camps. Freedom of conscience, freedom of thought, freedom of religion, freedom of speech, are all anathema to Communism. We also noted in an earlier chapter that Communism was responsible for a death toll of at least 94 million in the Twentieth Century. (Stephane Courtois et al, *'The Black book of communism'*)

On a range of other fronts, the Victorian era in Britain had a profound influence on the world, such as through the increased globalisation of production and consumption and all the fossil fuel use and pollution that went with it. I don't think Britain is to be uniquely blamed in this, wherever it led, other countries were close behind, or alongside.

Although much of the foundation of the secular worldview was laid out in the Victorian era, it had different consequences in different parts of the world. Many have wondered why Marx's ideas helped fuel revolutions elsewhere but did not trigger revolution and class war in Britain. I think that a major part of the answer is in the rise of popular Protestantism through the 1700s and 1800s including the Methodist revival that started in the mid-1700s. Many have noted this. By 1851 nearly 1.5 million people in Britain associated themselves with Methodism (see John Cannon and Robert Crowcroft, (eds) *The Oxford Companion to British History*), from a population of 27 million in England, Wales, Scotland and Ireland.

John Wesley laid much of the foundation for the return of huge numbers of people in Britain to a vibrant personal Christian faith, and that led on to the transformation of wider society.

> "Wesley's central understanding of Christianity was that individual redemption leads to social regeneration." (Vishal Mangalwadi, *The Book That Made Your World; How the Bible Created the Soul of Western Civilisation*, page 265)

The scale of Wesley's achievements is hard to take in. He made an immense contribution to the education of the masses in Britain and to social reform.

> "He wrote 330 books that were published in his lifetime. He composed English, French, Latin and Greek grammars. He edited many books for the general education of his preachers and congregations, which became the fifty volumes of his famous Christian library." (Vishal Mangalwadi, *The Book That Made Your World, How the Bible Created the Soul of Western Civilisation*, page 266)

He also insisted that Christian faith, based on the Bible must change society for the good.

"Thirteen years before the Abolition Committee was formed to end the slave trade, he published his Thoughts upon Slavery, a graphic, vehement and penetrating treatise denouncing "this horrid trade" as a national disgrace. He kept up his attack on slavery until the end of his life, the last letter he wrote being to William Wilberforce, an evangelical (Christian) member of parliament who led a lifelong campaign to abolish the slave trade." (Vishal Manga-lwadi, *The Book That Made Your World, How the Bible Created the Soul of Western Civilisation; how the Bible created the soul of western civilisation*, page 267)

He also supported fair prices, a living wage, prison reform, an end to medieval medical practices and the regulatory control of alcohol. He did all that whilst travelling a quarter of a million miles on horseback on poorly made roads all over Britain and preaching at least 45,000 sermons. (Vishal Mangalwadi, *The Book That Made Your World, How the Bible Created the Soul of Western Civilisation.*)

His preaching and advocacy had an effect. Britain had descended into a terrible social state by the 1700s potentially ripe for revolution like France, but Wesley's persistent preaching built up and drove a movement that radically re-shaped the country on Christian lines. When he first started publicly preaching in towns and villages all over England he was regularly attacked and had things thrown at him. His meetings were often disrupted even violently. But the message of faith in Jesus took root and re-directed the lives of millions.

"In the first decades of his service, his arrival and that of his followers in any town and village was the signal for a violent popular uprising. But for the last ten of his eighty-eight years, it is no exaggeration to say that Wesley was the most respected and beloved figure in Britain." (Vishal Mangalwadi, *The Book That Made Your World, How the Bible Created the Soul of Western Civilisation*, page 269)

As a direct result of Wesley's ministry, radical reforming zeal was directed towards social reform rather than armed class struggle. It has been said of the Labour Party in Britain that it *"owes more to Methodism than to Marxism."* (Reportedly a quote by Morgan Phillips then General Secretary of the Labour party[12]). The Methodist revival took Christianity from the straight jacket of formal state-controlled religion into something that transformed the lives of ordinary people with incredible results. Methodism expanded the Sunday Schools movement teaching people to read and write so they could read the Bible, bringing literacy to the masses. A society can never be the same again when most people can read.

> "Restoration of the authority of the Bible in the English world amounted to a civilization finding its soul." (Vishal Mangalwadi, *The Book That Made Your World, How the Bible Created the Soul of Western Civilisation*, page 270)

The Bible and Protestant Christian thought became the shapers of the worldview in Britain, even for those who did not become committed Christians, the influence was that pervasive and still is to a greater extent than most people realise.

Indeed, many have made the connection between democracy and Christianity, which it has become fashionable to deny.

> "All societies of men must be governed in some way or other. The less they may have of stringent State Government, the more they must have of individual self-government. They less they rely on public law or physical force, the more they must rely on

private moral restraint. Men, in a word, must necessarily be controlled, either by a power within them, or by a power without them; either by the word of God, or by the strong arm of man; either by the Bible or by the bayonet." (Robert C. Winthrop, Speaker of the House of Representatives (1847-1849) quoted in, Vishal Mangalwadi, *The Book That Made Your World, How the Bible Created the Soul of Western Civilisation,* page 353)

It may surprise many readers that Vishal Mangalwadi, an Indian author, who began life a Hindu, also discusses similar positive effects of the Bible and Christianity on India. He gives the example of the Hmars who were transformed by Christian faith, built on the Bible, from a tribal society of head-hunters so feared they were literally outcastes, that is outside the caste system, to becoming one of the most literate ethnic groups in India who have produced multiple notable figures in modern Indian public life. (See *The Book That Made Your World, How the Bible Created the Soul of Western Civilisation, chapter 19*)

History is as always complicated. At another level in society in the Victorian era, academics began questioning the reliability of the Bible as a believable record of the events they portrayed. Miracles were questioned. The strict materialism (i.e. the view that the physical and material is all there is to reality) that was central to evolution gained popularity and as a consequence, miracles recorded in scripture were questioned as never before. Never mind that strict materialism is easily falsified, the idea gained a strong foothold in popular culture with the view growing that there is no supernatural, or metaphysical, or non-material reality. Miracles were sneered at as primitive and backward superstitions.

There's another great Victorian idea, the belief in "progress", which in its Victorian manifestation was linked to the evolutionary claim of everything getting better, and of course if everything has evolved to how it is, it must be "right". Arguing from what is, to what ought to be, is fundamentally flawed (see for example, the work of Hume on this fallacy), but problems with the logic have not diminished its popularity. Marx also saw religion as a backward superstition, something for the ignorant masses who knew no better, from where it was a short step for communists to view religion as something to be eradicated and eradicating religion led swiftly to eradicating people. "Progress", as a vague undefined notion remains at the heart of political rhetoric to this day. It means whatever anyone wants to make it mean, and thus of course ends up meaning nothing.

Science was increasingly held up to be the only reliable source of knowledge and final arbiter of all disputes, as 'more right' than any other knowledge claims. (See for example the discussion in, John Lennox, *Can science explain everything?* And John Lennox *Gunning for God, why the new atheists are missing the mark*). We are still living with the legacy of that faulty reasoning in many areas of life.

The preservation and transmission of the text of the books of the Bible was questioned and undermined in the minds of many people. Science produced reliable knowledge; religion was based on myths. Britain came out of the Victorian era into the Twentieth Century with Darwinism (evolution), atheism, and secularism undermining the Christian worldview. This continued to unfold through the Twentieth Century with that century being probably the most violent on record. The result is where we started this book. Most people today have a range of things they believe they know as unassailable fact, which turn out to be built on shaky foundations.

Since these great challenges to the Christian worldview became prominent, there has been a steady and determined process of study and explanation such that each of the major challenges to Christian belief can be examined carefully and evaluated in the light of the evidence and rebutted. **The whole point of this book is to show that the evidence is there to refute the secular challenges and to have a robust Christian world view and belief.**

There were good ideas, and there were bad ideas, and there were some very pervasive ideas. And some of the ideas the Victorians gave us have been both bad and very pervasive. They constitute a collection of ideas that have led the world astray:

1 Evolution as explaining all life without God

2 Marxism, leading to Communism and mass oppression

3 the idea that we can't trust the Bible

Possibly the last of these has been the most destructive, because it is in the realm of ideas that the world is changed. Darwin understood that. Marx understood that. And the authors of the books making up the Bible understood that. What we think and believe always has consequences and history has repeatedly borne out that claim.

It will probably be clear to you from your own experience, that popular culture, the media and the school system in the west are still preaching loudly at society that the ideas of Darwin and others are right beyond any question. The push back against this has been very quiet in Britain, whereas it has been much louder and more noticeable in the US. Isn't it time you considered carefully whether a worldview arising from Victorian ideas that are so easily challenged and found wanting, might not be right after all?

So, we now move on from the shaky foundations of evolution

and by extension, secularism, to look at some of the claims of the Tubingen school, the Higher Critics and others in the 1800s, that have so effectively undermined any belief in the writings in the Christian Bible as being reliable. Surely, we need to understand the reliability and credibility of a book, the Bible, that has been identified as transforming whole societies. Is belief in its authority well founded?

Therefore, we will consider several key questions:

> Are the texts we have of the books in the New Testament what was originally written or were they changed later to make them say what Christians wanted them to say?

> Have the books been preserved reliably?

> Are the right books in the Bible, or were important ones suppressed and left out?

> In other words, are the critics of the Bible right, or is there good evidence to disprove their claims?

When we have dealt with those objections, we can move on to look in more detail at what those books in the Bible actually have to say.

If we had started this discussion much earlier in this book you might not have seen why it matters so much, or why the whole debate cannot just be ignored in the safe knowledge that everyone "knows" that everything just evolved without any God being involved. I have tried to not leave you that comfortable space from which you can dismiss this discussion as irrelevant or unimportant.

Some Christians reading this will object that they think they can believe in evolution and still be Christians. Well, yes, they can, but several things need saying in response. First and most fundamentally, are they really clear on what evolution is? Evolution relies on random undirected chance. If an element of direction is introduced into it, then you are saying that God uses death and competition to achieve His ends. That rapidly takes us to a pretty dark place.

People looking in from the outside, in my experience, see this more clearly than Christians who try to blend the two; if evolution is true, Christianity makes no sense. What are we needing saving from? If we are evolved, then what we are is just what we are. Talk of any need of salvation makes no sense. Unless we have a valid means to distinguish good from bad in nature, how can we do so in the realm of morals? Unless there was a fall from a perfect state, how can there be a restoration to one in the future? Attempting to blend Christianity and evolution may provide an emotional comfort to those challenged by the aggressive claims of evolution, but it really makes no sense of either perspective. If evolution is true, then death was part of God's method of making us and surely it makes God self-contradictory to later "save" us from death. (For a fuller discussion, see *Refuting Compromise* by Jonathan Sarfati).

I have met vastly more people who find in the "fact" of evolution something that prevents them from taking Christian belief seriously, (it appears to do away with need for a God), than people who are convinced by Christians trying to hold both views.

Other Christians, more so in Britain than in America, are terrified that if they don't buy into evolution no-one will ever listen to them. The harsh reality is that they don't appear to be listening anyway. And why should they if what you say is inconsistent? Christian belief then looks like wishful thinking against the apparent certainties of science; harmless but not very convincing. There is no need for the accommodation. There is no reason to cling to evolution, seductive though it is, since if it is fatally flawed, it is fatally flawed.

The reality is that many of the most ardent supporters of evolution hold to that position because the alternative is so obvious, a creator. In my experience, they really don't want to face up to the consequences of that being true.

We have also noted earlier that the hardest admission for many scientists to make is *"We don't know"*, or even worse *"We haven't the faintest idea how we would ever know"*. Science has put itself in the predicament, by insisting that the only reliable knowledge is from science, but then finds that there is much it can't answer. Clinging to a bad idea because you don't like the look of the obvious refutation of it, is more likely to prove a millstone than a life raft. If that is the situation for evolutionists, why should Christians feel the need to join them? For a hard-hitting discussion of the question of whether it makes sense for Christians to try to reconcile evolution and the Bible you could look at *Baptizing the devil, evolution and the seduction of Christianity* by Clifford Goldstein. We digress however, let's return to the question of the reliability of the books collected into the Bible.

Let's get straight to the point. After a more than a century of careful scholarship on the Biblical texts what can we conclude? Craig Blomberg sums it up this way.

> "(1) We have an extraordinarily high degree of probability of being able to reconstruct the original texts of the biblical books, much higher than for any other documents of antiquity.
>
> (2) Especially with respect to the New Testament books, where there is no disagreement among the major branches of the Christian church as to what the canon should contain, claims about the accuracy and value of apocryphal or noncanonical counter-

parts are dramatically exaggerated.

(3) Modern-language translations, including English, are demonstrably very reliable." (Craig Blomberg, *Can we Still Believe the Bible?* Page 214)

Or to put it as plainly as possible. We have enough evidence to know what was originally written. The right books were included in the New Testament, other books that could possibly have been included, such as the Gnostic Gospel of Thomas, were left out for good reason. And we have reliable accurate translations of the originals into modern languages that adequately gives the modern reader their intended meaning. We will now look at some of the evidence that supports Blomberg's claims.

I find that many people come to this whole discussion with quite unrealistic expectations. They expect God to have dictated down a microphone, word for word, what was to be written. They assume that unless there was direct verbal inspiration in this manner of dictation, that God had no hand in what was written. In addition, they don't spend time to understand a world before word processors, computers, databases, photocopiers and printing presses existed and assume that preserving accurate copies was simply not possible.

Many also seem to take the view that unless they can be shown the original handwritten scroll signed something like "Paul of Tarsus, Roman citizen, apostle to the Gentile world", they cannot know what was originally written. When it comes to historical documents such unrealistic and inaccurate expectations have to be modified.

It is important to be clear what it is that we are trying to reconstruct, when we seek to be sure we have an accurate version of the original texts. Having an accurate copy of something does not automatically mean that everything it says will be immediately accepted as true or right, but it does deal with one major objection that is often raised; that we can't know what the original authors wrote and therefore we have no chance to work out what they intended to say.

Christians *do* view the books that make up the Bible as inspired, that is that God had a hand in what was written. That does not mean direct verbatim verbal dictation is required, word by word. That is a straitjacket that meaningful and precise communication does not need. There are religions that claim they have that, but Christianity does not claim that about all the words in the Bible and it doesn't make much sense to try to either.

There *are* passages that do claim to be the literal words of God, most notably the Ten Commandments given to Moses, but that is the exception. What this means is that the *thoughts* were inspired and that the authors conveyed them as they were able. What results is an impressive array of literature from history to poetry and philosophical discussion.

This is not a cop out, or excuse for not having a dictated manuscript. The God who created everything in the first place and who also created the very possibility of communication can communicate true ideas in a range of ways. We can say that God is love. We can describe that from many angles and discuss its implications. The fact that God is love does not become any more, or less correct because of those discussions, or the language they are conducted in; it is a truth that stands no matter what. We don't need a verbatim quote from God himself to make the statement true, though of course that can exist as well.

If that last paragraph, above, is translated from English (in which I am writing) into French, German, Mandarin, Arabic or British Sign Language, it is perfectly possible for the thoughts contained in it to be accurately conveyed, although the words will vary. With careful study it is perfectly possible to work out what was originally meant in Hebrew, Greek, Aramaic or Latin. It is also perfectly possible to translate any of those languages into one another or into another such as modern English.

In contrast, if a Twentieth Century French philosopher (after the fashion of the post-modernists) were to have written to me, claiming that we cannot know what the author meant (the 'author is dead hypothesis') not only would I not agree, but the claim would be self-refuting; after all they are communicating with me. If I can read their objection, then clearly communication is possible including across language barriers. The bigger question is, why it is that word-based communication, indeed any communication exists at all?!

We can move on to other objections people raise. It is often claimed that there are so many copying errors in the transmission of the text of the Biblical books, that we have no hope of establishing what the original text was. This idea surfaces every decade or so, with new supporters who imagine they have just become the first to think that there might have been problems making and preserving accurate copies of documents in the days before the printing press. They then also jump to inaccurate conclusions, and job done, they can get on with ignoring what was written and encouraging others to do the same. Not surprisingly there has been a ready audience for such books.

A recent populariser of the idea that multiple copying errors have been introduced has been Bart Ehrman in, *'Misquoting Jesus: the story behind who changed the bible and why'*. He alleges 400,000 variants exist in the texts of the New Testament. (Cited in, Craig Blomberg, *Can we Still Believe the Bible?*). There are many early copies in existence, and he alleges this vast number of differences between them.

It sounds dramatic. The number taken in isolation gives the sense that the texts must be hopelessly inaccurate - prior assumption/prejudice confirmed, get on with life. The picture that will come to mind for many people is the game of whispers at a children's party. A message is passed round a circle person to person in whispers and everyone laughs when the message comes out completely changed at the end. The result is often hilariously different from the original. This is absolutely not the right analogy. In the game, children are incentivised to not pass the message on accurately, that after all is the point of the game. (John Lennox, *Can science explain everything?*)

The situation with the New Testament texts is very different.

> "A full 102 copies of individual New Testament books or portions of them have been recovered from the second and third centuries". (E.g. between AD 100 and AD 300. Jesus was crucified AD 30.) "And every single one of them is written with the very careful handwriting of an experienced scribe, not with the more careless scrawls of less literate individuals whom Ehrman postulates would have introduced many more errors in these earliest centuries." (Craig Blomberg, *Can we Still Believe the Bible?* page 27)

There are also over 25,000 manuscripts of parts of the New Testament available from before printing. Even if there were 400,000 possible variants between them, when spread across 25,000 manuscripts,

> "This is an average of 16, and only 8 if the estimate of 200,000 variants is the more accurate one." (Craig Blomberg, *Can we Still Believe the Bible?* page 17)

16 or 8 copying errors per manuscript suddenly sounds significantly less impressive, especially since most might be minor matters of spelling. The type of "variants" that exist are mostly small spelling differences or slight changes in word order or other easily explicable copying errors. They also tend to cluster on certain passages,

> "Paul Wegner estimates that only 6 percent of the New Testament and ten percent of the Old Testament contain the vast majority of these clusters." (Cited in Craig Blomberg, *Can we Still Believe the Bible?* page 17)

> "A large percentage of the variants cluster around the same verses or passages. Less than 3 percent of them are significant enough to be presented in one of the two standard critical editions of the Greek New Testament. Only about a tenth of 1 percent are interesting enough to make their way into the footnotes in most English translations. It cannot be emphasized strongly enough that no orthodox doctrine or ethical practice of Christianity depends solely on any disputed wording. There are always undisputed passages one can consult that teach the same truths." (Craig Blomberg, *Can we Still Believe the Bible?* page 27)

This is worth repeating.

> "A large percentage of the variants cluster around the same verses or passages. Less than 3 percent of them are significant enough to be presented in one of the two standard critical editions of the Greek New Testament. Only about a tenth of 1 percent are interesting enough to make their way into the footnotes in most English translations. It cannot be emphasised strongly enough that no orthodox doctrine

or ethical practice of Christianity depends solely on any disputed wording. There are always undisputed passages one can consult that teach the same truths."

Now I hope you are an exceptionally careful reader, because whilst the paragraph was repeated because the message it gives is so important, I also repeated it because there is one textual variant contained within it that makes absolutely no difference to its meaning and which most readers will simply not even notice. Got it yet? Try harder!

Well, there are some differences between standard American English spelling and standard British spelling of the same English words. In this instance the spelling of emphasized is varied to emphasised in the repeated paragraph. You get the picture why it is that the majority of textual variants are simply not significant enough to foot note in any reliable translation. (And before anyone objects, clearly this is an analogy in English because the majority of readers don't read New Testament Greek. For fuller examples from the actual Greek text see Blomberg, *Can we Still Believe the Bible?*).

It is worth mentioning more detail about the wealth of 25,000 documents that we have to work with. This is Craig Blomberg's summary.

There are 5700 manuscripts of portions of the Greek New Testament from before the invention of printing.

There are approximately 10,000 manuscripts of the Latin translation of the New Testament as well as manuscripts in Syriac, Coptic, Armenian, Georgian and Slavonic.

Then we have extensive quotations of the scriptures by the church fathers in the second and third centuries AD, (That is writings by notable early Christian commentators). In fact, Bruce Metzger contends that,

"We could still reproduce the contents of the New Testament from the multiplicity of quotations in commentaries, sermons, letters and so forth of the early church fathers." (Bruce Metzger quoted in Lee Strobel, *The Case for Christ*, page 62)

There is robustness in this diversity. It allows comparison across such a range of material, that with good knowledge of the languages concerned, plausible reasons for many variations are easily found: missing letters, accidental repetition of a syllable or word etc. Taken together it means that any one verse can be corroborated by many other texts, such that it becomes easier to construct a reliable original, rather than less so.

On the question of how frequently the opportunity might have arisen to make copying errors, most people wrongly assume that copies of the manuscripts would wear out quite frequently and need replacing. More copies in the chain from the original surely means more errors introduced they reason; they then assume many copies in the chain and go no further. George Houston's work on ancient manuscripts in libraries shows that,

"Manuscripts were in use anywhere from 150 to 500 years before being discarded. The fourth century Codex Vaticanus (B) was re-inked in the tenth century 600 years after it was produced." (Cited in, Craig Blomberg, *Can we Still Believe the Bible?* page 34)

Far from being reproduced every few decades,

"the original copy of a biblical book would most likely have been used to make countless new copies over a period of several centuries, leading to still more favourable conditions for careful preservation of its contents." (Craig Blomberg, *Can we Still Believe the*

Bible? page 34)

We should also look at how the Bible compares to other ancient literature. These are Blomberg's figures again.

Homer's Odyssey and Iliad had immense cultural significance to the ancient Greeks. The works were widely known and valued, and they are the next best attested ancient literature after the New Testament. Less than 2500 manuscripts of the two works remain.

For the notable early 2nd century Roman historians, we have less than 200 manuscripts.

Herodotus wrote in the 5th Century BC. There are 75 copies. Thucydides wrote around the same time, 20 copies remain.

Livy the Roman historian lived from the last century BC into the First Century AD. We have 27 copies of his works.

> "And the oldest surviving manuscripts for any of these authors dates from at least four centuries after the time it was first written, sometimes as many as nine centuries after, versus a gap of only one century, or less, for most of the New Testament books." (Craig Blomberg, *Can we Still Believe the Bible?* page 35).

We don't have time to detail all the controversy and discussion around the gnostic gospels that some have claimed should be included in the 66 books of the Bible as recently popularised by Dan Brown's *The Da Vinci Code*. (It is worth remembering it is a work of fiction and many of its claims are fictional). Suffice it to say, those other texts were not included in the list of books regarded as inspired, from very early on, because they had little merit. Blomberg covers the topic well.

To expand your research, you could look at the very substantial *'The Historical Reliability of the New Testament'* by Craig Blomberg (783 pages) and also, *'On the reliability of the Old*

Testament' by K. A. Kitchen (662 pages). There is plenty more to read. The picture that emerges is not the one promoted in popular culture. We can be confident of what was originally written.

The sensible conclusion to draw from this evidence is that it is time to stop pretending that we can't know what the Biblical authors originally wrote, and to instead read them and see what they have to say.

We can have confidence that we can know what the authors of the books collected in the Bible originally wrote

> "But these are written that you may believe that Jesus is the Christ, the Son of God, and that by believing you may have life in his name."
>
> The Apostle John referring to Jesus' acts and miracles in John 20 vs 30

20 MEASURING UP

Vital truths of Christianity
for secular people

S
o far in this book I have tried to open up the discussion to show that the secular worldview, in various ways, does not provide an adequate basis for rejecting Christian belief, nor does it have a very convincing basis for a world view in its own right. I think it would now be helpful to simply set out the broad framework of the Christian world view that this book has been making the case for.

Where then can we find answers?

In contrast to secularism, Christianity offers reasonable answers to our most fundamental questions, that are compatible with all the facts of our existence, based on the existence of God, His mind, His personality, His agency and subsequently ours. In fact, being made in the image of God places an immense value on every human being. Christian belief does not offer exhaustive answers to everything, but it offers answers that form the framework for a coherent understanding of ourselves and the world around us. It is worth remembering that something can be a true statement even if it is not an exhaustive explanation of every aspect of what it addresses. (See Francis Schaeffer, *The Schaeffer Trilogy*, for a fuller discussion).

The insights that form the Christian worldview are coherent. They do account for the physical material world but also the metaphysical reality we all experience: the world of things and the world of concepts. Both are given due weight, and both are valuable because both arise from a loving God.

These insights can be summed up as some basic statements of relevance to this discussion of origins that we have been looking at for several chapters:

God always existed before the universe and is its ultimate cause

He is the source of the laws of physics and chemistry that govern the universe

He is the source of the information needed to make life

He is the Designer behind the Design we see at every level

He made us to operate in more than just a physical way. Like Him, we are conscious, have a mind, appreciate beauty and have an inbuilt sense of right and wrong. We care about what happens to us when we die. In short, we are made in the image of God.

We understand reality through language, and we live in a language-based universe, even down to every cell in our bodies being programmed by DNA, a language-based code

We recognise that there is bad as well as good in the world and that everything is not perfect as it originally was

The important question is not whether God exists, but what is He like, and for that we must turn to the evidence He has revealed of himself.

Creation from the smallest creature to the vast universe shows a careful Designer

The moral law within us shows a moral God who is concerned with right and wrong but gives us genuine free will to make choices

We can then go on to other fundamental points discussed in upcoming chapters:

God's actions in history show a person who predicts events and is in charge of the direction of history. i.e. who is outside space and time as we experience them, but who acts into them

His revelations in scripture (the Bible) show a God who is concerned with every aspect of our wellbeing, and He promises a future without pain and suffering. He is the God who made a perfect world that has sadly rebelled, yet which He will rescue

The life of Jesus shows a God who shares our suffering, who understands that it is real and not an illusion and will do something about it

The resurrection of Jesus demonstrates not only the divinity of Jesus, but that God will deal with death

These are some of the main elements of the Christian world view. It takes full account of the evidence. It makes sense of who we are and what we see in all creation around us. It takes account of right and wrong, suffering and beauty, death and hope.

We can expand this set of statements further. So, here is a fuller set of statements that set out the dimensions of Christian belief and the Christian world view. They are propositional statements of truth about God, the Universe, the world around us and ourselves; propositional statements that can be true whilst not being exhaustive statements that tie down every detail. Indeed, anyone who claims to understand or have an answer for every aspect of everything frankly isn't credible.

Let's look at what these statements offer in overview first, then see how they measure up in practical reality[13].

There is a God

He is the ultimate cause of reality, but He Himself is not the result of any cause

He is not silent, He does communicate with us

He is good all of the time

He made everything; He is the source of reality

He has made a rational, ordered universe

He is the origin of personality and personality is not an illusion

He made us in His image; we are each immensely valuable

He has made a moral universe; right and wrong are real

We see from the nature and the Design of everything that He has made, that He is omnipotent and the creator of everything

He is the origin of communication and has communicated propositional truth to us; true but not exhaustive

He has revealed fuller truth about Himself, that can only come to us by direct revelation that He has given, for example in the Bible

He has shown what He is really like in the life, death and resurrection of Jesus

He communicates directly and profoundly with us by the leading and witness of His Spirit to lead us in the right direction if we will listen

What he has created is not now perfect as it once was, sin has marred it and the world is in rebellion against Him

He gives a new life to all who will receive it, and will make a new reality, a new heavens and earth which we can be in for eternity

The interlinked ways in which God reveals these truths to us are achieved through several areas of overlapping witness. They come together in a convincing whole that touches each part of our existence and our experience of ourselves and the world around us. Each of these statements could, of course, be expanded in a much fuller discussion and they introduce some of what we must look at in the remainder of this book.

He has revealed Himself in what He has made

He has revealed himself by His actions in real history

He has revealed Himself in scripture

He has revealed Himself in Jesus

He has revealed a true understanding of ourselves; we are, though now imperfect, still made in His image

He reveals Himself in the lives of those Jesus touches

He reveals Himself in our hearts

These areas of witness come together in the Christian **world-view** and the **experience** of living the Christian life. Together they form a compelling whole.

Measuring up

The statements of Christian belief given above may seem a bit abstract until we see how they work through into the practical reality of people's lives. So, here is a simple comparison that sets out in very basic terms where the Christian world view and the secular world view differ and crucially what life looks like if we live consistently with either worldview. This is not a criticism of all secular people, but an appeal to think through the basis for your worldview. Can you live consistently with the answers your worldview gives you and be happy about it? Do you have a basis for hope?

When considering other points of view, we tend to filter them against our basic assumptions or pre-suppositions. If they disagree with our existing pre-suppositions on some fundamental point, then we tend to dismiss them as wrong. This point bears repetition, it is so fundamental. However, by setting out the worldview of Christianity and the worldview of secularism in a structured way the contrasts between them become very clear and the issues to explore become equally clear. I believe the inadequacy of the secular world view is then cast into clear light. It just does not provide a basis for satisfactory answers to some of our most basic questions, such as 'Where have I come from?', 'Why am I here?' and 'How should I live?'

The fact is that very many people have given little thought to all this and aren't too troubled by it. They are, of course, welcome to live that. In Western Europe and North America, it has been possible for decades now, to simply set these problems aside and spend all your time endlessly distracted by money, possessions, hobbies, celebrity culture, sport etc. The distractions are endless; enough to fill a lifetime in fact. However, if you are reading this far then I trust you would like more than just distraction and for many people, life will reach a crunch point when they want something more hopeful and more certain to build their life on.

I fully understand that to simplify these two positions to such brief statements will not capture all the range of opinion within them, but the contrast between them is cast into clear light. The following table comparing the Christian worldview and the secular worldview sums up the situation.

The point of the comparison is to show that what we believe about questions such as where we came from and whether we are made in the image of God, have consequences right throughout our worldview and then if we are consistent, with how we live our lives. The discussion of how the basic presuppositions of our worldview work through into how we live our lives could be very lengthy, but there is a connection between them for individuals and societies. Different cultures around the world and throughout history have lived quite differently from one another, some of them being cruel, brutal, and miserable for many people within them, others allowing individuals and families to flourish.

Many secular people might be unhappy with the comparison that is being made. However, if you don't live in a manner that is consistent with the basic presuppositions of secularism and are in fact aligned with a Christian worldview on many points, then isn't it important to examine Christian belief and its basis very carefully. If it matches how you think life should be lived, such as being kind and loving to others rather than self-centred, that is a very very good thing. But remember that the Christian has a basis for why they should live like that, secularism does not rest on presuppositions that support that view. If life is lived entirely consistently with a secular worldview it can be very bleak indeed. Therefore, isn't it worth examining Christian belief more closely?

To explore these issues further, one suggestion worth reading would be Vishal Mangalwadi's book, *The Book That Made Your World, How the Bible Created the Soul of Western Civilisation* He makes a systematic examination of the impact and legacy of the Bible and Christian thought, especially Protestant Christianity since of the Reformation in Europe and he explores the cultural impact of Christian belief and the foundation it has laid in western societies that we are still living with.

Christian world view		Secular evolutionary world view
	Origin of the Universe and all of reality	
God has always existed and made everything		Everything spontaneously arose from nothing
	Origin of life	
God intentionally created life		Life arose by accident through Random Chance
The universe and all life are Designed		All appearance of Design is an illusion, we are just chemicals
	Origin of personality and mind	
God is a person and we are made in His image with personality		Personality is a construct; we are just a function of our genes
	The existence of right and wrong	
We are in rebellion against God after the first people rebelled: right and wrong do exist		Right and wrong are not absolute, they are just conventions and open to change. There is no basis for identifying what is right or wrong beyond social consensus
	The origin of knowledge and the basis of communication	
God has communicated with us and it is possible to know truly but not exhaustively. Truth exists and can be meaningfully communicated		All knowledge is relative, and communication is ultimately meaningless (Post-modernism) There is no truth

	The purpose of existence	
To know God, love Him and other people and to enjoy all He has given us and made us to be, for eternity		There is no ultimate point to existence, so get what you can while you can
	The future	
Peace of mind in this life, life after death and a bright future		This life is all there is
	The basis of hope	
God has dealt with our rebellion and has defeated death through Jesus if we turn to Him		There is no basis for hope, but the myth of human progress is insisted on anyway
	How should we live?	
Love God and love others		Do what you think is right, no-one can tell you what to do
	What is the outcome of our worldview, if lived consistently with its own terms?	
Loving people, families and communities		Self-centred, narcissistic individuals and social breakdown
Peace of mind, care for others, hope for the future, making the world a better place		Despair, hopelessness, selfish lives, harming ourselves and others

It is the final part of this comparison that really hits home. If we are the result of Random Chance and there is no ultimate basis for right and wrong and no basis for hope, then why shouldn't we just live for ourselves and not care about how that affects others? In contrast, if we are made in the image of God, know He cares for us and wants to restore that image in us, marred though it is at present and also wants to rescue us from a world of pain and difficulty, doesn't that change how we see ourselves and others? Doesn't that make other people of immense value as well? Believing those things gives us a basis for hope and a goal for our existence, both of which all people crave.

We must repeat that thankfully very many people do not live a life completely consistent with their secular worldview for which we must be tremendously grateful. We must also admit that many who have claimed to be Christians have not lived consistent with their worldview either. Anyhow, it is still the case that many, if not most secular people, continue to live on the cultural memory of the Christian worldview. But with each generation that memory is eroded, and the stark consequences of the secular worldview become more dominant in our culture with terrible results in people's lives.

If people are willing to concede that secularism poses problems for the worldview of individuals and thus for society, they then often shift the discussion rapidly sideways to suffering and pain. If that is not just an excuse to engage with the problems of secularism but is a genuine question, then it is worth remembering that in a secular worldview with evolution built in, it makes no sense to complain about pain and suffering because it has been through survival of the fittest and thus death of the less fit that evolution was supposed to have progressed. Whereas the Christian, knowing that they have free will and free choice can recognise a world that, though once made perfect, is now damaged and in rebellion against God with terrible consequences. They can also then choose to be part of God's solution of building a new kingdom based once more on kindness, consideration and love.

How unfortunate that many who call themselves Christians are muddle-headed on many aspects of the Christian worldview. They try to mix and match secularism and Christianity. The result, if looked at carefully, is incoherent to either perspective, and is typically quite unconvincing to secular people. Christian belief is not an add-on to the dominant secularism in western culture, but rather a fundamental repudiation of it.

Christianity created the tolerance within which secularism could arise and the thought space within which it formed. Tragically, secularism is increasingly intolerant of its Christian heritage and is too often pitted against Christian beliefs, partly because Christianity exposes the fundamental flaws in secularism, showing it up for the wishful thinking that it is.

Secularism is in fact nothing more or less than a Judaeo-Christian heresy, replacing a creator God with the secular origins myth of evolution and each individual as the final source of authority in their own lives, as opposed to any accountability to God. No doubt just as Christianity brought down communism in Eastern Europe, one day it will be Christianity that breaks the apparently monolithic consensus in the west on secularism.

If this comparison seems too stark to you, then I challenge you to continue to investigate your own world view and also the basis of Christian belief and ask yourself honestly, 'Do I have a solid foundation for meaning and hope in my life?' Many before you, have found that not only do Christian ideas make sense, but also that they offer a lived experience that has transformed their lives, because God is real, and Jesus is living and active and never turns away those who seek Him.

The secular world view claims to have an all-encompassing explanation of everything, without reference to God, but when examined carefully it explains little and offers nothing of lasting value

"Everyone on the side of truth listens to me."

Jesus of Nazareth to Pontius Pilate recorded in John's gospel 18 vs 37

21 THE LAST DISCIPLE

*The life and witness of
the first believers*

He sat in the quarry, in charge of the water, too old to heave blocks. Dust, hard work, and never-ending pain. The work the men were put to was unrelenting, with no days off, no sick leave, nor recreation. For most the grave was the only way out. He had done nothing wrong, nothing at all. Yet, here he was in the baking sun on hard labour. The soldiers knew he could be trusted and his serenity in a situation that should break a man had a profound effect on them. They knew he shouldn't be here and using this gentle old man to supervise others made his life more bearable and it made their lives much easier since the other prisoners respected him too. He had formed a friendship with several soldiers, and they even permitted him to write. He wrote letters for them, the day-to-day correspondence that criss-crossed the Roman Empire. He wrote his own letters too and the senior officers who could read, checked them before allowing them out with their own post.

Letter writing was a remarkable activity for a man in a penal colony in the First Century. The soldiers talked with him, about what he wrote and had written before. To their minds he had some strange ideas. He was, for example, consumed with the idea that there is only one God and that He is only loving, all of the time. As he put it,

> "God is light, in Him there is no darkness at all." (1 John 1 vs 5)

He said that the way to deal with injustice, ill treatment and oppression was to love those who did wrong to you. And he said he knew this because he had met the actual Son of God. He also claimed to now have visions from that same Son of God. Yet, there was something about him they couldn't ignore. Some scoffed at his ideas, but still respected his peace of mind, he was happier than them. Others came to believe as he did, that was the remarkable thing. Throughout John's life he told people that God is love, and he knew it because God had lived as a man, and John had met him, lived alongside him and been transformed by him.

John was the last one left of the original twelve apostles. All the others of the twelve special followers he talked about had been martyred or disappeared. Some details here are imagined into the situation of John's final years on Patmos, but the essential elements are known. Those twelve apostles and many others went out into the known world and beyond to tell people about God's son Jesus and the kingdom he is building. Eleven out of twelve paid the high price of martyrdom. Before we consider why that should be the case, let's consider some of what they achieved.

The Roman empire was brutal, cruel, bloodthirsty and built on slavery. Slavery only worked on the continued reinforcement of fear through pure brutality. Crucifixion was a punishment especially for slaves and here these Christians like John were worshipping a man who died a slave's death on a cross but was then found to be alive again. The practical outworking of that was Christian slaves and slave owners worshipping together on equal terms in the new Christian churches, as the Apostle Paul insisted they should. That was counter-cultural to say the least. Christianity fundamentally undermined the Roman economy and empire. (See Nick Page, *Kingdom of Fools, the Unlikely Rise of The Early Church*). Later organised Christianity has often swamped the teaching and witness of Jesus, the apostles and early Christians and I believe that is the case with the issue of slavery. People claiming to be Christian defended slavery right into modern times, such as in the American civil war. Jesus' own words address them directly,

> "By their fruit you will recognise them... a good tree cannot bear bad fruit and a bad tree cannot bear good fruit". (Luke 7 vs 16-18)

There have been people throughout history (and today), who have claimed to be Christians but simply are not. Even so, it was Protestant Christians who took seriously what the Apostles and St. Paul wrote, who were the ones who fought the long campaign for the abolition of slavery: William Wilberforce, John Newton, Lord Shaftesbury and others. We owe an immense debt to those who took Paul literally when he wrote that,

> "There is neither Jew nor Greek, male nor female, slave nor free." (Paul, letter to the Christians in Galatia; Galatians 3 vs 28)

They genuinely understood the equality of all people.

So, where does that leave John, the last of the twelve disciples to be alive. Why had it worked out as it did for the other apostles and many others. Why such violent opposition? Why does that violent oppression of Christians continue in many countries today? The answer is very simple and is in itself strong evidence for the claims Christians make: this world is in rebellion against God, and those who align themselves with Him, His Son Jesus Christ and the Kingdom of peace He is building. Thus, peaceful believers find themselves at odds with a world that does not want to live out the loving life that God wants us all to live.

Today that opposition is very intense in many countries around the world. In fact, whenever anyone becomes a Christian there is a real and genuine spiritual battle fought. Our rebellious hearts do not want to submit to God and the devil does not let anyone go easily. The good news is that not only is the power of God in Jesus greater than anything that opposes it, but also that following Jesus in this life means peace of mind now and it means a place in His eternal kingdom, a life after this one.

John was in a penal colony because he told people that God is good all of the time. The truth about Jesus was the antidote to the pagan culture of his day, just as it is the anti-dote to secularism today. John told people to meet hate with kindness, just as Jesus had. He said that no power on earth should claim our allegiance above God. He humbly lived out what he taught and through his teaching, many people did believe in Jesus as he did. That made this quiet old man dangerous, because he was helping turn the world upside down.

This world is in rebellion against God and Jesus shows us the way back to peace with Him

> "I am the way and the truth and the life. No one comes to the Father except through me."
>
> Jesus of Nazareth quoted in John's gospel 14 vs 6

22 AN ADVENTURE AT SEA

*Eyewitness accounts from
the First Century*

I love travel. I also love reading travel writing. I've travelled the world many times over through travel books undertaking several lifetimes of journeys through the words of others. Paul Theroux in the first chapter of 'The Old Patagonia Express', parodied the fake sincerity and straining for effect so prevalent in poor travel writing: the reader is suddenly parachuted into a situation of false jeopardy as the plane lunges over the jungle, towards the ground, will they make it? Anything that might be considered "other" compared to the reader's experience is used as a cheap dramatic device to carry the narrative when the author lacks any greater insight to offer. Thankfully Paul Theroux's travel writing is not like that at all.

One result of reading a huge number of travelogues is developing a keen nose for when the writer is being evasive or economical with the truth: glossing over facts, missing out parts of the journey or deliberately distorting for effect in the re-telling. What is not said is sometimes as poignant as what is. In Paul Theroux's early travel books, the nagging thought in the back of my mind was "What about his young family back home? What is all this travelling doing to them?" Then, with remarkable honesty in one of his later books, he tells how his long absences contributed to the breakdown of his marriage and the heartache it brought. In his younger works there seems to me to be a negative attitude to religion, and Christianity in particular, but in his 2017 travelogue 'Deep South', there is a deep sense of respect for the role of faith in other people's lives. Knowing his early work well, I valued all the more his appreciation of the role of church community and church services in the lives of the poorest people in the southern US. The youthful cynicism seemed excised, and he was meeting people on their own terms, trying to understand what church meant to them. His later travelogues, 'Dark Star Safari' and 'Deep South' are even better than his earlier work.

After being immersed in reading so much travel writing for so many years, I looked afresh at Luke's account of the Apostle Paul's missionary journeys around the Roman empire in his book that we know as 'The Acts of the Apostles', or just plain 'Acts'. What really struck me was how uneven the narrative is. In the passages where Luke is actually travelling with Paul, including his journey by sea across the Mediterranean, on the way to Rome as a prisoner to be tried by Caesar, the account is detailed, diary like, at times quite excited. It includes accurate details of shipping of the time, weather patterns, sailing routes, navigation practices, winds, bays and coastline, landing places and then shipwreck. In other places the account is terse, factual, brief, just reporting what he knows happened, but didn't experience himself, because he wasn't with Paul all the time on his journeys.

The geographical details of Paul's journeys are given meticulously and in the right order. We can't fault Luke for doing his research properly. The journey by boat after Paul had been arrested, across the Mediterranean Sea, is so precise in its details of shipping, sailing routes, weather conditions, coastlines and places, that we can accurately retrace the exact route.

Luke names so many places and puts them in correct geographical order in *The Acts of the Apostles*, that it is clear his narrative is anchored in geographical reality. One study looked at Luke's references to 32 countries, 54 cities and 9 islands and found no mistakes. (Norman Geisler and Thomas Howe, *When critics ask,* page 385, cited in Lee Strobel, *The Case for Christ*)

The journey in chapters 27 and 28 of Acts, starts at Adramyttium, stopping at Sidon, then heading west across the Mediterranean Sea. They sailed past Cyprus *"because the winds were against us"*, off the coast of Cilicia and Pamphylia, landing at Mycia in Lycia. Accurate information is given about the winds being against them, true to the location and time of year, and then they sailed to the lee of Crete,

> "opposite Salome. We moved along the coast with difficulty and came to a place called Fair Havens, near the town of Lasea." (Acts 27 vs 7,8)

Luke accurately notes,

> "Much sailing time had now been lost, and sailing had already become dangerous, because by now it was after the Fast." (i.e. Yom Kippur, in September.) (Acts 27 vs 9)

This is exactly the experience people had of sailing in the First Century, sailing was extremely difficult and dangerous into the autumn and winter. He also notes correctly that the harbour was not suitable to winter the ship in, so they decided to try to continue,

> "to reach Phoenix and winter there. This was a

harbour in Crete, facing both southwest and north-west." (vs 12), as is indeed the case.

Paul predicted disaster if they continued, with great loss and danger to their lives.

What follows is the very precise, diary like re-telling by Luke of how the ship couldn't make head way in a hurricane force storm, it was so fierce that they threw the cargo overboard and then the ships tackle to lighten it. After 14 nights they were still being driven by the storm, when they took soundings and found the water was getting shallower. They feared they would be driven onto rocks and the ship dashed to pieces and dropped four anchors.

> "When daylight came they did not recognise the land, but saw a bay with a sandy beach where they de-cided to run the ship aground if they could. Cutting loose the anchors, they left them in the sea and at the same time untied the ropes that held the rudders. Then they hoisted the foresail to the wind and made for the beach. But the ship struck a sand bar and ran aground. The bow stuck fast and would not move, and the stern was broken to pieces by the pounding of the surf." (Acts 27: vs 39-41)

Even here we see many details that fit exactly to the historical situation. The rudders which went below the hull on Roman era ships, needed loosening so that they did not run aground and jam as the ship went into shallow water.

Paul reminded them he had tried to prevent the disaster but encouraged everyone to eat something to get their strength up because for 14 days they had not eaten through the storm, and he again made a prediction.

> "Now I urge you to take some food. You need it to survive. Not one of you will lose a single hair from his head." (Acts 27 vs 34)

Worryingly,

> "The soldiers planned to kill the prisoners to pre-
> vent any of them from swimming away and escap-
> ing." (Acts 27 vs 42)

That would have been entirely consistent with Roman practice. The Centurion however had a favourable attitude to Paul,
and was no doubt impressed by Paul's accurate prediction of
the disaster.

> "But the Centurion wanted to spare Paul's life and
> kept them from carrying out their plan. He ordered
> those who could swim to jump overboard first and
> get to land. The rest were to get there on planks or on
> pieces of the ship. In this way everyone reached land
> in safety. Once we were safely on shore, we found
> that the island was called Malta." (Acts 27 vs 43-44)

All 276 of them abandoned ship. All survived as predicted.

The details in Luke's description of the voyage is so accurate
that it is possible to identify where on the coast of Malta the
shipwreck must have occurred. (See for example, *The Voyage
and Shipwreck of St. Paul* referenced in F. F. Bruce, *The New Testament Documents, are they reliable?*).

It can't be emphasised enough that this is not historical fiction,
this is First Century travel writing! It is worth reading the
whole episode through. It has stood up to the closest scrutiny
and is clearly the account of someone who was there himself,
experiencing the events for real. Luke goes on to describe the
remaining journey to Rome including landing at Puteoli then
taking the road, the Via Appia, to the Forum of Appius and
the Three Taverns (or shops) where a group of Christians met
them to continue with them to Rome. Again, Luke gets his
geography right. The remains of the Three Taverns have been
located, with a general store, an inn and a smithy.

"It was the last relay point before Rome for imperial couriers." (See C. Anderson and B. Edwards, *Evidence for the Bible*, page 174)

It was about 10 miles before Rome. In a world of horse and foot transport there were still service or rest stops!

Luke's record of events is what you would experience of an honest account. The loose ends aren't all tied up, because he doesn't make up what he doesn't know. The book of Acts ends without explaining Paul's fate in Rome. Other sources tell us he was executed. Luke says nothing about what happened to him, either because he didn't know, which is highly unlikely if Luke was writing a long time after Paul's death, or because Paul was still alive. That really struck me. The most likely reason for an incomplete and partial account was that Paul was still alive at the time of writing. That is entirely consistent with the book being what it claims to be, the carefully researched account of the apostles' activities in the very earliest days of the Christian church, including Luke's personal experience as Paul's travelling companion. This is eyewitness stuff.

Luke makes it clear that he is writing as an historian. He does not claim to be an eyewitness of everything, but to have carefully investigated it and written it down. He distinguishes in Acts between when he was present and part of the action and when he wasn't and is just reporting what he has investigated. This gives him a lot of credibility. He starts his earlier book, his biography (or gospel) of Jesus this way:

> "Since I myself have carefully investigated everything from the beginning, it seemed good also to me to write an orderly account for you, most excellent Theophilus, so that you may know the certainty of the things you have been taught." (Luke 1, vs 3,4)

And he starts *The Acts of the Apostles* with,

"In my former book, Theophilus, I wrote about all that Jesus began to teach and do." (Acts 1, vs 1)

Luke then continues with the narrative where he had left off in his earlier biography and records the history of the early church.

It is telling that in neither his biography of Jesus, (*Luke's gospel*) nor his book *The Acts of the Apostles*, does Luke mention the siege of Jerusalem and the destruction of the temple in AD 70. This was an event of such immense importance and was also predicted by Jesus himself, that if it had already occurred it would be almost impossible to think of Luke leaving it out. Luke had to be writing before AD 70 at the latest.

Paul was clearly aware of Luke's writing too, since he uses it as a source in his letters now known as 1 Timothy and 1 Corinthians, both of which we have preserved, placing Luke's accounts as earlier than his, and by implication as an accurate record in Paul's eyes. (see J. Warner Wallace, *Cold Case Christianity*, page 170). Paul's letters were probably written in the AD 50s.

Taken together, the fact that Luke does not mention either the destruction of Jerusalem or Paul's death places both of Luke's books as having been written early, the gospel in the AD 40s or early 50s and The Acts of the Apostles before the AD 70s. This is certainly early enough to allow him to have access to accurate eyewitness sources for events which he did not personally witness that are recorded in his gospel, and for the parts of The Acts of the Apostles (Acts) where he was not present. The way he is able to furnish more detail in Acts, on the events that he did personally witness, lends considerable credibility to his accounts. It is also reasonable to infer that the gospels of Mark and probably of Matthew were in existence and that Luke knew of them when he wrote because he says that,

"Many have undertaken to produce an account of the things that have been fulfilled among us." (Luke 1 vs1)

If we place the crucifixion of Jesus at about AD 30, these written records, by Luke, are very close in time to the events they record. (J. Warner Wallace, *Cold Case Christianity*).

If we dig deeper, we find that Luke has been borne out again and again as an accurate historian, in relation to the politics of his day, the Roman government, titles of officials, place names, the relative location of places to one another and in other more incidental details.

Luke accurately uses the correct titles for various Roman officials, which was a complicated business. For example, Cyprus changed from an imperial province in 22 BC, when it had an imperial legate in charge, to a senatorial province with a proconsul in charge. When Paul and Barnabas arrived in about AD 47 at Paphos, they met Sergius Paullus, the proconsul. Luke uses the correct term of address. (F. F. Bruce, *The New Testament Documents, are they reliable?*)

In 1877 an inscription was found near Paphos with the name of Sergius Paulus and his title as proconsul. There is also a boundary stone that was found in Rome dated to AD 54 giving evidence that he held office in Rome after three years as proconsul in Cyprus and that he was in Cyprus when Paul and Barnabas were there. (See C. Anderson and B. Edwards, *Evidence for the Bible*, page 156).

Luke calls the magistrates of Phillipi "praetors". But Phillipi was a Roman colony and so it officially had "duumvirs". It seems they affected the grander title of praetors. Cicero refers to other magistrates doing the same in another Roman colony, Capua;

> "Although they are called duumvirs in the other colonies, these men wished to be called praetors." (F. F. Bruce, *The New Testament Documents, are they reliable?*)

Luke calls the chief magistrates of Thessalonica "politarchs", a term which does not occur elsewhere in ancient literature, but which has been found in inscriptions as a title of magistrates of Macedonian towns in Thessalonica. (Acts 17 vs 6). He does not use the same name to refer to officials in every city and has been shown to be correct in his usage here for Phillipi. In 1876 a 2nd Century Roman arch was demolished in Phillipi, but the inscription was kept. It lists city officials and refers to them after the style politarch. (See C. Anderson and B. Edwards, *Evidence for the Bible,* page 158).

Herod Antipas who ruled Galilee when Jesus was alive was not promoted to royal status by the emperor. His subjects may have called him a "king", but his correct title was "tetrarch". Luke accurately uses tetrarch. (see for example Luke 3 vs 19) (F. F. Bruce, *The New Testament Documents, are they reliable?*)

In Acts 19 vs 22, when Paul is in Corinth, Luke refers to Erastus (a Christian convert) being sent by Paul to Macedonia on mission work. Paul in his letter to Christians in Rome, refers to an Erastus *"who is the city's Director of public works"* as someone sending greetings in his letter to the Romans (Romans 16 vs 23). In 1929 an inscription was found dating from the mid First Century , stating,

> "Erastus, in return for his aedileship, laid this pavement at his own expense".

The aedile was in charge of city finances. In Paul's letter he refers to an Erastus by a related title, oikonomos. It is correct to point out that this is a lower office, but it also had responsibilities as a treasurer. It is possible that Erastus was promoted after Paul wrote of him. Anderson and Edwards point out that,

> "In the view of the comparative rarity of the name – about one in eleven hundred at that time (from the Lexicon of Greek Personal names) – it is unlikely that two men of the same name would hold finan-

cial office in Corinth at the same time.... It is therefore more than likely that we are reading of the same man."

(See C. Anderson and B. Edwards, *Evidence for the Bible*, page 166)

In several instances where people have thought Luke was wrong in some detail, further evidence has come to light that has shown him to have been right after all. In Luke 3 vs 1, Luke uses the Greek method of synchronisms to give an accurate date. He refers to a series of important figures to achieve this,

"In the fifteenth year of the reign of Tiberius Caesar – when Pontius Pilate was governor of Judea, Herod Tetrarch of Galilee, his brother Phillip tetrarch of Iturea and Traconitis, and Lysanius tetrarch of Abilene – during the high priesthood of Annas and Caiaphas, the word of the Lord came to John." (Luke 3 vs 1)

Luke is clearly going to great lengths here to anchor his narrative in an exact date in real history and is inviting his readers to test what he writes. Various scholars used this passage to claim Luke didn't know what he was talking about because there was record of a Lysanias not being a tetrarch but ruler of Chalcis half a century earlier. However,

"An inscription was later found from the time of Tiberius, from AD 14 to 37, which names Lysanias as tetrarch in Abila near Damascus - just as Luke had written... it turned out there had been two government officials named Lysanias!" (John Mcray quoted in Lee Strobel, *The Case for Christ*, page 104)

Elsewhere Luke names three Roman emperors Augustus, Tiberius and Claudius and many other notable persons,

"In addition to the emperors, we meet the Roman

governors Quirinius, Pilate, Sergius Paullus, Gallio, Felix, Festus; Herod the Great and some of his descendants – Herod Antipas the tetrarch of Galilee, the vassal kings Agrippa I and II, Berenice and Drusilla; leading members of the Jewish priestly caste such as Annas, Caiaphas, and Ananias; Gamaliel, the greatest contemporary Rabbi and Pharisaic leader." (F. F. Bruce, *The New Testament Documents, are they reliable?*)

Clearly Luke was confident of getting his facts straight.

Luke is also accurate when describing events and people in context. He gets the local politics, culture and atmosphere right. Jerusalem is painted as with *"excitable and intolerant crowds"*. Whereas Syrian Antioch *"where men of different creeds and nationalities rub shoulders and get their rough corners worn away"*, is where the first non-Jewish (Gentile) Christian church is established, not surprisingly. (F. F. Bruce, *The New Testament Documents, are they reliable?*)

Other incidental details in Acts have been confirmed by archaeological research. When Paul and Barnabas came to Lystra in Asia Minor on their first missionary journey, Paul healed a lame man.

> "When the crowd saw what Paul had done, they shouted in the Lycaonian language, "The gods have come down to us in human form!" Barnabas they called Zeus, and Paul they called Hermes because he was the chief speaker." (Acts 14 vs 11,12)

Paul and Barnabas had difficulty in stopping the crowd from sacrificing to them and persuading them they were mere men, but men with a message about God, nonetheless. It is a very odd incident, why would the people jump to such a conclusion? Zeus and Hermes (or the Romans: Jupiter and Mercury) were traditionally associated with that region. Ovid the

Roman poet tells of a well-known story of how these came to that area in disguise and received hospitality only from one old couple called Philemon and Baucis. Zeus and Hermes destroyed everyone but turned the couple's house into a temple and them into priests. They were rewarded for their kindness, but their inhospitable neighbours were overwhelmed in a deluge. (See C. Anderson and B. Edwards, *Evidence for the Bible*, page 157 and F. F. Bruce, *The New Testament Documents, are they reliable?*).

In 1910 Sir William Calder discovered an inscription circa AD250 at Sedasa near Lystra,

> "recording the dedication to Zeus of a statue of Hermes along with a sundial by men of Lycaonian names." (F. F. Bruce, *The New Testament Documents, are they reliable?*)

So, here we have confirmation of Luke's accuracy as a historian even in incidental details.

Sir William Ramsay, the archaeologist who did much work in Asia Minor was originally convinced of the idea that Luke must have been written in the middle of the second century, that is long after the events described. His work as an archaeologist and historian convinced him he had been wrong. He says of Luke,

> "Luke is a historian of the first rank; not merely are his statements of fact trustworthy; he is possessed of the true historic sense; he fixes his mind on the idea and plan that rules in the evolution of history, and proportions the scale of his treatment to the importance of each incident, he seizes the important and critical events and shows their true nature at greater length, while he touches lightly or omits entirely much that was valueless for his purpose. In short, this author should be placed along with the very

greatest historians." (Quoted in F. F. Bruce, *The New Testament Documents, are they reliable?*)

F.F. Bruce makes his overall evaluation of Luke as a historian by pointing out that we have ample knowledge of the progress of Christianity before AD 60 and know little of it for many years after that.

"After Luke there arose no writer who can really be called a historian of the Christian Church until Eusebius, whose Ecclesiastical History was written after Constantine's Milan Edict of Toleration (AD 313)." (F. F. Bruce, *The New Testament Documents, are they reliable?*)

If Luke is an accurate historian, drawing on credible eyewitness sources and his own direct experience, it makes it possible to take him seriously in the other things he writes about in the life of Jesus and in the life of the apostles and the early church.

It became the fashion in the 1800s for academics to claim that the New Testament records were written long after the events and are thus not reliable. They also claimed they had been changed in transmission and that the oldest surviving copies were written so long after the events that they could not be regarded as reliable. Put these two claims together and the conclusion offered was that we can't trust the New Testament books. That view has entered the public consciousness. It has been promoted by the media and is promoted in countless classrooms. The result is that many people think they "know" that the Bible is unreliable and made up later. Nothing could be further from the truth. Since the attacks of the sceptical academics, more than a century of careful scholarship leaves us with the opposite conclusion. The New Testament books are the best attested texts from antiquity, and it is possible to be confident that we have an accurate text preserved. The evidence for early authorship of the books has also grown immensely.

If we are to write off the New Testament books as unhistorical and unreliable, then we must be consistent and write off everything we thought we knew about history from less well attested sources than these from before the invention of the printing press in 1440. (See J. Warner Wallace, *Cold Case Christianity*). No-one seriously proposes giving up on most of history prior to the last few centuries, so we similarly cannot be consistent and reasonable if we refuse to accept the evidence for the historicity of the New Testament.

No single corroborating fact seals the case for being convinced that the New Testament books are accurate and based on contemporaneous evidence of the life of Jesus and the early church. As we have seen with this brief look at the work of Luke, it is the steady accumulation of multiple corroborations that leaves us with the most reasonable conclusion being that he was writing reliable history, drawing on eyewitnesses' testimony, or from those who talked to them.

In the media, in school, in novels, in fact right across secular culture, a different picture is painted. It is not uncommon for the historical reliability of the whole of the New Testament books to be cast into doubt, quite wrongly. This may well be what you have received as the accepted view of most people. Well, if you read more and realise that you have not been given an accurate or frankly even a truthful view of this subject, I hope it will encourage you to question more deeply what else you think you know and to read into the New Testament yourself.

Since it would call so much of secular culture into question, it really does seem that for many people, there is no desire to do anything than keep repeating the convenient claim that the New Testament is unreliable because then, of course, it is easier to ignore.

Jesus really lived, and he inspired a generation of his followers to take the good news of His gift of life to the then known world, as recorded in *The Acts of the Apostles* by Luke

The Apostle Peter spoke for all the Apostles when he said,

> "We did not follow cleverly invented stories when we told you about the power and coming of our Lord Jesus Christ, but we were eyewitnesses of his majesty."

The second letter of Peter 1 vs 16

23 THE WRITING IS ON THE WALL

Daniel and history

D aniel was just a teenager when he was taken prisoner of war. Nebuchadnezzar sacked Jerusalem and looted the temple of its treasures and took prisoners back to Babylon. A national humiliation was visited on the tiny state of Israel as it was incorporated into the Babylonian empire. Not only was there terrible bloodshed and loss of political independence, but because the vessels used in the Jewish Temple were carried off to Nebuchadnezzar's treasury the temple services ended, causing a religious crisis as well as a political one. The Middle East has seen an almost endless cycle of turmoil and warfare since, with empires clashing over this region more than anywhere else on earth. At the time of writing the two devastating Iraq wars had barely subsided before Syria was engulfed by terrorism and a more than decade long multi-faction civil war. Again, and again, this region has been a focal point of world history and a crucible of conflict. For the last 3 millennia at least, it has remained at the centre of human affairs.

Daniel found himself on a 1600 mile (2700 Km) forced march to Babylon. On arrival, since he came from a noble family in Israel, he was taken into training in Nebuchadnezzar's palace. He quite possibly endured the humiliation and pain of being made a eunuch and he was enrolled in what we might call a 3-year equivalent of a degree programme for administrators. Nebuchadnezzar trained up administrators and officials from all over his empire, to then in turn help run the empire. Making them eunuchs helped ensure they could not set up dynasties of their own and would remain loyal to the king.

The events that unfolded in Daniel's life have given rise to many phrases that are embedded in the English language to this day, a collective memory whose meaning secularism has obscured: such as to be "Thrown to the lions", "Feet of iron and clay", "In the fiery furnace" and "The writing is on the wall".

We will look briefly at some of the episodes in Daniel's life that give rise to these memorable phrases, starting with his being taken prisoner of war as a young man by Nebuchadnezzar, through to his serving as an old man of around 90 under Darius the Mede in the kingdom of Medo-Persia, and we will relate these events to history.

Daniel, and the friends who were taken prisoner with him, refused to worship false gods, even to the point of risking their lives. Daniel was also called upon repeatedly to interpret dreams for Nebuchadnezzar and Daniel also received a series of dreams or visions of the future. In Babylon, the "wise men" or Chaldeans in Nebuchadnezzar's service claimed to foretell the future and to be able to divine the right decisions for the king. The fact that multiple scenarios arise in the book of Daniel where interpretation of dreams is central to events, fits exactly to the historical context.

Several themes emerge from Daniel's life and experience. The strongest is that who we worship matters immensely. It also becomes clear that God acts into and directs the course of history.

Many have sought to write off the book of Daniel as having been written after the fact, that is after the events it portrayed and thus being faked. They think they know for certain that no-one can tell or be told the future. They typically ascribe to unknown Jewish authors/ scribes/ editors, in the last few centuries BC, the role of editing Daniel to make it fit history. Such cynicism is easy to voice, but it doesn't fit to the evidence within the text of Daniel itself for some compelling reasons. In particular, this is because the prophecies in Daniel accurately predicted the coming of the Messiah (Jesus) despite the fact that the majority of the Jewish religious hierarchy rejected him as the Messiah when he appeared. A tampered with text would be much more convenient if it didn't point so clearly to the Messiah which the custodians of that text then rejected. When we say that we must however remember that initially, nearly all the early Christians were Jewish, clearly many Jews did not take the same view as their religious leaders.

The prophecies in Daniel also reach way past the late centuries BC and even the Messiah, in AD 1 to AD 33, right down to our own time. This has implications for any evaluation of the authenticity of the book of Daniel and its reliability as a record of God's revealing of history to him and to us.

Ancient Babylon may seem remote, almost unknowable history. However, you can visit the Pergamon Museum in Berlin and see the immense rebuilt blue Ishtar gate, covered with decoration. Numerous archaeological artefacts remain from Babylon in many other museums as well as in situ in present day Iraq, so we start from a solid historical foundation. We can also pin down many key events of relevance such as the date Babylon was invaded by the Medes and Persians (539 BC) towards the end of Daniel's life. The book of Daniel is built on historical bedrock.

So, to return to some of the key events in Daniel's life and the implications they have for history. Nebuchadnezzar was an absolute ruler. It is hard to grasp today what that meant, but it literally gave him the power of life and death over all his subjects in his vast empire. One night he had a dream that troubled him. In it he saw a vast statue.

Nebuchadnezzar suspected that the dream was something of great importance, but what did it mean? He didn't want to be misled, he wanted to know for certain what it meant. It seems he was suspicious that his wise men, who claimed to commune with the gods to tell him the future, were in fact charlatans who made things up. So, he set a clear and surprisingly scientific test. They were to first tell *him* what he had dreamed and then interpret it. They protested, they complained that if only the king would tell them the dream, they would interpret it. He said to them,

> "You have conspired to tell me misleading and wicked things, hoping the situation will change." (Daniel 2 vs 9)

Nebuchadnezzar did not believe their claims to have a hotline to the gods and ordered that unless they told him the dream and then interpreted it, they would be put to death. I did mention he was an absolute ruler and not apparently a patient man or one who took no for an answer.

Daniel was counted as one of the wise men, so he was caught up in the situation. When he heard of the death decree he asked for a stay of execution and then prayed that the one true God would reveal it and its meaning to him, which He did.

Daniel then went into the king and offered to do the impossible and tell him what he had dreamt and then what it meant. He had Nebuchadnezzar's full attention, who promptly got much more than he was expecting.

Daniel proceeded to recount the dream showing he really was in communication with God, unlike the other wise men who worshipped a variety of pagan deities.

> "You looked, O king, and there before you stood a large statue – an enormous statue, awesome in appearance. The head of the statue was made of pure gold, chest and arms of silver, belly and thighs of bronze, legs of iron, feet partly of iron and partly of baked clay. While you were watching, a rock was cut out, but not by human hands. It struck the statue on its feet of iron and clay and smashed them. Then the iron, the clay, the bronze, the silver and the gold were broken to pieces at the same time and became like chaff on a threshing floor in the summer. The wind swept them away without leaving a trace, but the rock that struck the statue became a huge mountain that filled the whole earth." (Daniel 2 vs 31-35)

Daniel then explained what it meant. The dream set out the broad sweep of history going forward from Babylon to the end of time. Babylon was the head of gold, then,

> "After you another kingdom will arise, inferior to yours. Next a third kingdom, one of bronze will rule over all the earth. Finally, a fourth kingdom, strong as iron – for iron breaks and smashes everything – and as iron breaks things to pieces, so too it will crush and break all the others. Just as you saw that the feet and toes were partly iron and partly clay, so this will be a divided kingdom: yet it will have some of the

strength of iron in it, even as you saw iron mixed with clay. As the toes were partly iron and partly clay, so this kingdom will be partly strong and partly brittle. And just as you saw the iron mixed with baked clay, so the people will be a mixture and not remain united, any more than iron mixes with clay." (Daniel 2 vs 39-43)

Then came the punch line. After this succession of human kingdoms, the final one is of a quite different character.

"In the time of those kings, the God of heaven will set up a kingdom that will never be destroyed, nor will it be left to another people. It will crush all those kingdoms and bring them to an end, but it will itself endure forever. This is the meaning of the rock cut out of a mountain, but not by human hands – a rock that broke the iron, the bronze, the clay, the silver and the gold to pieces. The great God has shown the king what will take place in the future. This dream is true and the interpretation is trustworthy." (Daniel 2 vs 44,45)

Not only did Babylon give way to a succession of other kingdoms but the last one broke all the previous ones to pieces "at the same time". It was clearly not a human kingdom and its breaking of previous kingdoms that had already passed away in history shows it ending history as we know it too.

Nebuchadnezzar recognised the dream and was overwhelmed, falling prostrate on the ground in front of Daniel – an absolute ruler was humbled. Daniel was made ruler over the entire province of Babylon and put in charge of all the "wise men". And so began the extraordinary rise and public life of Daniel.

If we start with Babylon and look to the succeeding kingdoms or empires that impacted on the Middle East and Israel, the statue is taken to represent the succession of Babylon to Medo-Persia (Silver), then Greece (Bronze), then Rome (Iron), then the divided territory of the Roman empire with some strong countries and some weaker ones (Iron and Baked clay) never being united again into one mega empire. Every attempt to reunite Europe and the Middle East into such an expansive empire since Rome has failed, from Charlemagne to Phillip of Spain, to Napoleon, to Hitler. It is sobering that after Rome broke apart, the nations have remained as predicted to Daniel, divided, some weak, some strong, to this day.

Through a series of other dreams and events the conversion of Nebuchadnezzar from autocratic tyrant to believer in the true God continued. Daniel through the rest of his lifetime also received a series of dreams or visions which set out the broad outline of history down to the Messiah, "the Anointed One" and on to the present day.

A generation ago, most people heard these stories and knew something of the outline of the events they portray. Sadly, with the demise of Christianity in much of the western world many people don't know them anymore, so permit me to outline a few more key events in the life of Daniel.

Nebuchadnezzar clearly liked the idea of being the "head of gold", but he didn't like the idea of Babylon ever being replaced. So, he set up a huge statue of gold all the way down (no succeeding kingdoms) and called his nobles together and commanded them to fall down and worship it when music was played. We can imagine his logic. He didn't want them thinking that since the dream had predicted that after his kingdom had ended another would arise, that they would be the ones to build that kingdom. He sought to set the record straight; his was the only kingdom and they were to show him absolute loyalty. If they didn't, they were to be thrown into a fiery furnace, which was stoked and ready nearby as an incentive to comply with the king's commands.

Three Hebrew young men, friends of Daniel and also in Nebuchadnezzar's service, refused to bow down. They were warned to comply, and they refused again because it meant worshipping something other than the true God in heaven. Nebuchadnezzar was absolutely furious in a way that perhaps only an absolute ruler can be, and so they were bound with ropes and thrown into the furnace. What happened next once more shocked Nebuchadnezzar to the core. Three young men were thrown into the furnace, but that is not what he saw in there,

> "He said, 'Look! I see four men walking around in the fire, unbound and unharmed and the fourth looks like a son of the gods'." (Daniel 3 vs 25)

They were brought out unharmed without even the smell of fire on them.

Later, Nebuchadnezzar went on to receive another dream of a great tree growing to fill the earth then being cut down, that Daniel interpreted as a warning that he must change his ways or be humbled and driven away from people as a mad man for "7 times." (Daniel 4 vs 16)

It came to pass after a 12 month stay of execution that it did happen to Nebuchadnezzar. He was mad for 7 years until,

> "At that time, I, Nebuchadnezzar, raised my eyes towards heaven and my sanity was restored." (Daniel 4, vs 34)

For many if not most people today, these stories would seem destined to remain interesting stories, infused with the supernatural, but scarcely credible. Miraculous deliverance from fire is not exactly an everyday occurrence and many would insist it is not possible. However, it is a curious phenomenon in western societies that on the one hand, we find hard-line secularists who insist there is no supernatural, and on the other increasing numbers of people who are quite credulous and prepared to believe almost any supernatural phenomena is possible, though curiously that typically doesn't include anything miraculous that could point them to God and require them to live differently.

The thing that makes it hard to dismiss Daniel so easily is that the prophecies he interpreted for Nebuchadnezzar and which he received himself, set out the flow of history from his day till now.

Let's look briefly at the last of the phrases mentioned at the start of this chapter. We have encountered "Feet of iron and clay" and "In the fiery furnace". We now turn to "The writing is on the wall" and "Thrown to the lions".

Nebuchadnezzar's successor Belshazzar did not pay attention to the lessons Nebuchadnezzar had learnt; to acknowledge the one true God in heaven and worship him alone. In fact, he went much further than ignoring Nebuchadnezzar's experience even though he knew about it, and organised a mass orgy of drinking and debauchery with 1000 of his nobles plus his wives and concubines (e.g. harem) all joining in at which he ordered that the vessels from the temple in Jerusalem be brought in for people to get drunk from. The scene has become a by word for debased behaviour. It has been painted by many classical painters often as an allegorical warning to those in power. It was a deliberate act of defiance of the one true God, though he knew better.

During the banquet a hand appeared and wrote on the plaster of the palace wall,

> "The king watched the hand as it wrote. His face turned pale and he was so frightened that his knees

knocked together and his legs gave way." (Daniel 5, vs 5,6)

But no-one could read what it meant. It read:

"Mene, mene, tekel, parsin" (Daniel 5 vs 25)

The riddle plays on the multiple meanings of the words. Mene can mean numbered, or it can mean a Mina, a unit of currency. Tekel can mean a shekel another unit of currency or weighed. Parsin is the plural of peres which can mean divided, or half a Mina or half a Shekel. It also sounds like Persian. It is unlikely that no-one could read Aramaic, but it made no sense when they looked at it. Was it -

Numbered, numbered, weighed, divided?

or

Mina, Mina, Shekel half a Shekel?

It really appeared to make no sense!

Eventually Daniel was called for, to read the inscription in Aramaic and interpret it. Once more God gave him its meaning. The message was extremely serious. Daniel reminded Belshazzar that he had failed to learn the lessons that Nebuchadnezzar had learned, even though he knew all about Nebuchadnezzar's experience. He was deliberately defying God. Daniel interpreted the words and gave their meaning.

"Mene; God has numbered the days of your reign and brought it to an end.

Tekel; You have been weighed on the scales and found wanting.

Peres; Your kingdom is divided and given to the Medes and Persians."

(Daniel 5 vs 25-28)

That very night the Persians invaded Babylon by a clever strategy. They diverted the flow of the river upstream and broke in under the city wall. Belshazzar was killed and Darius the Mede took over the kingdom. Daniel saw the first succession predicted in the dream of a statue come true with the fall of Babylon and another kingdom succeeding it. Medo-Persia was the next kingdom, the kingdom of silver.

The incredible life of Daniel is not quite over yet. Darius had clearly heard of Daniel's interpretation of dreams and his role in governing under Nebuchadnezzar and placed him in a senior government position. Daniel was by now approaching 90 years old. He was so pleased with Daniel that he planned to make him head over all the kingdom. Others were immediately jealous. They wanted rid of Daniel but couldn't find any basis to accuse him because he wasn't corrupt and did his job incredibly well, so in the end they schemed to get at him through his religion. They persuaded Darius to pass a decree that if anyone worshipped any god or man but the king for the next 30 days he must be thrown into the lion's den. This flattered Darius' ego and he agreed. Then the crunch came. Daniel was spotted praying to God three times a day as normal. Darius did not want him executed, and tried to avoid it, but the Medes and Persians held that the law once made could not be changed, even by the king, and so by sunset Daniel was "*Thrown to the lions*". The entrance was sealed to avoid any interference in the situation and amazingly Darius wished Daniel God's protection. Darius, like Nebuchadnezzar many years before him, had set a test. Whatever Daniel was thrown into, it would break the bones of a man of 90 and the lions would devour him. After a sleepless night, by first light of morning Darius rushed to see if Daniel was still alive. He was not only alive but unharmed in anyway. Darius was overcome! Those who had accused Daniel and plotted his demise were themselves thrown to the lions and devoured. Darius wrote throughout the kingdom that,

> "I issue a decree that in every part of my kingdom people must fear and reverence the God of Daniel, 'For he is the living God and he endures forever; his kingdom will not be destroyed, his dominion will never end." (Daniel 6 vs 26)

Darius understood that it matters who you worship and that the one true God is in charge of history. No doubt he was also impressed to learn that his own succession after Babylon had been predicted.

There is much more that could be said about Daniel and about the visions he received, this short introduction cannot cover it all. We will finish with returning to the time prophecies in Daniel.

When Daniel interpreted the dream of a tree that grew to fill the earth and was then cut down, he used the phrase "seven times". It turned out that Nebuchadnezzar was mad for seven years. Time was not expressed directly as "seven years".

In one of the visions given to Daniel an angel appeared to him and gave him the interpretation of something he had seen in vision earlier.

> "Know and understand this: From the issuing of the decree to restore and rebuild Jerusalem until the Anointed One, the ruler comes, there will be seven 'sevens' (or weeks) and sixty-two 'sevens (or weeks)'. It will be rebuilt with streets and a trench, but in times of trouble. After the sixty-two sevens, the Anointed One will be cut off and have nothing (or no-one)." (Daniel 9:25) (Comments in brackets supplied)

The prophetic interpretation continues for a few verses and

there is much more that could be said about it. (For more on the book of Daniel see for example, Michael Makowski *The book of Daniel, Prophecies for our Times, Simply and Clearly Explained*).

The decree to rebuild Jerusalem issued in 457 BC by Artaxerxes provides a starting point. Since the reformation, from Martin Luther onwards, people have puzzled over what these verses should be translated as and what do they mean. Seven sevens, or seven weeks or seventy weeks. If, as with Nebuchadnezzar's dream, the times, or days, or weeks are symbolic of longer time periods and if we count forward 70 weeks or 490 years from 457BC we arrive at the lifetime of Jesus the predicted Messiah, the Anointed One. It is intriguing that the dates fit exactly to when Jesus was alive and the time of his ministry.

Jesus was aware of the parallels, referring to himself repeatedly as the "Son of Man" a name for the Messianic figure in the book of Daniel.

> "In my vision at night I looked, and there before me was one like a son of man, coming with the clouds of heaven. He approached the Ancient of Days and was led into his presence. He was given authority, glory and sovereign power; all peoples, nations, and men of every language worshipped him. His dominion is an eternal dominion, and his kingdom is one that will never be destroyed." (Daniel 7 vs 13,14)

This is paralleled by many references made by Jesus of Nazareth such as,

> "No-one has ascended into heaven except he who came from heaven - the Son of Man." (John 3 vs13)

> "Then Jesus said to them, 'The Son of Man is Lord of the Sabbath'." (Luke 6 vs 5)

"Again the High Priest asked him, "Are you the Christ (or Messiah), the Son of the Blessed One?" "I am," said Jesus. "And you will see the Son of Man sitting at the right hand of the Mighty One and coming on the clouds of heaven." (Mark 14 vs 61,62)

It is also intriguing that however you count out the other time periods prophesied in Daniel they have all run out. For example, the 2300 days in Daniel chapter 8:14. In fact taking the starting point of Artaxerxes' decree in 457 BC to rebuild Jerusalem, adding 2300 years we reach 1843, then missing out the year zero that didn't exist we get 1844. The implication is clear. History from Daniel would see a succession of kingdoms, the appearance of the Messiah and then at some point the time prophecies (whatever they mean in detail) would run out, leaving an unspecified remaining end time before God wraps up history. Daniel himself was struggling to understand what he had been shown and was told,

"Go your way, Daniel, because the words are closed up and sealed until the time of the end." (Daniel 12 vs 9)

After reviewing the remarkable life of Daniel, we must finish with this deeply intriguing thought. God had revealed to Daniel a succession of kingdoms that fits the broad sweep of history right up to the present day, including the period when the Messiah would be on earth. What does it mean for us? As you work though what you believe, maybe it is worth coming back to Daniel and spending some more time on this ancient book. Maybe you will find that it contains not just great allegorical stories, but something of much greater importance.

God has acted into history

To quote Daniel one last time,

"The Most High is sovereign over the kingdoms of men."

Daniel 4 vs 25

And,

"His dominion is an eternal dominion; his kingdom endures from generation to generation."

Daniel 4 vs 34

24 DIDN'T ANYBODY SEE IT COMING?

Isaiah and the Messiah

Most of us have dreamt of finding treasure at some time or other. That treasure hunting impulse is something many have shared down the centuries, though sadly not always exercised in a benign way. The tomb robbers in Egypt, for example, deprived future generations of historical artefacts and historical knowledge of immense value because the real value of discoveries often lies in what they show us of the past.

In Staffordshire, England, in 2009 two amateur metal detectorists located an unbelievable find. From a ploughed field they uncovered coins, exquisite jewellery, horse buckles, sword pommels. In total more than 3500 items were found. It was the largest hoard of Anglo-Saxon gold ever discovered, with more than 5 kg of gold. The sheer quantity and variety shocked everyone. (See https://www.staffordshirehoard.org.uk/)

It became known as the Staffordshire Hoard. It includes items with Christian and pagan motifs and shows a society in a period of profound change. One intriguing item is a gold strip about 17 cm long with an inscription from the Old Testament book of Numbers chapter 10 vs 35. In modern English it reads,

"Rise up O LORD! May your enemies be scattered: may your foes flee before you".

There was a significant external threat from Viking raiders that may have led to the burial. For whatever reason, at some point in the Dark Ages an unknown person or persons hid a treasure trove of immense value and it lay undiscovered for 1400 years. Parts of the hoard are now on display in museums in the Midlands whilst conservation work is carried out on many other items. It was estimated to have a value of £3.2 million, but the real value is in the insights into a period of history with little in the way of written records. When examined closely under 2- or 3-times magnification, the intricate detail and quality of workmanship on so many of the small objects is scarcely believable and the average quality of all the objects is very high.

We turn now to other treasure in a dry desert. In 1946/47, some Bedouin herdsmen threw small rocks into the mouth of a cave in the desert of Qumran near to the Dead Sea. The impulse of curiosity is understandable. Rather than the sound of rock on rock however, they heard what sounded like breaking pottery. When they had climbed to the cave entrance, they found pots containing pieces of scroll with writing on. Eventually when archaeologists were alerted further investigation found a considerable number of pots in several caves. In all 11 caves were discovered with scrolls in. The herdsmen had stumbled across what is now known as the Dead Sea Scrolls. The scrolls contain all kinds of information that give insights into the lives of the those who hid them, usually believed to be the Essenes, an obscure Jewish sect, during the last three centuries BC and First century AD. The Dead Sea Scrolls contain fragments of nearly every book of the Old Testament. The most significant find was an almost complete copy of the book of Isaiah, the Great Isaiah Scroll. It has been dated to about 100 BC. (J. Warner Wallace, *Cold Case Christianity*)

The Isaiah scroll was about 1000 years older than the oldest Masoretic copy of the book of Isaiah which Bible translators had relied on until then. Even more important than its value as an object was the discovery that it

> "proved to be word for word identical to our standard Hebrew Bible in more than 95% of the text." (Gleason, Archer, *A survey of Old Testament, Introduction*, quoted in, J. Warner Wallace, *Cold Case Christianity*, page 233)

Where differences do occur, they are largely minor matters of spelling, or occasional insertions of a word for clarity such as at the end of the verse "they shall see" (Isaiah 53 vs 11), where "light" is added.

> "None of these grammatical variations changed the meaning of the text in any way." (J. Warner Wallace, *Cold Case Christianity*, page 233)

I have referred to the book Cold Case Christianity here as a very readable source to explore these issues further, but there are of course many more academic and heavy weight texts looking at these same issues in more detail which come to the same conclusion. (For another very readable overview see, Craig Blomberg, *Can we Still Believe the Bible?*).

Why does this matter? Well, simply put, **Christian belief hangs on the historical acts of God into real history.**

We encounter the same problem with the written records of Jesus life and the lives of the apostles in the New Testament books. You can look at the teachings of Confucius on their own merit without needing to establish whether he really lived, though there is no reason to doubt that he did, but the teachings of Christianity make no sense without the life, death and physical resurrection of Jesus. If you attempt to separate the two, his real life and his teaching you are doomed to failure. Similarly, if God did not act into history, predict history and predict the Messiah, much of the case for accepting that Jesus was who he claimed to be falls apart too.

Those who do not want to accept that God could ever possibly act into history have set out to rubbish the various books collected into what we now call the Old Testament section of the Bible. One of the lines of attack has been to claim that the text we have is so changed that we cannot possibly know what the original was like. They assert, without proof, that the text has been changed over time to add the messages people wanted to get from it. The Dead Sea Scrolls, however, paint a different picture of very careful preservation and transmission of the text.

Let's look at some of what is in the Isaiah scroll, because it turns out to be quite inconvenient and not be what everyone would like it to be.

Several themes emerge in the book of Isaiah. There are repeated warnings to the nation of Israel and the surrounding nations to change their ways or disaster of various forms would come upon them. There is a repeated call to abandon idols and other 'gods' and to turn to the one true God who made everything. The language and logic in Isaiah are shockingly modern, sometimes downright sarcastic and surprise many readers. Here is an example, pointing out the stupidity of making idols.

"Half of the wood he burns in the fire: over it he prepares his meal... From the rest he makes a god, his idol; he bows down to it and worships. He prays to it and says, "Save me; you are my god".... No one stops to think, no one has the knowledge or understanding to say, "Half of it I used for fuel; I roasted meat and I ate. Shall I make a detestable thing from what is left? Shall I bow down to a block of wood?" (Isaiah 44 vs 16-19)

In contrast Isaiah uses the same argument we have considered in earlier chapters; that all of nature around us argues for a Creator and a Designer, one omnipotent pre-existent being. He repeatedly identifies the one true God as the one who made everything.

"For this is what the LORD says – he who created the heavens, he is God; he who fashioned and made the earth, he founded it." (Isaiah 45 vs 18)

Isaiah leaves it as self-evident that there is an ultimate cause to reality and that the cause is the one and only God. However, he moves beyond stating his existence to something much bolder. He says that God declares,

"Remember the former things, those of long ago; I am God, and there is no other. I am God, and there is none like me. I make known the end from the beginning, from ancient times, what is still to come.... What I have said, that will I bring about; what I have planned, that will I do." (Isaiah 46 vs 9-11)

Many predictions are made in Isaiah. Sceptics insist they were edited in later after the event, because they insist that no one can predict the future. It isn't so easy to dismiss Isaiah, however. He predicts by name that Cyrus the Persian emperor will allow Israelites to return from captivity to rebuild Jerusalem and the temple (Isaiah 44 vs 28 and 45 vs 1,2). Isaiah predicted Cyrus by name more than 150 years before he reigned. Many have insisted this cannot be true and must be a later insertion, they claim there must have been a later Isaiah or a committee of scribes editing the book of Isaiah at a later date. All they do, however, is create a greater problem for themselves because the text we have of Isaiah is the same as that of the Dead Sea Scrolls which is solidly known to be from before Jesus lived, and yet throughout the book there are predictions of the Messiah which did come true in the life of Jesus of Nazareth. So, instead of having just one prophet called Isaiah accurately predicting the future, they end up with two Isaiahs or a whole group of people accurately predicting Jesus' life and work, which is probably an even greater miracle. As we shall see, the prophecies of the Messiah that we will come to present a greater challenge to dismiss than trying to write off one reference to Cyrus.

The fall of Babylon is predicted, (see for example Isaiah 47) along with the demise of various other nations. However, as with the book of Daniel the prophecies in Isaiah reach much further forward into history with predictions of the Messiah. The Messiah (Jesus) came after most of the Dead Sea Scrolls were written out. With the Great Isaiah scroll, we have a text of Isaiah that predates Jesus, yet he fits exactly to the predictions it makes. We have the same text of the book of Isaiah in the Bible today. This is not what many people wanted to find, because it is very inconvenient to their attempts to write off the idea that God had any hand in what Isaiah wrote. The section in Isaiah from chapter 52 vs 13 through to the end of chapter 53 predicting the life and ministry of the Messiah, is worth reading in full, although predictions of the Messiah occur in many places through Isaiah.

I'm not sure what most people are expecting from a book like

Isaiah but judging from the line most secular people have been fed, the last thing they are expecting is solid evidence that we have a reliably preserved text, or accurate predictions. Thanks to the Dead Sea Scrolls we can be confident we have a text that accurately reflects what was in circulation as the book of Isaiah, well before Jesus of Nazareth was born, lived, taught, was persecuted then executed. Here, in Isaiah chapter 53, in Hebrew poetry, from over 2500 years ago we have a remarkable portrait of an individual that fits shockingly well to Jesus' life and ministry. If you read and take in the biographies of Jesus in the gospels, then return to read this section of Isaiah it is truly remarkable.

It was passages like this that helped the Jewish followers of Jesus to set aside the idea they had received from their religious leaders, that the Messiah was to be an all-conquering military hero who would kick out the Romans who were occupying Palestine at the time, and to see that the life, suffering and death of the Messiah were exactly what was predicted. And along with that they came to understand that Jesus was God *"embodying himself in human form."* (N.T. Wright, *The Resurrection of the Son of God*).

If we look at what Daniel predicted, and Isaiah predicted as well as other prophets recorded in the books compiled into the Old Testament, we find a quite incredible picture emerges.

> "Imagine someone predicting that the 68th president of the United States will be born in Riverside, California. If that single prediction came true, that would be amazing enough. But what if additional predictions were added? Not only will the 68th President of the United States be born in Riverside, CA, he will begin his presidency in 2030, and then 3 ½ years into his presidency he will be assassinated, and the

assassination will be carried out with a 22-calibre handgun, by one of his close political allies. Now we have moved beyond the realm of amazing into the realm of impossible. There is simply no way that all of these converging features could be foretold years in advance without foreknowledge. And yet this is precisely what the Bible does." (Of the Messiah). (Ty Gibson, *The One*)

Here are some comparisons between Isaiah (plus a few other Old Testament prophets) and the records of Jesus' life in the gospels.

Isaiah says,

"See my servant will act wisely; he will be raised and lifted up and highly exalted. Just as there were many who were appalled at him – his appearance was so disfigured beyond that of any man and his form marred beyond human likeness." (Isaiah 52 vs 13,14)

We find similar in the Psalms. Long before the Messiah, David wrote:

"A band of evil men has encircled me, they have pierced my hands and my feet. I can count all my bones; people stare and gloat over me. They divide my garments among them and cast lots for my clothing." (Psalm 22 vs 16-18)

Jesus was arrested, tried, flogged nearly to death (the intention was to nearly kill someone) and then raised up on a cross and crucified even though Pilate the Roman governor declared,

"I find no basis for a charge against this man." (Luke 23 vs 4)

"When they had crucified him, they divided up his

clothes by casting lots." (Matthew 27 vs 35)

Isaiah predicted,

> "He was despised and rejected by men, a man of sorrows and familiar with suffering. Like one from whom men hide their faces, he was despised, and we esteemed him not." (Isaiah 53 vs 3)

Jesus was rejected by the religious authorities as the "Wrong Messiah" (see Nick Page, *The Wrong Messiah, the Real Story of Jesus of Nazareth* for more discussion).

Christians came to recognise that Jesus died the death we should die so that we might have the life that he can give. He taught it and the temple service they had been following predicted it. We could say much about that, but at the simplest level, the Temple service had a sacrificial lamb at the Passover festival, the very weekend when Jesus was crucified.

Isaiah claims,

> "Surely he took up our infirmities and carried our sorrows, yet we considered him stricken by God, smitten by him and afflicted. But he was pierced for our transgressions, he was crushed for our iniquities; the punishment that brought us peace was upon him, and by his wounds we are healed. We all like sheep have gone astray and the LORD has laid on him the iniquity of us all." (Isaiah 53 vs 4 – 6)

In the biographies of Matthew and Luke we find,

> "When they came to the place called the Skull, there they crucified him." (Luke 23 vs 33)

> "Those who passed by hurled insults at him, shaking their heads and saying, "You who are going to destroy the temple and build it in three days, save your-

self! Come down from the cross, if you are the Son of God!" (Matthew 27 vs 39,40)

Centuries before crucifixion was even invented it was alluded to in piercing and raising up, in Isaiah 52 and Psalm 22.

With the crucifixion and resurrection of Jesus, God was showing that right and wrong are real. Sin, that is rebelling against God and doing wrong, is a problem only God himself can fix and at immense cost. In fact, a cost so great we can only begin to understand it. The way in which Jesus did not resist his execution, as recorded in all four biographies (gospels) but instead calmly and quietly went to the cross, is also made clear in Isaiah.

> "He was oppressed and afflicted, yet he did not open his mouth; he was led like a lamb to the slaughter and as a sheep before her shearers is silent, so he did not open his mouth." (Isaiah 53 vs 7)

The gospel of Matthew records:

> "The chief priests and the whole Sanhedrin were looking for false evidence against Jesus so that they could put him to death. But they did not find any, though many false witnesses came forward. Finally two came forward and declared, "This fellow said, 'I am able to destroy the temple of God and rebuild it in three days'". Then the high priest stood up and said to Jesus. "Are you not going to answer? What is this testimony that these men are bringing against you?" But Jesus remained silent." (Matthew 26 vs 59-63)

Isaiah predicts his burial place.

> "He was assigned a grave with the wicked, and with

the rich in his death." (Isaiah 53 vs 9)

Luke records that Jesus was buried in a rich man's tomb borrowed because there was no alternative at short notice,

> "Now there was a man named Joseph,... Going to Pilate, he asked for Jesus body. Then he took it down, wrapped it in linen cloth and placed it in a tomb cut in the rock, one in which no one had yet been laid." (Luke 23 vs 50-53)

Even the resurrection is portrayed,

> "After the suffering of his soul, he will see the light of life and be satisfied, by his knowledge my righteous servant will justify many, and he will bear their iniquities... he poured out his life unto death, and was numbered with the transgressors. For he bore the sin of many and made intercession for the transgressors." (Isaiah 53 vs 12,13)

Matthew records:

"After the Sabbath, at dawn on the first day of the week, Mary Magdalene and the other Mary went to look at the tomb.... Suddenly Jesus met them. "Greetings," he said. They came to him, clasped his feet and worshipped him." (Matthew 28 vs 1, 9)

Many Jewish people have come to recognise Jesus as the Messiah by comparing Isaiah 53 with the biographies of Jesus life. The parallels are so powerful. There is much more to consider here, and this book is only an introduction, so do take your time to evaluate the book of Isaiah and the prophecies of the Messiah contained in it. There is no need for a snap judgement, dig deeper and let the evidence speak for itself.

Isaiah was not alone in making predictions about the Messiah. Multiple unconnected writers over more than 1000 years made predictions about the Messiah in books now collected into the Old Testament. Here are some more.

He is predicted to be born of a virgin,

> "Therefore the Lord himself will give you a sign: The virgin will be with child and will give birth to a son and will call him Immanuel." (Immanuel means God with us). (Isaiah 7 vs 14)

He will be a descendant of Jacob,

> "I see him, but not now; I behold him, but not near. A star will come out of Jacob: a sceptre will rise out of Israel." (Numbers 24 vs 17)

He will be of the tribe of Judah and born in Bethlehem,

> "But you Bethlehem Ephrathah, though you are small among the clans of Judah, out of you will come for me one who will be ruler over Israel, whose origins are from of old, from ancient times." (Micah 5 vs 2)

He will be of the family line of Jesse,

> "A shoot will come up from the stump of Jesse; from his roots a Branch will bear fruit. The Spirit of the LORD will rest on him- the Spirit of wisdom and of understanding, the Spirit of counsel and power, the Spirit of knowledge and of the fear of the LORD." (Isaiah 11 vs 1-3)

He will be a descendant of David,

> ""The days are coming," declares the LORD, "when I will raise up to David" (or from David's line) "a righteous branch, a King who will reign wisely and do what is just and right in the land. In his days Judah will be saved and Israel will live in safety. This is the name by which he will be called: The LORD Our

Righteousness." (Jeremiah 23 vs 5,6) (Comments in brackets supplied)

Jesus fulfilled all these predictions by where he was born and who was in his family tree. His genealogy is in Luke 3 vs 21-37.

He took the prophecies very seriously. For example, Zechariah 9:9 says,

"See, your king comes to you, righteous and having salvation, gentle and riding on a donkey, on a colt, the foal of a donkey."

Matthew records that Jesus intentionally fulfilled this prophecy entering Jerusalem on a donkey. "When Jesus entered Jerusalem, the whole city was stirred and asked, "Who is this?"." Matthew 21 vs 10

Nick Page points out that in the run up to the Passover festival the Roman governor entered Jerusalem from the other direction in great pomp and military might with cavalry. Jesus entering from the opposite direction on a donkey was making a vivid point about the nature of true power and the kingdom of God versus the brutality and oppression of the Roman authorities. (See Nick Page, *Whatever happened to the ark of the covenant?*)

One obvious question is, what did Jesus himself make of all this? Talking to his disciples after his resurrection he said,

"This is what I told you while I was still with you: Everything must be fulfilled that is written about me in the Law of Moses, the Prophets and the Psalms." (Luke 24 vs 44)

We have looked at just a small selection of the prophecies of the Messiah in the Old Testament books. It is worth bearing in mind that the religious hierarchy of Jesus day largely did not accept him as the Messiah, but to those with an open mind the prophecies were convincing proof, along with his resurrection. This is a reasonable counter argument against those who claim that Christians later modified these ancient books to make them fit to Jesus as the Messiah; Jewish people were making that claim right from the start. It was central to who he was and what they believed.

The Apostle Peter made this the central point of his first large scale public address after the resurrection.

> "Men of Israel, listen to this: Jesus of Nazareth was a man accredited by God to you by miracles, wonders and signs, which God did among you through him, as you yourselves know." (Acts of the Apostles, 2 vs 22)

If that wasn't solid eyewitness testimony and true, then his Jewish audience in Jerusalem would have known and ignored him. After more discussion he says,

> "Therefore let all Israel be assured of this: God has made this Jesus, whom you crucified, both Lord and Christ (Messiah)." (Acts of the Apostles 2 vs 36)

His lengthy speech led to 3000 converts in one day.

Later, after his conversion on the road to Damascus the Apostle Paul (or Saul by his Jewish name) taught the same message in the Damascus synagogues. (We will look at this in another chapter).

> "At once he began to preach in the synagogues that Jesus is the Son of God... Saul grew more and more powerful and baffled the Jews living in Damascus by proving that Jesus is the Christ (or Messiah)." (Note - Christ derives from Greek, Messiah from Hebrew, they mean the same thing). (Acts of the Apostles, 9 vs 20 and 22)

The point is that the prophetic context for the Messiah mattered right from the start of people believing in Jesus as the Messiah.

It is extremely helpful that copies of these Old Testament texts survive independent of the Christian tradition, preserved by Judaism, that still contain these same verses and prophecies, and we must be immensely grateful for that. They provide a corroboration of the predictions of the Messiah that Jesus fulfilled.

Sometimes I wonder what modern people are expecting to find when we talk about prophecies of the Messiah. They were written so long ago by diverse authors spanning over a thousand years, all in such different circumstances to our own, or even to the time when Jesus lived, and yet we have:

> predictions of his family lineage,
>
> his place of birth,
>
> the essentials of his ministry,
>
> his sacrificial death,
>
> his resurrection,
>
> the exact time of his life and crucifixion (Daniel 9 vs 25 see previous chapter).

They point unmistakably to Jesus of Nazareth.

Can this all be coincidence? When good evidence of the reliability of the texts lies also with Jewish not just Christian sources, how reasonable is it to claim they have been modified by Christians after the fact? When does a long series of "coincidences" stop being coincidence? How many things about Jesus' life need to accurately fit to the line of descent, location, and ministry predicted for the Messiah, before someone is prepared to say, 'Ok, this is more than any reasonable person can call coincidence'?

Jesus fulfilled the prophecies of the Messiah, and the manuscripts that we have show us that the predictions were exactly that, predictions given before the events they outline occurred

Isaiah says that God declares.

> "I make known the end from the beginning, from ancient times, what is still to come."
>
> Isaiah 46 vs 10

Isaiah gives a purpose for why these things are revealed. Is that why so many don't want to see the evidence for what it is, because it has clear implications?

> "Seek the Lord while he may be found; call on him while he is near. Let the wicked forsake his way and the evil man his thoughts. Let him turn to the LORD and he will have mercy on him, and to our God for he will freely pardon."
>
> Isaiah 55 vs 6,7

Five centuries later Paul of Tarsus quoted Isaiah extensively and wrote:

> "For everything that was written in the past was written to teach us, so that through endurance and

the encouragement of the Scriptures we might have hope."

Letter to the Christians in Rome; Romans 15 vs 4

25 HOW DO YOU EVER KNOW?

The truth vs competing claims

J ust up from the harbour sat a modest house with a flat roof with a couple of additional rooms built onto it and fish were drying in the sun. A piercing Mediterranean light shone through the open window that faced the sea, catching the sea breeze. Most windows were shuttered against the midday heat. The street had fallen quiet after the fish market and an unassuming middle-aged man now sat at a simple desk writing on small pieces of parchment, laboriously in large handwriting. This habit of writing on small pieces and then sewing them together to make portable documents rather than using the traditional scrolls was a cutting-edge innovation of its day. (Nick Page, *Kingdom of Fools, the Unlikely Rise of The Early Church*). The ships, large and small, visible in the harbour connected the empire across the sea at the centre of the known world. Ideas flowed along with goods and wares. You could set off to anywhere from here. The man writing had nothing of note in terms of personal possessions, he was writing in a friend's house, composing one of his many letters where he explained his beliefs and thinking to new believers.

The threads of his life all wove together towards this same issue that he was presently writing about. What was the key in explaining his belief to others that made it totally distinct from all the other religious claims made across the Roman world? What made it clear that this was *the* truth? The issue had consumed much of his adult life and he always came back to the same answer that he had found at the beginning:

the physical bodily resurrection of Jesus from the dead.

The experience of sharing what he believed had been traumatic. He had been flogged, beaten with rods, chased, prosecuted, shouted down and thrown out of town. In Athens he had been called to explain himself before the learned council of the city the Areopagus. Paul had talked with anyone he came across who would listen, and he knew the issues inside out. (Note that whilst the setting here is imagined, to take our thoughts to the context where Paul wrote, we do have reliable copies of what he wrote).

If from the comforts of the 21st Century we look back to the 1st Century world and think it unsophisticated we simply show our own ignorance. It was possible to obtain a first-class education then, that compares well with any available now. Paul almost certainly spoke and wrote Hebrew, Latin and Greek as well as speaking Aramaic. He was a Roman citizen but had grown up a devout Jew. His education had included studying the great Greek philosophers as well as the Torah and its interpretations. He was well travelled and well connected. He also had a brilliant mind.

Here is the nub of the issue he faced. If he were to debate with an educated Greek about the existence of God and indeed of only One supreme God, he would be potentially setting himself up for a conversation that could last a lifetime. All the issues that are rehearsed in these discussions today, were in some form or other, already matters of debate and discussion then. On the basis of argument alone, he could set out a reasonable basis for his beliefs but that was not enough to convince people. There had to be a further ingredient and he saw that could only be God choosing to act directly into history to reveal himself in an incontrovertible way that breaks the philosophical and theological deadlock. God acting into what He has made from the outside, but in a way that made it clear that it was Him acting. This is the unique aspect of Judeo-Christian thought; a real God acting into real history, not wishful thinking, religious sentiment or philosophical discussion.

As well as being well rehearsed in the philosophical debates of the day, Paul had received an extensive orthodox Jewish education under a renowned tutor, Gamliel. He had served an apprenticeship, that is a discipleship, and come out the other end able to recite the Torah and quote every authority on its interpretation and application. He had joined a religious reform movement that sought to implement to the letter, all that they believed God required of them, by becoming a Pharisee. He had given himself to good works helping the poor and sick. He had also sought to zealously protect what he had been taught and believed and persecuted the followers of a new movement known at that point as followers of The Way. Then, unexpectedly, he left all that behind and became a follower of The Way, that is a Christian. When he talked with other Jews about his belief in Jesus as God revealing himself in human form, he knew exactly what they would be thinking in response; this was not what they believed God would do. (See for example Nick Page, 'The Wrong Messiah, the Real Story of Jesus of Nazareth'). Some believed, but many opposed and persecuted him viciously. What could possibly get through to them?

Paul was as we noted of two camps. He had grown up in Tarsus.

He straddled the Roman/Greek and Jewish worlds and could see how people thought in both. He wondered endlessly what would get through to them?

The answer in both cases, for Jews and Greeks/Romans was the fact of the resurrection of Jesus and the consequences that fact then had in his life and others. This was philosophically, theologically and practically, the key point he had known from the beginning, and it had lost none of its force over many years of sharing it. When he had first heard of Jews following Jesus, he wasn't surprised. Popular leaders arose from time to time. They developed a following, then they annoyed the Romans, they died, and their followers were scattered and that was that. This Jesus had been a miracle worker, some said a prophet and he had a noticeable popular following, but when he died, in his case, his followers didn't melt away. They insisted that he had risen from the dead with a real physical body and after appearing to many people over a period of weeks, then went up to heaven. As a well-read Jew it had made no sense. The Messiah was not expected to be Divine, so Jesus' claims to divinity were offensive. His rising from the dead made little sense from a Jewish or Roman/Greek perspective. Dead people don't come back to life again, everyone knew that. (For a good discussion of the resurrection see N. T. Wright *The Resurrection of the Son of God*).

So, Paul's initial course of action had been to persecute the early followers of The Way as they were called. He simply could not bear seeing their heresy, as he understood it, spread any more.

The one thing that he had not counted on was that Jesus might actually have risen from the dead. That was to him the one unthinkable possibility. As he put it in a letter he later wrote to believers in Corinth,

"We preach Christ crucified: a stumbling block to the

Jews and foolishness to Gentiles." (Paul, First letter to the church in Corinth, 1 Corinthians 1 vs 23)

It was foolishness to the Greeks (that is the Greco-Roman culture) because dead people stay dead, always, everyone knew that. It was a stumbling block to Jews because whilst the *Book of Daniel* bore witness to the possibility of resurrection at some future point, as he understood it, it was not expected to happen to the Messiah in advance of anyone else. Nor for that matter was the Messiah supposed to go around claiming to be equal with God or the embodiment of God (See N. T. Wright, appendix to Flew, *There is a God; How the World's Most Notorious Atheist Changed His Mind*). But if it was actually true that he had risen, then everything Paul believed would have to be rethought, because it proved the claims Jesus had made of himself. He had after all publicly said,

"I am the way and the truth and the life." (John 14 vs 6)

Then it happened. Paul met him. He was on the way to Damascus from Jerusalem to find these heretics and drag them back to Jerusalem to answer for their corruption of the Jewish faith, when he met him. A blindingly bright being appeared and asked him by his Jewish name

"Saul, Saul, why are you persecuting me?" "Who are you?" he asked. The answer was, "I am Jesus whom you are persecuting." (Acts of the Apostles 9 vs 4,5 ESV).

Paul was left blinded.

It is a fascinating incident and to Paul it must have seemed a very curious question. Saul (as Paul was known at that point) was persecuting the early followers of Jesus before anyone had even coined the name Christians. But the question he was asked made it clear that his actions against them were really against this person, who now confronted him. He was clearly taking on something much bigger than a few followers of a new Jewish sect. This blindingly bright being then instructed him to go into the city of Damascus where he would be told what he must do, which he duly did. After three days Paul was prayed for by a believer in this Jesus and he miraculously received his sight back.

His immediate reaction to this event was to preach in the Damascus synagogue that Jesus is the Son of God and the Messiah. Now from a Jewish perspective that is a big one. God is one. No-one was expecting Him to have a son. Clues were there in the Old Testament scriptures, to use their common name today. For example, right in the first chapter of Genesis God is referred to in the plural,

"Let us make man in <u>our</u> image." (Emphasis added)
(Genesis 1 vs 26)

Even so, it was not the expected thing that God would have a son.

Paul baffled the Jews in Damascus by proving that Jesus is the Messiah from reference to their own scriptures. Actually, to say they were baffled is serious understatement. They were totally taken aback by this unexpected turn of events, the persecutor of these followers of Jesus was now making claims that proved the new faith. Yet, Jesus simply did not fit what they expected the Messiah to be. Saul now calling himself Paul, then appears to have disappeared from view for a number of years. He was probably considering his position very carefully. I suspect he was simply overwhelmed and took quite a time to work out what it all meant and to relate what had happened to him to what he already knew.

The writings of Paul that we still have preserved in the New Testament, are better attested than just about any other ancient literature, so we can't wiggle off the hook by suggesting it was all made up later, a point we looked at in another chapter. In those writings it comes clear what Paul did in response to meeting the risen Jesus. He made contact with other eyewitnesses to Jesus' appearances after his resurrection. He reviewed the Torah and prophetic writings to work out where this fitted in with his Jewish faith and he debated with everyone who would listen, in synagogues and in any venue that would let him, and he had boiled it all down to one essential point as being more important than any other. He repeats himself for emphasis,

> "If Christ has not been raised, your faith is futile....If only for this life we have hope in Christ, we are to be pitied more than all men"! (Paul's 1st letter to the Corinthians 15 vs 17, 19)

Why? Firstly, unless God had acted into history in an unmistakable way to reveal his power, by appearing and living as a man and then after being unjustly killed, rising from the dead by his own power, proving his power over death, then everything else that Paul and others claimed followed from that was complete nonsense. Paul knew that and he staked his own life on it. When the enormity of what had happened with the resurrection fully sank in, Paul knew that this was the turning point of everything. Secondly, Paul and other believers including Jesus special group of disciples were paying a very high price for their new-found faith. If the resurrection wasn't real, they were crazy.

No matter what your background, prior beliefs, education or bias, Jesus rising from the dead is bigger than everything else. By coming to life again he leaves people with no option but to move beyond any other arguments or preconceptions to work out what his resurrection means.

Be assured that it is not as if getting their heads around this was something the early believers did easily either. They clearly took quite a while to work out what it all meant as is discussed well by N. T. Wright (see his appendix to Anthony Flew 'There is a God; How the World's Most Notorious Atheist Changed His Mind' as well as Wright's fuller book on the resurrection, 'The Resurrection of the Son of God').

However, if the resurrection happened, then it is simply the biggest thing that has happened since the beginning of time, because it shows the power of God over death. If it didn't, then we are left with possibilities, inferences, lines of argument and well-meaning religious activity. If there was no resurrection of Jesus, it means there is ultimately no absolute basis for the belief that God is knowable and interested in us, rather than remote and unreachable. The resurrection is the seal of proof on Jesus' claim to be the saviour of the world.

So, Paul helps us refine our questions about belief to one supreme question. Did Jesus rise from the dead? And if the answer is yes, then it changes everything. There are an infinite number of other questions you can absorb your life with. You can philosophise from now to eternity, but if Jesus did rise from the dead, working out what that means becomes the single most important thing you will ever have to deal with because it is the basis of His claim to be the source of life and the one who can give life to those who believe in Him.

Jesus' resurrection changes everything

Paul explains what this means very directly. Many people are amazed to find he was so candid.

> "If Christ has not been raised from the dead, our preaching is useless and so is your faith."
> Paul of Tarsus, 1st letter to the Christians in Corinth; 1 Corinthians 15 vs 14

It is just what Jesus claimed too.

> "I am the resurrection and the life. He who believes in me will live, even though he dies; and whoever lives and believes in me will never die."
>
> Jesus of Nazareth, quoted in John 11 vs 25

26 THE WAY, THE TRUTH AND THE LIFE

The resurrection and what it means

I f the resurrection happened, it is literally the biggest thing in history. What we are going to do is look at some of the evidence that is available for the resurrection of Jesus. There is no analogy that can be made to help discuss this. Compared to anything else we consider it is so far off the scale that illustrations won't get us close. However, we must first of all take a more fundamental look at how it is that we know anything at all.

Most of what we think we know we share with others in our culture and times. Our upbringing and the cultural influences around us shape our world view and from them we absorb most of what we "know". If someone wants to convince us of something new, they may try one of various ways of doing so.

It is possible to appeal to authority. For example, 'Teacher says', so it must be true. Or, how about, 'An expert says', so it really must be true. Or even better, 'Many experts agree'. Surely that makes it even more certain! However, experts can be wrong. In fact, they are often wrong. There is a place for expertise, it can contribute to our understanding, but an appeal to experts will not of itself resolve arguments about the resurrection because we can often line up people who claim to be experts on both sides of an argument. The problem then is that people tend to believe the 'expert' who most closely fits their prior assumptions, or worldview, not necessarily the one who lines up with the evidence.

We can look to science to try to resolve an issue. If something is labelled as 'science' or 'scientific' it is popularly held to be more true than other knowledge. A lot of Christians have fallen into the trap of being brow beaten by the claims that science makes to be the preeminent source of knowledge. Thus, as Francis Schaeffer put it, they think that the Bible is true, but science is "more true". That is a logical fallacy as well as an unsafe assumption, but it is still very widespread. (Francis Schaeffer, *'Escape from Reason'*). When recognising tensions between the supposedly more reliable knowledge of science versus the Bible, many Christians have taken the route of separating belief from any rigorous evidence base. They may think it sounds very holy, but it is very dangerous. Often, they say in effect, 'Well just believe any way' and belief becomes a leap of faith away from the evidence. Soren Kierkegaard the Danish Theologian is credited rightly or wrongly with promoting that approach. Belief becomes a metaphysical experience not anchored in reason or evidence. And most people rightly reject it on those terms when they encounter it presented that way.

There are immense problems with a 'leap of faith' away from the evidence, not the least of which is that such claims to knowledge are untestable and are therefore potentially little more convincing than delusions. The fact that many Christians persist in seeing faith and belief as a leap away from the hard world of evidence has meant that people looking in from the outside are quite rightly very sceptical. It looks like willing yourself to believe. Those same people then fall back on the messages they have received from western culture over the last century and a half that science is more reliable than any other knowledge, and they are fully equipped to dismiss out of hand Christianity and claims such as Jesus rising from the dead. Sadly, many Christians and churches have fed this problem by retreating from arguing for the solid evidential basis for Christian belief and they have failed western countries where Christianity was previously much more widespread. There is a place for the subjective experience of Christianity, it is essential, but it is not the primary basis for belief.

We must keep remembering that a significant lesson of the 20th and 21st centuries regarding science, has been a growing realisation that there is a lot that science simply can't address, even though in the media science and scientists are still often rolled out as the final arbiters of any debate. It is a false and lazy argument to appeal to science as the ultimate authority to resolve any issue. It is an equally lazy and false argument to label any "non-scientific" explanation as false or unreliable, or "less true". We can't travel back in time and do scientific tests to evaluate the resurrection. This is a question that must be addressed on the basis of other evidence. That means primarily treating it like any other historical event and examining documents, eye-witness accounts and evaluating claimants' lives and actions.

There is another problem if you want to convince someone of something new, they have to be willing to hear you. We have seen that it is always a sure bet to appeal to their previously held assumptions or presuppositions (i.e. their existing worldview). If what you say matches those prior assumptions, they are likely to receive what you say and believe it. To argue for the solid historical basis of Christianity means that someone who isn't a Christian, has to be willing to look beyond their existing pre-suppositions and consider the possibility of there being more than they were previously aware of. The whole point of this book has been to encourage people to do just that.

If we limit ourselves to only being willing to accept as true things which fit our pre-existing assumptions or pre-suppositions about what is or can be right, then we are basically saying that whatever we absorbed as children in our upbringing must pose an absolute limit to what we are able to know. That is clearly not satisfactory.

If we are prepared to take it a bit further, then we may find that we are limiting what we know and can know, to what the majority of the culture around us agrees with or believes. That position also has problems, not the least of which is that the cultural consensus drifts over time and is different in different places. Some commonly held views of today are not the same as those of a century or two ago.

If we are more brave, we can follow the evidence and argument wherever they lead. Previous chapters have shown in a range of ways that the evidence points to the existence of a God who made everything and is able to act into history, space and time and to reach out to us. The question then becomes, whether He did so or not. If you are willing to set aside the barriers that have previously held you back from considering this question, then the most feasible way to explore it is to look at the historical evidence for the resurrection. If the resurrection didn't happen, then Christianity is just a moral code based on wishful thinking. If the resurrection did happen no-one can safely ignore it.

It is no accident that there has been an intense attack on the historical reliability of the Bible as a record of real events in the last 150 years, because if its historical reliability is destroyed, Christian belief crumbles with it. Christianity unlike any other belief is not a philosophical system, although philosophy can be helpful in pointing to the existence of God. Christianity rests on the claim that God acted into history, appeared as a man (Jesus), died and came back to life thus conquering death for everyone who believes in him. If you do not believe that you are not a Christian.

To evaluate this claim of Jesus being God in human form, dying and rising again, we will need to examine these claims as we would any historical event. Without the history it remains just abstract ideas. We will also need to establish the credibility of the records that we have, just as we would examine any other eye-witness testimony; can we trust them?

I'm going to anchor this discussion first of all in Lee Strobel's book 'The Case for Christ', and in J. Warner Wallace's, 'Cold case Christianity'.

Lee Strobel, a journalist, examined the evidence for Jesus' life, death and resurrection in the way he would examine any court case he was covering, by looking at all the evidence he could turn up and interviewing experts. He started an atheist wanting to disprove Christian belief, he ended up a Christian. He began with the records of Jesus life, his biographies (the gospels) and the eyewitness testimony they contain. This is something that anyone can relate to and understand.

Here is some of the evidence that emerges.

When the eyewitness records of the resurrection are examined forensically as though for a court case the details do stand up to scrutiny, showing them to be credible records of real events from actual eyewitnesses. For example, if you were making up claims about the resurrection at a later date, you would not record the first witnesses to the resurrection as being women. In First Century Jewish culture, women were not considered reliable witnesses. This is simply not something that men

(Matthew, Mark, Luke and John) writing biographies of Jesus would choose to include if they wanted to convince sceptics, unless it was true. In their time it would simply have been embarrassing. To modern eyes we trust a woman's testimony. Their culture didn't. Yet they truthfully recorded what happened and what happened was not convenient, but they told the truth anyway.

To give a measure of quite how much this went against the culture we can read Luke's account for example. At the start of his biography of Jesus he says,

> "since I myself have investigated everything from the beginning, it seemed good to me to write an orderly account." (Luke 1 vs 3)

When the account comes to the resurrection Luke writes,

> "On the first day of the week, very early in the morning, the women took the spices they had prepared and went to the tomb. They found the stone rolled away from the tomb, but when they entered, they did not find the body of the Lord Jesus....
>
> When they came back from the tomb, they told all these things to the Eleven and to all the others.. But they did not believe the women, because their words seemed to them like nonsense. Peter, however, got up and ran to the tomb. Bending down he saw the strips of linen lying by themselves, and he went away wondering to himself what had happened." (Luke 24 vs 1,2 and 9-12)

However, when the Apostle Paul later writes about the same event he says,

> "For what I received I passed on to you as of first importance; that Christ died for our sins according

to the scriptures and that he was buried, that he was raised on the third day according to the scriptures, and that he appeared to Peter, and then to the Twelve. After that he appeared to more than five hundred of the brothers at the same time, most of whom are still living." (1 Corinthians 15 vs 3-6)

What happened to the women in the account? Well, it seems that Paul compressed the events to a more culturally palatable summary and edited the inconvenient women out of the story as he retold it. He jumps straight to Peter, a 'reliable' man in his cultural context. This places his account firmly in the First Century when he lived. It also speaks volumes for Luke's accuracy as an historian that he recorded that it was women including Mary Magdalene who were the first to witness the empty tomb and the risen Jesus, even though it was inconvenient to do so.

N. T. Wright comments on the place of women in the four gospel narratives of the resurrection, especially Mary Magdalene.

"She is chosen as the prime witness: there she is in all four accounts. As historians we are obliged to comment that if these stories had been made up five years later, let alone thirty, forty, or fifty years later, they would never have had Mary Magdalene in this role. To put Mary there is,... like shooting themselves in the foot. But to us as historians this kind of thing is gold dust. The early Christians would never, never have made this up. The stories – of the women finding an empty tomb and then meeting the risen Jesus – must be regarded as solidly historical." (N.T. Wright in Flew, 'There is a God; How the World's Most Notorious Atheist Changed His Mind', page 207)

The fact that all four of the gospels place the women in such a central position, places their record before Paul's in terms of chronology. Also, the gospels simply record the fact of the resurrection. They do not lay a theology of resurrection for Christian believers on the account in the way that Paul does later. N. T. Wright again,

> "So, we have to conclude that these narratives go back way behind Paul to a time when we see the very, very early church reeling in shock from this totally unexpected event of the resurrection and figuring out what it means."

And,

> "I discover, as I look for historical explanations, that two particular things must have happened: (1) there must have been an empty tomb that was known to be the correct tomb; it couldn't have been a mistake; (2) there must have been appearances of the risen Jesus. Both must have occurred." (N.T. Wright in Flew, *'There is a God; How the World's Most Notorious Atheist Changed His Mind'*, page 209)

These accounts are soaked through and through with the culture and historical context of their time and speak to us today as reliable records of what they describe.

Let's consider the empty tomb a bit further.

The easiest way to stop any crazy ideas (from the Roman authorities' perspective) about Jesus having risen from the dead would be to produce the body. The problem was they couldn't. They had even anticipated this problem since Jesus was on record as saying that he would rise from the dead *"on the third day"*, (Luke 18 vs33) so they had sealed the tomb and posted a guard in case the disciples should take the body and claim he had risen from the dead. The guard would be potentially executed for failure to keep the tomb safe from interference, but they did indeed fail to keep the tomb secure. Jesus died on a Friday, but by Sunday morning the body was gone. The authorities then paid off the soldiers and told them to say that the disciples had come and stolen the body to make up a story about him coming to life again. That story never was going to be credible. Grief stricken disciples who were showing every sign of giving up on the idea that Jesus was the Messiah were not in a position to overpower Roman guards.

> "There is simply no plausible natural explanation available today to account for how Jesus' tomb became empty. If we deny the resurrection of Jesus, we are left with an inexplicable mystery." (William Lane Craig, *Reasonable Faith, Christian Truth and Apologetics*, page 377).

Also, there was nothing in Judaism that would have led the disciples who were all Jewish, to expect the Messiah to be resurrected, it was simply not what they thought would happen. (See N.T. Wright, *The Resurrection of the Son of God*).

> "As Wright nicely puts it, if your favourite Messiah got himself crucified, then you either went home or else got yourself a new Messiah. But the idea of stealing Jesus' corpse and saying that God raised him from the dead is hardly one that would have entered the minds of the disciples." (William Lane Craig, *Reasonable Faith, Christian Truth and Apologetics*, page 372)

Many people have come forward with theories that try to undermine a straightforward reading of the four gospel accounts. Another common one is to claim that Jesus must have only looked dead on the cross and so somehow have revived in the tomb and escaped.

This kind of theory abounds with problems. (See for example,

Lennox, '*Can science explain everything?*' chapter 8). First, the Roman soldiers charged with executing him on a cross along with two others on crosses at the same time were professional executioners. They knew when a man was really dead. Crucifixion kills eventually from suffocation and to speed this up, if needed, they would break the legs of the victim, so they could no longer raise themselves up to breathe. The Jewish authorities asked the Romans to break Jesus' legs to make his death quicker so that he wouldn't still be on the cross over the Sabbath (Saturday)(John 18 vs 31). However, when the Roman soldiers checked, they did not need to do this since he was already dead. (The beating he had before crucifixion alone would have nearly killed him). But to make sure one of the soldiers thrust a sword into Jesus side. This would puncture the diaphragm and ensure asphyxiation. It is recorded that a sudden gush of blood and water came out.

> "One of the soldiers pierced Jesus' side with a spear, bringing a sudden flow of blood and water." (John 19 vs 34)

This is the kind of eyewitness detail that adds much credibility to the accounts. A First Century witness would not know what they were seeing with that liquid gushing out, but modern medical knowledge recognises it as the result of the trauma Jesus had already suffered and that He was dead. This would not necessarily happen to someone pierced by a sword under other circumstances.

> "The spear apparently went through the right lung and into the heart, so when the spear was pulled out, some fluid – the pericardial effusion and the plural effusion – came out. This would have the appearance of a clear fluid, like water, followed by a large volume of blood, as the eyewitness John de-

scribed." (Alexander Metherell quoted in Lee Strobel, *The Case for Christ* page 214)

Jesus was really dead when he was taken down from the cross.

The theory of Jesus not being dead after crucifixion is medical nonsense. If he had just swooned, been carted to a tomb, then somehow later been dragged from his tomb, and also survived the terrible lack of medical knowledge of the day, it would be a miracle in itself. To survive the scourging, beating and crucifixion and sword in the side today would be nearly impossible, if the victim were taken immediately to the best medical facilities available in the world with extensive surgery, massive blood transfusions, life support machines etc. Their chances of living would be virtually non-existent. In the First Century those chances would be an absolute zero. Crucifixion may have been a lengthy painful process, but it was execution. Nonetheless, people do continue to repeat such implausible theories.

There is another problem. The disciples basically hadn't believed Jesus when he had foretold his death and resurrection. They would need some serious convincing. A nearly dead man clearly not long for this world, would not be the convincing evidence of coming back to life that they would need to believe in resurrection. They weren't idiots, they would be able to distinguish a healthy man come alive again from a near corpse only just breathing. Such a pathetic figure would simply not have been the risen Messiah who inspired the disciples to spread out around the world to witness to his life, teaching and resurrection.

Jesus had in fact had real difficulty getting across the idea of what the resurrection would be and mean. We shall digress to consider how Jesus had attempted to explain what was going to happen and also consider some of what it means for us, before returning to the discussion on the evidence for Jesus' resurrection. Jesus used the experience of his friend and follower Lazarus to try to show what it was all about.

Mary, Martha and Lazarus were brother and sisters and disciples of Jesus. Lazarus got sick. The sisters sent word to Jesus hoping he would come and heal their brother, they had seen and heard of Jesus healing many others, but Jesus who was just a short distance away from their home in Bethany just outside Jerusalem waited. Lazarus died. Jesus delayed.

> "Our friend Lazarus has fallen asleep; but I am going to there to wake him up. His disciples replied, "Lord if he sleeps, he will get better." Jesus had been speaking of his death, but his disciples thought he meant natural sleep." (John 11 vs 13)

By the time he got to them, the sisters were full of questions, overcome with grief. Jesus talked with them about the resurrection life and Mary affirmed her belief in a future resurrection at the end of time. But Jesus wanted to show them more. He asked to go to the tomb, but they protested,

> "by this time there is a bad odour, for he has been there four days." (John 11 vs 39)

Lazarus was well and truly dead by now. Yet Jesus said he was sleeping! It sounds cryptic, but it isn't, he was teaching something of vital importance. Jesus then prayed out loud and called out,

> "Lazarus, come out!" (John 11 vs 43)

The dead man, now alive again, came out still wrapped in the grave cloths.

Rather than give a lengthy discussion and explanation, Jesus waited until he was dealing with a demonstrably dead man, then described his state as *sleeping*, then called him out from the grave to life. Lazarus died, his body began to decay, then

Jesus called him back to life. Lazarus knew nothing of the intervening 3 days, it was the same as sleep to him. The apostle Paul referred to God,

"who alone is immortal." (1 Timothy 6 vs 16)

Immortality is a property of God himself and is not something we inherently have in ourselves as created beings. Eternal life is the gift of God, not something we have in and of ourselves.

Many people, Christian or not, think they know what Jesus taught about what happens when you die. They think when they die, they will go straight to heaven. Surprisingly neither Jesus nor the Biblical authors taught that. Those same people think that they have an immortal soul, but that is an imposition of a pagan idea. The Jewish concept of existence had no soul that could be separated from the body and have its own conscious separate existence. We are an integrated whole, body and soul together. Death is like sleep, since we know nothing, and for us in death, time ceases to exist. Only when God calls us out from the grave at the end of time and gives us a new resurrection body do we know anything again. Eternal life is the gift of God (John 3 vs 16). We have no eternal existence unless God gives it.

Similarly, there is no eternal soul to dispose of in an eternally burning hell. In fact, when Jesus referred to what modern readers often think is a reference to hell, he was alluding to the rubbish dump outside Jerusalem in the valley of Hinnom, arriving through Greek to English as Gehenna, that became the Medieval model of hell. His language is metaphorical. I believe it is not pushing the point too far to paraphrase him as in effect saying, 'Do you want to end up on the rubbish heap or up there beyond the sky?' It was a vivid metaphor for his immediate hearers who would not miss the point at all. Only those to whom Jesus gives life will live for eternity. Absolutely nothing in all creation has an independent life of its own, separate from God. Only He is pre-existent and eternal. Even the devil is destined for total destruction and non-existence. John in Revelation talks of a lake of fire reserved for the devil and his angels (Revelation 19 vs 20 and 20 vs10), signifying total destruction, not dominion over a competing eternity in hell whilst God presides in heaven. There is no rival to God for eternal existence and only He can confer it on anyone. At the resurrection at the end of time, those Jesus has saved are re-made with new resurrection bodies and are once again conscious living beings, but this time in a perfect new heavens and new earth.

> "Do not be amazed at this, for a time is coming when all who are in their graves will hear his voice and come out - those who have done good will rise to live, and those who have done evil will rise to be condemned." (Jesus quoted in John 5 vs 28,29)

Even the idea of going to heaven needs challenging, since the promise in the Bible is of a new earth not some non-specific un-located heaven.

> "Then I saw a new heaven and a new earth, for the first heaven and the first earth has passed away." (Revelation 21 vs 1)

The Apostle Paul is also clear on this. (See 1 Corinthians chapter 15)

Those ideas are very challenging for many people because they have been conditioned, either as Christians or not, to think they know that Jesus taught something quite different; they think that he taught that they go straight to heaven (wherever it is) as soon as they die. It is very shocking to them when they look more carefully and find that he didn't teach that after all. N.T. Wright is a recent figure in a long line of people who have made that discovery (see for example Tom Wright, *Surprised by hope*). I don't agree with everything he writes such as on purgatory, however, he is, I believe, absolutely correct in identifying that a Greek, non-Jewish idea infiltrated Christian thinking by the Middle Ages, namely that we have an immortal soul capable of separate existence in its own right.

All of this in no way reduces or undermines Christian faith or the concept of salvation from a sinful state, but it puts a quite different colour on it. And it shows how important it is to think things through and look at the evidence for yourself.

So, Jesus offered citizenship in an eternal kingdom and though our present bodies are temporary, they will after one short sleep be replaced with still physical, but eternal ones. As John Donne put it in poetry 400 years ago in his sonnet '*Death be not proud*',

> "One short sleep past, we wake eternally,
>
> And death shall be no more; Death thou shalt die.'

A large minority of Christians have been quite clear on this point all through the centuries, but unfortunately an inaccurate view has become the most widely promulgated one. Much more could be said about this, but if you read the New Testament authors with an open mind you will find clarity on this.

We must return to the evidence for Jesus' resurrection, which is the guarantee of our own later resurrection by the same power of God.

When thinking what the resurrection meant to the earliest Christians, we must note that Jesus' resurrection became the central point of Christian belief right from the start. (See N. T. Wright, *The Resurrection of the Son of God*). It didn't assume that position later. It was not an add on to a philosophical system. It was totally unexpected in Judaism and without precedent in pagan religion (See the lengthy discussion in N.T.

Wright *The resurrection of the Son of God*). It was a new thing and a huge challenge for Jewish followers to get their heads around, but they could not avoid it, because they knew it to be true.

The resurrection of Jesus was the whole point of Christianity right from the start

The Apostles, plus other disciples of Jesus, as well as a group of more than 500 believers claimed to have seen Jesus after his resurrection. (See The Apostle Paul in 1 Corinthians 15 vs 6). This number of people in multiple locations and times becomes too great a number to orchestrate in a conspiracy and cannot be explained by claims of delusions or hallucinations.

The 12 apostles told everyone who would listen all about it. When Peter was speaking to a large crowd in Jerusalem at Pentecost just weeks after the resurrection, claiming that Jesus was raised from the dead and alive again, then if Jesus' tomb were not empty and the body was available, anyone could point to it to disprove his claims.

The disciples of Jesus continued to make the resurrection the centre point of their claims about Jesus even though it got them into a lot of trouble. Eleven of those twelve disciples were killed for what they did because their teachings directly challenged the pagan religions of their day and the Roman empire. Maybe one of them, if he knew it was all made up and just a lie, would be mad enough to die for it. But 11 out of 12? Then the twelfth one, John, died in a penal colony still insisting Jesus had risen from the dead. This just isn't the psychological profile of a group of fraudsters and con men getting together and agreeing a made-up story.

For an in-depth consideration of the evidence for the resurrection of Jesus, William Lane Craig's discussion in *Reasonable Faith, Christian Truth and Apologetics* is good. He summarises three historical facts that can be established independently, that need to be accounted for:

> "the empty tomb, the resurrection appearances, and the origin of the Christian faith."
>
> (William Lane Craig *Reasonable Faith, Christian Truth and Apologetics*, page 360)

He considers each in detail and the attempts that have been made to explain them away and why those attempted explanations are lacking. When taken together, the most reasonable inference from these three facts is that Jesus rose from the dead.

Since the resurrection of Jesus is essential to Christianity and unique, it has been subject to endless attempts at explaining it away or to prove it did not happen, so of course this discussion could be much longer if we were to try to deal with every objection raised. However, we have looked at some strong lines of evidence that show that Jesus' resurrection is the most reasonable explanation of the evidence that we have, and that is something that comes as quite a shock to most people.

If you read further on this in the sources mentioned in this chapter, you can follow the evidence and see the credibility of belief in the resurrection stand firm. J. Warner Wallace, *Cold Case Christianity* is a good place to start. Do dig deeper. You may well be amazed at what you find.

Jesus' resurrection means victory over death and new life for us; a new way to live now and a physical bodily resurrection in the future to an eternal life. It is a new life that starts now and lasts for eternity

Jesus of Nazareth, speaking to Martha one of his disciples (yes, women were his disciples too) said,

> "I am the resurrection and the life. He who believes in me will live even though he dies; and whoever believes in me will never die."

John 11 vs 25,26

Jesus after his resurrection spoke to his disciples,

> "He told them, "This is what is written: The Christ will suffer and rise from the dead on the third day, and repentance and forgiveness of sins will be preached in his name to all nations, beginning at Jerusalem. You are witnesses of these things."

Luke 24 vs 46-48

27 THE STRONGEST ARGUMENT FOR CHRISTIAN BELIEF

Lives transformed

E verything discussed in this book would remain just an interesting set of ideas, arguments, inferences, illustrations and debates unless it has the power to make a difference for good in people's lives. We have noted how it transformed the lives of the followers of Jesus after his resurrection, but what about after that? Has Jesus embodying God and coming to show us what He is really like, then dying and rising from the dead, made any difference in people's lives since then? For surely, if it hasn't what is the point of looking into all this? The world is full of religions. Is Christianity different and does it make any difference? The simple answer is yes and in every way.

Let's look at some other lives to see what difference the life, death and resurrection of Jesus has made. However, we must first understand in the simplest possible terms what Jesus claimed it all meant and what the apostles and early Christians understood it to mean.

Religion in all its forms makes demands on its followers to do something to earn something. That is the formula. Do something, earn something. (Summed up well in, Lee Strobel, *The Case for Grace*). Follow these rules and you will be alright with God on judgement day. Or follow these disciplines and you may be reincarnated to a better state. Or keep these rules and you will be able to earn enough good points to outweigh the bad points in your life and you will go to paradise.

The central problem that religion of every form tries to address is that all people have a sense within them that this life is not all there is. They have a desire for something better, but they are also aware of their own failings and are concerned that they are somehow not good enough to obtain that something better. That much seems to be innate within all human beings. To deal with this, religion, in its multiple forms, proposes to show the right way to live to earn or achieve a better outcome - somehow. That also seems innate; we all want to earn something better. The details vary but that is the basic formula across religion; just about all religion, even secularism if you look carefully. Do something, earn something.

Thank goodness Christianity is not like that.

Now, it is true that a lot of what has been called "Christianity" is sadly just religion. It sets out rules and how to follow them and promises heaven as the reward. It is vital that we make it clear that that is religion, not Christianity. Jesus' teaching and life and then the teaching of the apostles shows something very different. Jesus and then the apostle Paul, made it very clear that we cannot earn anything of God, by any means, ever.

Some Christians reading this will be deeply shocked, because many people have been taught the formula of religion in some way; do something earn something. Even if that is not exactly what they were taught, it is often the message they have received. Others know the theory that it is not like that but are still stuck at an emotional level in keeping rules trying to <u>earn</u> something from God.

This is why it is vital to read what Jesus and the apostles taught for yourself, don't rely on what other people tell you to believe. They made it very clear that Jesus showed us what God is like and He is good all of the time. He loves and cares about everyone.

> "For God loved the world that he gave his only Son, that whoever believes in him should not perish but have eternal life. For God did not send his Son into the world to condemn the world, but in order that the world might be saved through him." (John 3 vs 16,17)

> "Truly, truly I say to you, whoever hears my word and believes him who sent me has eternal life. He does not come into judgement, but has passed from death to life." (John 5 vs 24)

Jesus (and therefore God) is concerned about right and wrong and He does hold people accountable for their actions.

> "Not everyone who says to me, 'Lord, Lord', will enter the kingdom of heaven, but only he who does the will of my Father who is in heaven. Many will say to me on that day, 'Lord, Lord, did we not prophesy in your name, and in your name drive out demons and perform many miracles?' Then I will tell them plainly, 'I never knew you. Away from me you evil doers!'" (Matthew 7 vs 21-23)

Those are some of the most alarming words in the Bible. It is clearly possible to "do religion" in Jesus' name but not be right with him.

So, the crucial difference between Christianity and any religion based on what we can achieve, is very powerful. Christianity makes it clear that we can never, ever, in a million lifetimes (even all eternity) do enough good to outweigh any bad we have done and because of that we are guaranteed to fail if we try. We cannot work our way to heaven. We cannot improve ourselves enough to be acceptable to God, even with his help. We have to face up to our helpless condition. Compared to an infinitely good God we stand no chance of being counted good enough by any measure. Our only possibility is for Him to do something we can't do ourselves. We need a change of status from rebel outcast to loving family member. And vitally we must recognise our absolute need of that transformation being done by God in us.

If what God requires of us so that we can be with him for eternity is to have no bad in us at all, we are all doomed. Thankfully, He knows that and has done what we cannot do ourselves. He has dealt with all the wrong we have done and all the wrong we have the potential to do. He has paid the cost of that and is then prepared to make us part of His family, His kingdom, as if we never had anything bad in us at all. All we can do is recognise our need of that transformation in status and ask for it and receive it. It is what Christians mean by sin, and forgiveness. It is much more than any specific thing we have done wrong; it is about who we all are, in our very inner selves and God forgiving that and making us new. He starts a process of working on us from the inside out, but crucially it is a change of status that He confers on us that takes us into citizenship of His eternal kingdom.

This is so counter-intuitive, *so unreligious*, that it literally takes a gift of God to open your heart and mind to see it and understand it. Otherwise, you will either dismiss it and carry on your life, or you will in some way keep trying to earn it.

"What happens now to human pride of achievement? There is no more room for it. Why?... because the whole matter is now on a different plane – believing instead of achieving. We see now that a man is justified before God by the fact of his faith in God's appointed Saviour and not by what he has managed to achieve under the law." (Roman 3 vs27,28 J. B. Phillips' translation)

Every analogy is imperfect, but here is a simple illustration (I am not the first to use this illustration, I think I first encountered it in a talk by Lee Strobel). If I want to become a citizen of the United States for example, but I was born elsewhere, then unless that citizenship is conferred on me, I will never have it. I can try to live the best life possible; it won't make any difference. I can enter the country illegally, but it won't make me a citizen. I could then make endless positive contributions to society, but I still would not be a citizen. Citizenship is not something I can give myself. If, however, the President chooses to grant me citizenship, it is then a fact. What if the President also gave me a house to move to, and personally said he now regarded me as family and hoped to see me any time I wanted to drop by, all the while knowing I have taxes outstanding in my home country? It would be an act of immense kindness, accepting me, imperfect as I am, and giving me things that I could never earn. We could call it grace, because it is one person with the power to do something for another person, choosing to do so for no reward or payment, but doing it just because He can and wants to. I hope I would then strive to be the model citizen and give back all I could to the country that was so kind to me.

Citizenship in the kingdom of God is given by God because He wants to! He does it on the basis of you or I wanting it, recognising we can never deserve it, and then receiving it with gratitude from the bottom of our heart. We will be so grateful we will want to live differently, for the rest of our lives. It is God's grace that transforms us; we do not live better to somehow deserve God's grace.

> "Sin used to be the master of men and in the end it handed them over to death; now grace is the ruling factor, with its purpose making men right with God and its end bringing of them to eternal life through Jesus Christ our Lord." Roman 6 vs 20,21 (J. B. Phillips' translation)

What Jesus did was to take upon himself the consequences and just reward for all the bad in us. The just reward for that is death because there is no place for any bad in a perfect eternity. You may not want to accept that claim, but you too will have to face up to your own mortality, we all do. Remember however, that because Jesus was God embodied as a man he could not stay in the grave. His resurrection declares that he has power even over death, he has power to give life.

> "The reason the father loves me is that I lay down my life – only to take it up again. No one takes it from me, but I lay it down of my own accord. I have authority to lay it down and authority to take it up again. This command I received from my Father." (John 10 vs 17,18)

The apostle Paul explained the implications this way,

> "This righteousness from God comes from faith in Jesus Christ to all who believe." (Romans 3 vs 22)

This is the crucial difference between Christianity and dead religion that cannot bring life. Jesus gives life as a free gift to those who realise they need it, ask for it, and will receive it. Christians call this the grace of God. Even though we don't deserve it, He will give us life if we believe He is who He claims to be and has the power to give it and we recognise our need of it.

Summing up. The pathway to receiving that new life given by the grace of God is through true sorrow for the wrong we have done and a genuine heartfelt desire for forgiveness and a willingness to let Jesus work in our lives. We don't deserve it, we can't earn it, but through Jesus we can become part of God's family for eternity. It is a new citizenship in an eternal kingdom, that we could never buy or achieve from anything we can do. That's why Jesus talked all the time about the kingdom of God.

So, Christianity recognises the problem that all religion recognises; that we need something we don't have, but it makes it clear we can't earn it no matter how hard we try. We don't do something and therefore earn something. Jesus gives life, we believe and receive it. He does what we can't do. You will know that you have received it because as the emotional reality hits home, you will have a gratitude that nothing can shake. The grace of God changes people, forever. Following Jesus is not "do as you like". We may not be able to be good enough to earn a place in eternity, but He wants us to live in a loving and kind way and He will help us to do so, it is the whole point of the kingdom of heaven that he is building. People who follow Jesus will seek to avoid wrong and do right and He wants to transform their lives and others through them.

I have read objections to the cross and the idea that God could want Jesus to die on it, claiming that surely, He could just forgive us anyway. There is much that can be said about that, but if we recognize Jesus as God embodying himself in human form, to then be treated so appallingly by the people He created, we could see no more vivid illustration of a world in rebellion against God. It explains the mess we are in.

It also becomes clear that forgiveness is not a trivial thing and that somehow, in a profound way that we can only partially understand, God himself pays that cost. This is the creator of everything rescuing what He has made <u>at His own expense</u>. Jesus rising from the dead then makes a stronger statement than any argument or declaration ever could. He showed he had power over death and has life within himself and that he has dealt with our rebellion and with death. In effect He says, 'Would you like to join me in eternity too?'.

The very fact that people resist accepting their need of forgiveness by God and the need of the life that Jesus offers, validates the fact that this is a world in rebellion against its maker. That battle in your heart over trying not to ignore God, and also trying not to earn anything from God by your own efforts, is powerful testimony that what you are reading is true.

That inner struggle over your will, that battle with personal pride in not wanting to submit to your need of forgiveness, is the battle everyone who is a Christian has had to go through and is powerful evidence to you that you need what Jesus will freely give. The good news is that millions have made it past that resistance and given in to Jesus and the grace of God.

It must be repeated that the amazing thing about God's grace, is that it transforms the people who receive it. Let's meet a few, but I must give a note of caution first. I am concerned not to fall into telling stories of what has become a stereotype: 'Bad person meets Jesus and becomes good person, and you should copy him'. It is unhelpful to single out only people that many will think were living "bad" lives. Every one of us is in the same situation, there are no truly "good" people in their own right, we all need forgiveness and we all can receive it. God's grace is not limited.

I must give another note of caution too. We must be very

careful what we ascribe to God as His doing. It is too easy to write the narrative of our own lives and ascribe a greater plan to everything that happens to us, good or bad. We should be clear: do not ascribe a greater purpose to evil, it diminishes it[14]. Whatever trouble or mess we have been in or are in, Jesus reaching out to rescue us is the crucial thing. He originally made a perfect world and never wanted all the pain, hurt, destruction and death to happen.

How low can you go?

Where does empathy spring from?

Where in the human heart does concern for others displace callous indifference?

How does a person totally fixated on themselves finally look in the mirror held up to their very soul and desire to be different?

Perhaps some part of an answer starts on a tiny sandy island off the coast of Africa. He was trapped against his will, enslaved in fact, always fearful, always hungry, always thirsty, badly sunburnt and dressed in rags, forced to endure the threat or actual use of violence. How long could you look at the horizon, longing for deliverance and your spirit not be crushed by never finding it?

Yet when he escaped, John went back to the trade he knew best, being a slave trader.

How low can you go? (I heard this question of John Newton posed very powerfully by David Neal).

To be forced by your own misfortune to endure slavery yourself, then on gaining your freedom, to simply return to enslaving others, takes some doing. Where in such a hard heart does God begin? But He did.

Eventually John Newton left the slave trade and became a

church minister and a powerful advocate for the abolition of slavery. His first-hand testimony of the realities of slavery helped convince others to stand against it too. His famous hymn, *Amazing Grace* is seen by many as autobiographical.

"Amazing grace, how sweet the sound, that saved a wretch like me.

I once was lost, but now am found, was blind but now I see."

The Apostle Paul was determined to wipe out Christianity until Jesus met him on that road to Damascus. For such a complete and permanent U-turn to occur, testifies to what he really saw.

The word "conversion" has a bad name in some people's eyes. What exactly is it? Well, every time human pride and self-sufficiency is put aside, and Jesus is allowed to realign the thoughts, dreams, hopes, priorities and crucially worship of a human heart and mind, He makes a conversion.

Some of the more dramatic stories are impressive. Saul of Tarsus, from persecutor of the faith to its most effective advocate. John Newton, from slave trader to campaigner for the abolition of slavery. However, even when it seems less dramatic it is still a complete realignment of everything; Jesus changing people from the inside out.

What about those millions of less dramatic beginnings to the Christian life? Each in its own way is no less amazing because it is equally significant. Christian belief is a life changing matter of eternal consequence. It is so radical that Jesus described it as going through another birth, but this time to a life that will last for eternity.

In his book *The Case for Grace*, Lee Strobel looks at a series of lives transformed. He talks to an orphan in Korea, a University

Professor and others about their encounter with life changing grace. God got through to them and they were changed.

You can read more of Lee Strobel's own journey from atheist to Christian in his book *The Case for Christ*. He was a legal correspondent on a leading newspaper, then his wife became a Christian. He was angry and set out to prove it all nonsense. He interviewed every relevant witness he could find, and he did not end where he expected. He too became a Christian.

One of the bestselling books on Christian belief in the last century, *Mere Christianity*, was written by C.S. Lewis who was an atheist professor who became a Christian. His Christian books are so convincing because he spent so long trying to prove the opposite. He is now well known for his children's books on Narnia, but *Mere Christianity* is well worth a read. Some of his other works such as *The Problem of Pain* have helped millions.

These life stories should give everyone serious pause for thought. In contrast, when did you come across an evolutionist telling their life story thus?

> 'I was feeling hopeless and struggling with addiction. Then I met Random Chance. Random Chance worked in my life and gave me the power to get off the substances that were wrecking me. I found Random Chance a fulfilling and convincing explanation of all aspects of my existence and reality around me. I found a sense of community and purpose with other believers in Random Chance. Randomness has transformed my life. Since then, I have been helping in many projects to help other people build more randomness into their lives. Randomness has met my existential needs for peace of mind, hope and purpose. Try Random Chance.'

Isn't it reasonable to question the power of Random Chance to which evolutionists attribute the origin of all of life and all of reality?

So many people have looked at the evidence for who Jesus is, his life teaching and resurrection, and have come to faith in him. How about you? Each person's journey to faith is individual. Some require more convincing on some points than others, but it is a curious phenomenon, that so many talented people who have tried to find convincing proof for their disbelief, have ended up believing instead. We have looked at the evidence and lives touched by it. Where have we ended up?

There is a God, Jesus is His Son and He gives life to all who will believe Him and take Him at His word.

When this world breaks you, only Jesus can truly put you back together

> "For I am convinced that neither death nor life, neither angels nor demons, neither the present nor the future, nor any powers, nor anything else in all creation, will be able to separate us from the love of God that is in Christ Jesus."
>
> The Apostle Paul in his letter to the Christians in Rome; Romans 8 vs 38, 39

28 THE EXTRAORDINARY LIFE OF JOSHUA SON OF JOSEPH

*Take a fresh look at the life
and teaching of the world's
most famous rabbi*

A show down between Joshua and the religious authorities had been coming for a while. What was at stake was the understanding of what God wants of us. In the unfolding drama a disabled man became a central figure. Even with modern legislation to protect disabled people, life can be very tough if you have to live with some form of physical or mental disability. In the 1st Century life was much harder. For most people then with any significant disability, the only opportunity for income was begging and they depended totally on the generosity of family, friends and strangers.

Joshua picked a fight with the religious authorities. Sadly, they saw disability as a punishment from God either for what a person had done wrong, or maybe for what their parents had done. That placed an additional stigma on disabled people. The religious leaders also thought that the way to be acceptable to God was following the law of Moses and being ceremonially clean. This required ritual purity which was achieved by following complex rules. The rules had started with the laws of Moses, but they were amplified by 613 additional rules that were added to ensure that the primary rules were kept properly. This rule keeping encompassed the whole of life. Joshua saw things differently.

Some of the rules sound ridiculous to modern sensibilities, such as some of the rules concerned with how to keep the Sabbath. Devout Jews followed many restrictions unless by not keeping them they had unintentionally done work on the Sabbath and broken the commandment to rest and cease from working. This could include, for example, not pulling a chair across a soft floor lest its chair legs unintentionally plough the dirt[15]. The Sabbath was meant to be a day of rest and time for prayer and study and family. It had become an exercise in rule keeping that prescribed the minutiae of what could and could not be done. You could only walk a certain distance: a Sabbath day's walk. You could only eat food prepared the day before. You could see a justification for some of the rules but taken all together they became very exacting and restricting. Joshua however seemed to make a habit of making his own interpretation of how to keep the law of Moses.

So, he picked a fight to wind the religious authorities up; he healed a disabled man on the Sabbath. Many people mis-read Joshua's actions as showing that the Sabbath didn't matter. His actual words give a very different picture,

> "The Sabbath was made for man, not man for the Sabbath." (Mark 2 vs 27)

In other words, understand what it was intended to be and make it a blessing not a burden, because physical and spiritual rest are essential.

The story starts with Joshua visiting a location known as the pool of Bethesda. For many years critics claimed this was an example of the story being fiction, since no such pool existed. John describes it as being surrounded by 5 covered colonnades. When it was discovered and excavated, it turned out to fit the rather odd description. (See Clive Anderson and Brian Edwards *Evidence for the Bible*, page 128). It was a real location after all.

Jesus saw the man lying there and asked him, *"Do you want to get well?"* John 5 vs 6. He had in fact been disabled for 38 years. He was probably there due to a belief that the waters could in some way bring about healing, as witness his reply to Joshua that there was no-one to help him into the waters. Joshua responded,

"Get up! Pick up your mat and walk." (John 5 vs 8)

And he did and was healed.

Once the religious authorities found out they were indignant, because the healing had happened on the Sabbath. They weren't overjoyed at a bona fide miracle, just miserable because Joshua was breaking the rules. They classed his actions as "work". You might be thinking, 'Surely healing someone is more important than keeping rules?' That was not how they saw it; to their minds, it seems, there were six other days to do the healing on!

They found Joshua and confronted him, and he promptly went much further than challenging their view on Sabbath keeping. Responding to their complaint at breaking the Sabbath he said,

"My Father is always at his work to this very day, and
I, too, am working." (John 5 vs 17)

They understood exactly what he was really saying,

"Not only was he breaking the Sabbath, but he was even calling God his own Father, making himself equal with God." (John 5 vs 18)

That wasn't enough for Joshua. He now had their full attention and he piled on the claims.

"I tell you the truth, whoever hears my word and believes him who sent me has eternal life and will not be condemned; he has crossed over from death to life." (John 5 vs 24)

And lest they miss the point, he underlines it and adds highlighter so to speak,

"Do not be amazed at this, for a time is coming when all who are in their graves will hear his voice and come out – those who have done good will rise to live, and those who have done evil will rise to be condemned." (John 5 vs 28, 29)

All eyes were on him to see if there was any evidence that what he claimed was true and the rest of his life was an amplification of his credibility to be making those claims.

You will realise that Joshua was Jesus of Nazareth. Joshua is simply another rendering in English of the same name, I only used it to encourage you to try to look at him with fresh eyes. So, let us look at some of the other things he taught and did to try to make sense of him. As I write this, I am intensely aware of the weight of responsibility to represent truthfully and accurately the picture the gospels paint of Jesus. There has been a range of views across Christianity on many subjects, including what some of Jesus' teachings and actions meant, but the core basics come through loud and clear if you are willing to investigate them with an open mind. So, don't just take my word for anything, check it out for yourself, this is all too important for anything I write to get in the way of your understanding in anyway at all. If there is any inaccuracy in this discussion, it is mine and I strongly suggest you measure what is written here against the four biographies of his life, known to most people as the gospels.

There are some interesting defining characteristics of the events and teachings of Jesus as recorded by his four 1st century biographers, Matthew, Mark, Luke and John. He spent a lot of time with the sort of people whom the religious authorities looked down on. He repeatedly wound up the religious authorities of his day by refusing to agree that the way to being accepted by God was keeping all their rules. He loved telling memorable stories. And he kept doing things that forced people then and now to think radically about who he was.

To understand the story of the paralysed man healed at the pool of Bethesda, we must note again that Israel at that time, lived under strict religious law, taught and administered to the people by the rabbis, teachers of the law, scribes and priests. Following the law of Moses, they had added many supplementary rules and regulations to help people be sure they would be keeping the law. Every Jew understood that keeping the law was what God wanted and their total duty. It is very hard for modern people to imagine how all pervasive this law was, there was no escaping it, every aspect of life was regulated by it; literally every aspect of it. Your imagination may be wandering to a range of topics and, yes, they would also fit within the description of "everything"; it really was all-encompassing.

Several things were unusual with this man Joshua. He had developed quite a following but not by being conventional. He was not teaching in a way that the temple authorities or the established religious teachers (Rabbis, Pharisees, Scribes) approved. In fact, the Temple authorities wanted rid of him because he threatened their grip on power and the incredibly lucrative flow of offerings that went with it. The temple, you see, had become big business. The temple authorities and the priesthood had a monopoly on offering forgiveness for anything people had done wrong and the law was so comprehensive and exacting that no-one could get through the year without breaking it. If they were to remain right with God, they needed forgiveness, and that was in effect to be purchased by buying offerings and sacrifices and bringing them to the temple. In a theocracy like this the temptation to abuse that power was, it seems, irresistible, so the temple authorities developed every money-making scheme they could find. They over-charged for sacrifices such as lambs or birds. They ripped people off with an outrageous commission when they changed their own currency into the special temple coins that they needed to pay the temple tax. Religion had become big business and religion was about power and control. (See Nick Page, *The Wrong Messiah, the Real Story of Jesus of Nazareth*)

Jesus however, had been performing miracles, and healing without their permission. He had been forgiving people for free, without requiring them to purchase their temple offerings and sacrifices. He had simply not been keeping to "the rules" and he had even harshly criticised them, the purveyors of God's forgiveness, so they wanted a way to get rid of him. He even taught in the public courts of the temple right under their noses as though he was deliberately trying to wind them up.

Jesus was a captivating speaker, nothing special to look at, but his words had the ring of truth. People who went to listen to him came away changed and the stories he told were so memorable that they went and told all their friends, such as the one about the man travelling from Jerusalem to Jericho.

Everyone knew it was a dangerous road with many bandits. The man was set upon by robbers and left for dead. A Jewish priest and a teacher of the law both came by and found the man but wouldn't help him, because their religious rules that meant it would make them "unclean" if they touched him, so each crossed to the other side of the road and left him there. Amazingly the one who rescued him and took him to an Inn and even paid for him to be nursed back to health was a Samaritan of all people. A Samaritan! One of their despised non-Jewish neighbours. Joshua finished the story by asking,

"Which of these three do you think was a neighbour to the man who fell into the hands of robbers?" (Luke 10 vs 36)

The story really struck a chord, because anyone listening could identify with the situation and yet would be shocked at the punch line, whilst recognizing the essential truth it was teaching them. A ceremonially unclean person was the one who did the right thing. The "religious" people didn't help, but an "unclean" outsider did. Did Jesus really mean what he had just said, that how you treat other people is what matters not your religious activities? The audience would know the law of Moses stated that you should love the Lord your God with all your heart and love your neighbour as yourself. However, Jesus was saying that your neighbour was also a Samaritan who didn't follow the right rules. He was saying God wants us to treat everyone as our neighbour and that was very challenging then and it still is now. (See Mark 12 vs 28-31)

He told many stories, some short, some longer. A considerable proportion of what he is recorded as saying comes in a poetic form; he made it memorable for an aural culture. The genius of his stories is that they are easily remembered and re-told. You don't even need to understand them to accurately re-tell them, then the listener can puzzle out the meaning for themself. They work across cultures and centuries; they are truly timeless. Here are some more of his teachings and stories. The metaphors he employs are embedded in the very fabric of our language. The stories and illustrations came from everyday life: sheep, gates, houses, farming. They still speak to us now.

> "Suppose one of you has a hundred sheep and loses one of them. Does he not leave the ninety-nine in the open country and go after the lost sheep until he finds it? And when he finds it, he joyfully puts it on his shoulders and goes home. Then he calls his friends and neighbours together and says, 'Rejoice with me that I have found my lost sheep'. I tell you that in the same way there will be more rejoicing in heaven over one sinner who repents than over ninety-nine righteous persons who do not need to repent." (Luke 15 vs 4-7)

Jesus was clear that everyone is valuable to God.

He talked about the need to make an effort to find the right way in life and foresaw that most people won't seek out truth,

> "Enter through the narrow gate. For wide is the gate and broad is the road that leads to destruction, many enter thought it. But small is the gate and narrow the road that leads to life, and only a few find it." (Matthew 7 vs 13, 14)

However, he emphasised that it is possible to find the right way.

> "Ask and it will be given to you; seek and you will find; knock and the door will be opened to you. For everyone who asks receives; he who seeks finds; and to him who knocks the door will be opened." (Matthew 7 vs 7,8)

He was also directly challenging to those who heard him but did nothing with what they heard,

> "Why do you call me 'Lord, Lord' and not do what I tell you. Everyone who comes to me and hears my words and does them, I will show you what he is like:

he is like a man building a house, who dug deep and laid the foundation on the rock. And when a flood arose, the stream broke against that house and could not shake it, because it had been well built. But the one who hears and does not do them is like a man who built a house on the ground without foundation. When the stream broke against it, immediately it fell, and the ruin of that house was great." (Luke 6 vs 46-49 ESV)

His teachings still surprise people. A lot of people think being a Christian is about being judgemental, not according to Jesus. He was tough on the religious who claimed to know better, especially if they were hypocritical and yet was easy on those caught up in all kinds of difficulties and trouble. He did make judgements about right and wrong, but he was not judgemental towards the struggling.

"Do not judge and you will not be judged. Do not condemn and you will not be condemned. Forgive and you will be forgiven." (Luke 6 vs 37)

He was also realistic about how others after him would distort what he taught and misrepresent God;

"Watch out for false prophets. They come to you in sheep's clothing, but inwardly they are ferocious wolves." (Matthew 7 vs 15)

He made it clear that any idea of perfecting ourselves and being good enough by our own efforts was guaranteed to fail. He did it by raising the standard that God requires of us so high that we can only be accepted by Him on the basis of forgiveness and believing, not on achieving a certain level of performance.

"You have heard it said, 'Do not commit adultery'. But I tell you that anyone who looks at a woman lustfully has already committed adultery with her in his own heart." (Matthew 5 vs 27)

He insisted that being right with God ("righteous") cannot be found on the basis of rule keeping. The Pharisees were the best rule keepers around, yet he said of them,

> "Unless your righteousness surpasses that of the teachers of the law, you will certainly not enter the kingdom of heaven." (Matthew 5 vs 20)

He taught a radical passive resistance that eventually broke the power of the Roman empire,

> "You have heard that it was said, 'Love your neighbour and hate your enemy'. But I tell you, love your enemies and pray for those who persecute you, that you may be sons of your Father in heaven." (Matthew 5 vs 43-45)

He prophesied the fall of Jerusalem to a Roman army in AD 70. (He was speaking some time AD 27-30).

> "When you see Jerusalem being surrounded by armies you will know that its desolation is near. Then let those who are in Judea flee to the mountains, let those in the city get out, and let those in the countryside not enter the city." (Luke 21 vs 20,21)

When the siege came, the Christians who listened to his prophetic advice fled and survived. Those people who stayed suffered terrible slaughter at the hands of Rome.

He did multiple healings and exorcisms and as we saw in an earlier chapter, raised Lazarus from the dead. This is only the beginning of a consideration of his life, work and teaching. The people he got through to were, on the surface of it, often unlikely characters. They were the people whom religion had written off, the people society looked down on; tax collectors who collaborated with the Romans, prostitutes, thieves and very many ordinary peasants. The only ones who were excluded were those who excluded themselves because they thought they were good already and had no need of any for-giveness or healing that he had to offer. The same is true today.

If you know you need help from Jesus, then ask and keep ask-ing. Pray and you will find answers.

When Jesus was asked how to pray, he said some of the most memorable words in history,

> "When you pray do not keep on babbling like the pagans, for they think they will be heard because of their many words. Do not be like them, for your father knows what you need before you ask him. This then is how you should pray:

> 'Our Father in Heaven, hallowed be your name, your kingdom come, your will be done on earth as it is in heaven. Give us today our daily bread. Forgive us our debts as we have forgiven our debtors. And lead us not into temptation, but deliver us from evil, for yours is the kingdom and the power and the glory forever. Amen.'" (Matthew 6 vs 7-13)

Lives have been transformed by just praying that one prayer every day.

If anyone had been listening carefully this same Jesus had said before,

> "For God so loved the world that He gave his one and only Son that whoever believes in him should not perish but have eternal life. **For God did not send his Son into the world to condemn the world but to save the world through him.**" (John 3 vs 16, 17)

And he was talking about himself.

He changed the people he met then, and he still does today. That is the same offer Jesus, as the Son of God makes to every-one.

You may think you know what Jesus was like and what Christians believe. Are you sure? Have you, like the religious leaders of Jesus' day, mistaken religion for the reality of how God really sees us and deals with us? You won't be first to have made that mistake and you needn't be the last to decide to move your understanding beyond "religion" to find out more about Jesus and what He means for your life.

We can't summarise adequately the whole life and teaching of Jesus in such a short space. I hope that these short excerpts are enough to fire your curiosity to read more for yourself. I suggest you read at least one of the biographies or gospels and have the courage to ask Jesus to reveal himself. Watch out he will not ignore your request!

This book started with the image of a ladder to belief. It has been a short book if we consider the range of issues that have been covered, so it can only introduce many of the ideas we have touched upon. I have set out where I believe you may find an adequate basis for belief and how you can test the rungs on that ladder and I sincerely hope you will do so, but you will never know if the ladder is reliable unless you test it out for yourself.

Christian belief is more than a set of ideas or arguments. It is more than evidence; it is a living experience. If you want that, then have the courage to simply pray for God to reveal Himself to you, because He surely will. Then take the first step on that ladder. It is not a leap in the dark, but a reasonable step of faith because God is there, and Jesus is living, powerful and active.

Jesus' life, teaching and resurrection is the answer to your most fundamental questions and needs

> "Come to me, all you who are weary and burdened, and I will give you rest."
> Jesus of Nazareth quoted in Matthew 11 vs 28

29 INTO THE LIGHT?

Which way will you turn?

s a small child I once stood beneath the stained-glass windows of York Minster[16] thoroughly entranced. Standing at the centre of the transept I could turn and see immense windows in each of the directions of the compass, as though I was at the centre of everything and was looking out to a world of colour. As the light changed outside and clouds passed by something new was always being revealed in the glorious patterns. Thousands of pieces of irregularly shaped coloured glass are held together in a lattice framework, a testament to the faith and hope of the craftsmen centuries ago. Even as a child I understood intuitively that the vast stained-glass windows were saying that through the stories portrayed in them we look out on to the wider world and the light that shines through them illuminates our understanding.

Any individual piece of stained glass may be notable for its brilliant colour or the way it corresponds to other pieces and their colours. However, looking at the glass one piece at a time, we might admire its beauty and the craftmanship involved in its creation, but it is almost impossible to imagine the whole window and all the images within it from one piece alone. When we have more pieces, each in correct relation to one another, the fuller picture and the stories and truths they convey begin to emerge.

This is a valuable metaphor for the process of exploring the possibility of Christian belief, because we need to necessarily look at one piece at a time, but we also need to develop a picture of how they fit together to make a beautiful and compelling whole. The complete picture is greater than the sum of its parts. It has more beauty and meaning, and more power to speak to us than is achieved by any sub-set of pieces. (Surely something of this interpretation was intended by the original creators of such masterpieces and many authors have noted the metaphor including C. S. Lewis).

People living in a secular culture, when they begin to think about Christian belief, typically have in mind a picture that is similar to a broken stained-glass window. From the inevitable heritage of western society and from the structure of reality itself, you will be aware of some of the pieces that make up the overall picture of belief. I hope you are beginning to see enough pieces with clarity that you will begin to discern the overall pattern and want to know more. Be encouraged, the breathtaking picture that is emerging will be more and more clearly seen and understood as you let the light behind it shine deeper into your mind, into your being, into your very soul.

The wonderful thing is that if you seek truth, it reveals itself to you. Seek Jesus and you will find him. As you look intently at some of the pieces and begin to figure out how they fit together, they shine more brightly. As more pieces fall into place a greater light is discerned shining through them all and the parts you have paid careful attention to are lit up and transformed by a source of light that is beyond them and shines through them. Each element of evidence turns out to have no colour of its own, it simply allows us to appreciate the qualities of a greater light that gives it its colour and beauty. White light can be transformative but as it refracts through the coloured glass it reveals more of what was within it all along, because it always carries the potential for every possible colour of the rainbow.

The Bible is full of light metaphors; light is fundamental to existence and comprehension. The first specific thing God is mentioned as creating is light,

> "And God said, "Let there be light," and there was
> light. God saw that the light was good, and he separ-
> ated the light from the darkness." Genesis 1: vs 3,4

The challenging thing with light is that it brings both beauty and illuminates darkness. Light warms us and draws us to itself, but it also shows up the darkness within us and can repel us from its intense glare. For many people, it is when they are in a very dark place that they finally begin to see the light and move towards it, and they know in the very core of their being that they can also turn away from it and maybe, just maybe, never find it again and be lost in the darkness for ever.

Yet, no matter how expansive the darkness or how total it seems, once even one tiny amount of light becomes visible, it transforms the situation.

> "In him was life, and that life was the light of men.
> The light shines in the darkness, but the darkness has
> not understood it." John 1: vs 4,5

On your journey into knowing Jesus you may have many questions still to resolve, but if you can see some of the pieces of the picture clearly, and recognise your need of help to understand more, then keep those pieces you do see clearly in mind. Let more light shine through them and you will in time be able to put many other pieces into place as well. The multi-coloured complex image that emerges will have different shades and hues of light that will touch every part of your mind and being, your hopes, your fears, your dreams and aspirations, your weaknesses and your failings. As you experience the transforming power of the light of truth you will be able to know with unshakeable conviction that the picture you see is the right one and it makes sense because it is the picture through which the source of all light itself is shining on you. Belief becomes more than truth, or knowledge, it becomes lived experience. It becomes the knowledge that God, through Jesus, is looking at you, knows everything about you and still loves you!

That experience is often both deeply reassuring and profoundly uncomfortable. We are forced to face up to the capacity right there within us to harm ourselves and others, and we are put on the spot and know that we must co-operate with the transformation that God wants to work in us. Everyone who seeks the light faces that experience at some point.

Jesus described it this way,

> "For God did not send his Son into the world to condemn the world, but to save the world through him. Whoever believes in him is not condemned, but whoever does not believe in him is condemned already because he has not believed in the name of God's one and only Son. This is the verdict: Light came into the world, but men loved darkness instead of light because their deeds were evil. Everyone who does evil hates the light, and will not come into the light for fear that his deeds will be exposed. But whoever lives by truth comes into the light, so that it may be seen

plainly that what he has done has been done through God." John 3 vs 17-21

You don't have to remain stuck in the dark confusion of secularism. Secularism presents itself to us as an all-encompassing worldview, but we have explored some of its weaknesses and shown many things it cannot explain. We have also begun to explore an alternative view of how our lives look through the lens of Christian belief.

Or, to return to the metaphor of a ladder that we have used throughout this book. There is no point in knowing that a ladder exists between you and belief, between you and a better place, unless you are prepared to try stepping onto it. If you reach a point where you decide the ladder looks trustworthy then isn't it time to try it out? If it is not stretching the metaphor too far, remember that it takes deliberate action and some determination to climb a tall ladder.

It's important not to misunderstand the nature of belief. You don't have to pass an exam to believe. You don't have to have a lot of qualifications. There is enough evidence that anyone can evaluate for themself to be able to believe. Nor, as I have said before, is belief a leap in the dark as it has become popularly viewed. Belief is a reasonable step based on a full consideration of all relevant evidence, even though no-one has answers to everything.

Some of the arguments and ideas we have looked at can seem difficult or even irrelevant to some people. That's fine because they are included to help those who need evidence on those points. I also recognise that the path into Christian belief is not one of intellectual argument and philosophical reasoning for most people, but most people do find a few sticking points they need to clear up to be able to make progress. They need solid answers on those particular questions.

In the first chapter we noted that the typical secular world-view, when summed up in plain language, looks something like this:

> "The Universe came from a big bang a very long time ago. Somehow by Random Chance life started and evolved, ending up with us. There's no real meaning to life other than the meaning we make for ourselves. The Bible is made up stories. Jesus was no more than a good teacher with some interesting insights on ethics. There is no absolute right or wrong. Anyone who has faith in God is basically involved in wishful thinking, which most of the time is fairly harmless, but not based on anything reliable, or on any kind of solid evidence."

All of which turns out not to be established fact. Secularism is built on shifting sands. When we look at the evidence, we find a quite different picture. It is essential to note that in pulling apart secularism we have included contributions from authors who are not Christians. Fundamental weaknesses in atheism, evolution and secularism, (which are not all identical but significantly overlapping), are apparent to many people, not just Christians.

We have however, pursued the argument and the evidence further than identifying the weaknesses of secularism to look at the dimensions of the positive case for Christian belief.

Some of the essential pieces of the evidence that support Christian belief as reasonable and credible include:

> The Universe and all reality around us point to a Designer and an ultimate cause: God.

> Random Chance can explain nothing of our origins because it can create nothing.

We experience a moral dimension to our existence; all people everywhere do.

There is a moral law within us and there is a non-material reality of right and wrong that we all experience.

We have minds and we experience that non-material reality. Our own thought processes are proof to us that we are more than just physics and chemistry.

We have reliable versions of what was originally written in the books making up the Christian Bible and they are anchored in history.

Jesus existed as an historical figure.

Jesus was God embodying himself in human form.

Jesus' death and physical resurrection proves his victory over death and makes his offer of life to us meaningful and believable.

Christian belief turns out to be true to all the evidence available to us and it offers in the life, teaching and resurrection of Jesus, real and lasting hope.

To make further progress with your thinking it can help to talk with believers. However, I must add some strong caveats. Sitting in a hen house does not make you a hen. Similarly, many people claim to be Christians with little understanding of what that really means. Some in fact, are Christian in name only. Sadly, they may associate with the activities of Christian religion, without it being a spiritual reality in their hearts and minds. We must remember that Christendom and Christianity are not the same thing. Christendom was the name for the area under the control of nominally Christian kings. Much that has been called Christianity over the centuries, simply hasn't been

Christianity at all.

So, I suggest, it is important when talking with Christians, to talk with those who do read their Bible, who do engage with the culture around them and who are willing to discuss belief in a constructive and non-judgemental way and who turn to God's self-revelation in Jesus for answers.

Don't look for the person with all the answers. Real Christianity has no gurus. Genuine believers must humbly acknowledge how little they understand and how much they don't know. People who know their limitations are much more credible than those who think they have an easy answer for everything. No one knows everything except God alone. The Apostle Paul recognised the limitations on our understanding this side of heaven, his description of the situation led me to the metaphor of a stained glass window we started the chapter with.

> "Now we see but a poor reflection as in a mirror; then we shall see face to face. Now I know in part; then I shall know fully, even as I am fully known." (The Apostle Paul, 1 Corinthians 13 vs 12)

No believer is more privileged than any other in seeking out and knowing truth. Real Christianity is not about being told what to believe top down on the basis of claimed authority. That is one of the core insights of the Protestant Reformation. Truth is also meant to be experienced in community with other believers because individually we only see part of the whole, but together we help and strengthen each other and share new insights that we don't gain alone.

So, do talk and discuss and read and ask Jesus for help. Prayer is just honest communication with God. And do seek out others on the same journey. It might seem obvious to go to a church to find out more. However, I realise that many people are deeply reluctant to do so. We must honestly admit there are no perfect churches, because they are full of imperfect people, in whose lives God is working. There are, however, welcoming churches that allow people to explore truth and belief, hope and disappointment, meaning and frustration. I am a conservative Protestant Christian. I have been genuinely blessed with being able to be part of friendly and supportive congregations. I also have Christian friends, whose faith I greatly respect, who attend quite a range of Christian churches. All I can suggest is that you evaluate truth for yourself and ask Jesus to lead you to Him first and foremost, and that He then leads you to other believers and further into truth. Remember that truth matters, not just community. Measure everything by God's revelation of Himself in Jesus and in the writings that He has inspired collected together in the Bible. Something may be believed by many people, including many Christians, but if it is not in God's revelation in the Bible it may also not be true. Many Christians have studied for themselves and found that things they thought they knew such as an eternally burning hell, turn out to not be the truth after all.

Many people go through a stage in their journey into faith when they want definitive answers to every question they have. They tend to gravitate towards people or groups who appear to have an answer for everything. That usually ends in disappointment. Some organisations that claim to be Christian offer neatly packaged answers to everything whilst denying core aspects of the Christian faith. Be careful. No-one in this life has all the answers. Then comes a deeper realization, that whilst it is important to have solid answers to important questions, the thing that really matters is to know Jesus, the Son of God, as alive and active in your own life and others. Truth and belief are then seen to be much more than just ideas or arguments, or propositional statements and they become a relational reality, a day-to-day experience. Truth matters immensely and should not be ignored, but it must always relate back to knowing Jesus as Saviour and Lord.

Conversely, many Christians don't take the time to build their faith on a solid historical and evidential basis and want to only offer the relational operation of faith to others. They become fixated on the experience of doing church, having the right music, the right level of excitement and stimulus. Christianity easily becomes a performance. Not surprisingly that just does not work in the long term. Heads and hearts need to be satisfied, it's not one or the other. That is why I have written this book. You don't have to stop thinking and questioning to believe in Jesus, but you also need more than just reasoning and knowledge about the truth. This is why Jesus said,

"I am the way and the truth and the life." (John 14 vs 6)

Christian belief is focused on a person, Jesus, not abstract ideas. He is a real historical person and the Son of God, whose actions in history make clear who He is and what He has power to do.

It is not necessary to understand or agree with every single argument in this book or other books on Christian belief, to be able to believe in Jesus as the Son of God. This book has simply tried to show you that objections to belief can be overcome because Christian belief is true to all the evidence available to us about ourselves, from our in-built recognition of right and wrong to our desire for meaning and eternity. It is true to the evidence all around us of Design and order. We have also looked at the credibility of the documents that give more detail on what God has been revealing through history and we have looked at the life and resurrection of Jesus, who was God embodying himself in human form to give us a clear picture of what He is really like. Christian belief has a robust basis.

Yet, as we have already noted, there is still one more thing missing; to know God for yourself. This is not something that comes at the end of a long process, like a graduation. It ought to grow as your understanding grows, but each person's journey is unique, so I can't prescribe an exact path to follow.

Jesus talked about revealing himself to people. The cast of characters he revealed himself to, who eventually became his followers, could not be a wider cross section of society. They include Mary from whom Jesus cast out multiple demons, Peter a fisherman, Matthew a collector of taxes for the Romans, Nicodemus, possibly the most senior Jewish teacher of his day, John a teenage boy, Joanna a mother, a unnamed Roman Centurion, Paul an academic and religious fanatic and many others. Social and educational background was clearly no barrier to understanding who Jesus was and following him then, and it isn't now.

Remember however, it is an active process, it requires us to seek, ask and listen. So, I encourage you to recognise the blocks that stand between you and belief, measure them on the evidence and be willing to move on beyond them.

I am challenging you to investigate further, with an open mind, because you have been fed a false claim by secular culture; the claim that belief isn't possible on any reasonable basis. Recognise that claim for what it is, just plain wrong and resulting from a refusal to engage meaningfully with the evidence, and then there is no reason to not check out the evidence for yourself.

> "Ask and it will be given to you; seek and you will find; knock and the door will be opened to you. For everyone who asks receives; he who seeks finds; and to him who knocks the door will be opened." (Jesus quoted in Matthew 7 vs 7,8)

Secularism will be like every ideology before it, a passing phase. When people are in the midst of a world view, they experience it as largely unchallenged. It is so dominant that it seems obvious and beyond question. Then it falls, just like the Berlin wall. It is highly likely that what dominates next will be some form of religion in response to the weaknesses of secularism. It may even call itself some form of Christianity. It is also quite possible for it to not really be Christianity at all. Jesus repeatedly warned against false Messiahs claiming to be Him returned and He gave many warnings against religion going wrong. However, that takes us into another discussion, but the essential point is that secularism is simply not the end of the story. It is not the final self-evident world view supplanting all others. The secular consensus in western society presently considers itself unquestionable, the unassailable culmination of history, and it will be wrong just as every preceding ideology was wrong.

In contrast Jesus said,

"My kingdom is not of this world." (John 18 vs 36)

Ideologies come and ideologies go, but citizenship in Jesus' kingdom starts now and lasts for eternity.

If after everything we have considered, you are with me in recognising that Christian belief is possible and built on a reasonable basis then the further reading section starts with several suggested books to read next, each is short and easy to read.

To be willing to have your entire worldview challenged along with all the assumptions that go with it is a very big thing. To be willing to consider re-building it on a different basis is literally life changing. The good news is that you are not expected to do this on your own. Jesus promises to be right there with you.

"Whoever comes to me I will never drive away." (John 6 vs 37)

You can climb a ladder to belief in God and Jesus as His Son and our Saviour, because it is reasonable, rational, and is true to all the evidence about yourself and the world around you

So, finally, thank you for coming with me on this journey. I hope these short discussions have helped you make steps toward understanding Christian belief and that they will help you in some way to find the satisfying and sufficient answers that you are seeking. But remember that we have only come to the beginning of many more discussions and insights. All we have done is clear away some of the reasons people think they have for not investigating Christian belief. There is so much more to discover. Have the courage to ask Jesus to lead you.

Everything in this life is temporary. The only enduring thing is to know God and Jesus His Son

"Heaven and earth will pass away, but my words will never pass away."

Jesus of Nazareth quoted in Luke 21 vs 33

SOURCES AND FURTHER READING

Where to find out more

T he reason this book was written is because there is compelling evidence to support an adequate and reasonable basis for belief in God and Jesus as His Son and our Saviour.

I have deliberately tried to write this book in a style that makes it easy to read. I have tried to distil complex issues to as simple a form as I feel I reasonably can. That of course means that you will almost certainly have many more questions, so this section shows you where you might go next to find out more.

The sources given here back up the ideas discussed in this book, and you can use them to the explore issues raised in more detail. I am heavily indebted to all these sources and many more. I have written nothing new in this book. The truth is not a new invention.

Please note however, that these books look at different parts of these arguments in varying levels of detail. Some of them are easy to read. Some are quite demanding. Not all are written by Christians. However, it is important to include these sources to acknowledge their contribution.

You might wonder why I have only included sources helpful to the arguments I have discussed. The answer is simple. We live in a culture that shouts out loudly with a mega-phone, that belief isn't possible unless you close your mind to the evidence, and it pushes that view in so many places, that that side of the argument is easy to find. I have focused on offering the side of the debate that has so often been pushed aside.

Many of these books have sold in their millions but are still marginalised by secular culture. Millions of people before you have not been willing to be told what to think by the prevailing culture around them. They have checked out Jesus for themselves and they come to belief in him as the Son of God and the one who gives them new life.

Before you get to any other books however, if you have not simply read through one of the records of Jesus life in the gospels of Matthew, Mark, Luke and John, then why not go straight to the source material and read one through. It will only take you a few hours at the most. It really is worth it.

The **English Standard Version (ESV) of the Bible** is available for free online and as a free download and mobile phone app.

Some quick reads

After everything we have discussed, here are some suggestions for a quick read:

More Than a Carpenter by Josh McDowell. He makes Jesus very accessible.

Epic, The Story God is Telling by John Eldredge. This book paints the big picture of what Christians believe God has been doing.

Steps to Christ by Ellen White. If you are already with me as far as wanting to step out in faith and know Jesus for yourself, then consider this classic.

The sources listed below will allow you to explore the issues raised in this book in more depth. I don't agree with every claim in every one of these books, no doubt you won't either, but I hope you too may find them helpful. The suggested reading is grouped under a series of themes.

Evolution, the limits of science and the existence of God

Axe, D (2016) *Undeniable. How Biology Confirms Our Intuition That life is Designed*, Harper Collins 290 pages
This book simply makes the case that the intuitive reaction we all have to Design around us in nature, that it is Design and that therefore there must be a Designer, is absolutely right.

Behe, Michael (1998) *Darwin's Black Box,* Simon and Schuster 329 pages
Michael Behe sparked a huge and ongoing discussion. He has encountered bigotry and closed minds who have been determined to silence him. Yet the issues he raised are still pertinent. He discusses the incredible complexity of structures at the level of single cellular organisms, such as the flagellum motor that some use to move about. His basic claim is that it is one of many examples of "irreducible complexity", that is that no part can be taken away and keep its function. That would mean that Natural Selection would not be able to produce the structure, because every intermediate stage would not function and would confer no advantage to the cell so would not be passed on. Basically, there are structures at a cellular level that have to be all or nothing.

Behe, Michael (2019) *Darwin Devolves: The New Science About DNA That Challenges Evolution*, Harper One 343 pages

This is I believe his best book. The strength of the argument is that when we go beyond somewhat abstract and philosophical discussions to look at what is actually going on within cells when organisms change and adapt, we find hard evidence of random mutations and Natural Selection doing exactly the opposite of what was believed they could achieve. They fit organisms into their environmental circumstances mostly by degrading pre-existing genetic information. Natural Selection does not originate life, it just helps it adapt to its environment.

Berlinski, David (2009) *The Devil's Delusion, Atheism and its Scientific Pretensions*, Basic books, 237 pages

David Berlinski is a philosopher and agnostic. He can be a bit demanding to read, but he ruthlessly cuts though the nonsense that is often pedalled as science. The main thing I gained from the book is that there are real limits to what we can know on the basis of our own efforts through science. There is much about reality that science really has no reasonable basis for saying anything about. That is not a popular idea for many scientists.

Carter, R (Editor) (2014) *Evolution's Achilles Heels, 9 PhD scientists explain evolution's fatal flaws – in areas claimed to be its greatest strengths*, Creation book publishers 270 pages

The fascinating thing with this book is that you have a series of scientists at the cutting edge of their subjects saying that the more they look at the evidence the more convinced they are that evolution from nothing up to us is simply not plausible. Quite readable.

Denton, Michael (1985) *Evolution a Theory in Crisis,* Adler& Adler 368 pages

Michael Denton is a biochemist. He reviews a range of problem for evolutionary explanations. His conclusion is that evolution is a belief *against* the evidence. He says evolution is "the great cosmogenic myth" of our time. In the same way that cultures around the world tell stories about the origin of life that bear little connection to observable facts, our modern western culture tells itself the evolutionary origins myth. Denton updated his book more than 20 years after the original:

Denton, Michael (2016) *Evolution: Still a Theory in Crisis*, Discovery Institute Press

Flew, A (2007) *There is a God; How the World's Most Notorious Atheist Changed His Mind,* Harper One 222 pages

Simply one of the best argued books you will ever have the privilege to read. There is no excuse for atheism in any form after reading this.

Goldstein, Clifford (2017) *Baptizing the Devil, Evolution and the Seduction of Christianity, Pacific Press publishing association* 250 pages

Goldstein argues the incompatibility of evolution with Christianity.

Gish, Duane (1995) *Evolution: The Fossils Still Say No*, Institute for Creation Research 391 pages

The evidence to fill the gaps in the fossil record that Darwin expected to find to support his theory of endless gradual change has simply not appeared. The fossil record is not able to sustain the idea of endless intermediate forms between species.

Johnson, Phillip E (2010) *Darwin on Trial*, Inter Varsity Press 247 pages

Phillip Johnson explores evolution as a lawyer and finds its claims over-reaching and unproven. He basically claims that evolutionary theory is naturalistic philosophy not empirical science and its main claims are simply unproven. They are not the "facts" they are presented as. To quote him,

> "The argument of Darwin on Trial is that we know a great deal less than has been claimed. In particular, we do not know how the immensely complex organ systems of plants and animals could have been created by mindless and purposeless natural processes, as Darwinists say they must have been." (Page 191)

Latham, Anthony, *Mind the Gap – An Outline of the Philosophical Positions Held about the Mind.* Centre for Intelligent Design UK, c4id.org.uk/ accessed 22/11/20

Lennox, John C (2007) *God's Undertaker, Has Science Buried God?* Lion 224 pages

John Lennox makes a convincing case that there is much that evolution simply cannot address. A rationally ordered, designed universe is compelling evidence that there is an ultimate intelligence behind it.

This excellent book was updated in 2021 with a new edition:

Lennox, John C (2021) *Cosmic Chemistry* Lion 400 pages

Lennox, John C (2011) *Gunning for God, Why The New Atheists are Missing the Target*, Lion 254 pages

This is an incredibly well written and well-argued book. If you are concerned that science has done away with God, this book pulls atheism apart very convincingly.

Lennox, John C (2019) *Can Science Explain Everything?* The Good Book Company 127 pages
A very readable discussion of the limits of what science can address and the implications of that for Christian belief.

Meyer, Stephen (2009) *Signature in the Cell,* Harper One 611 pages
This is a fairly heavy weight book. Its main conclusion is very simple. We see such evidence for Design within cells that it is absurd to not accept that there is a designer. DNA contains information that is not determined by its chemistry. The information had to come from somewhere else, therefore there is a designer. The book sparked quite a furore. Yet why should the scientific establishment be so scared of simply following the evidence?

Meyer, Stephen (2013) *Darwin's Doubt, The Explosive Origin of Animal Life and the Case for Intelligent Design,* Harper Collins 548 pages
Here Stephen Meyer takes the discussion further to see if there is evidence for the tree of life that Darwin proposed, (common descent) all evolving by Natural Selection through Random Chance alone. He concludes there isn't.

Meyer, Stephen (2021) *Return of the God Hypothesis, Three Scientific Discoveries That Reveal the Mind Behind the Universe,* Harper One 568 pages
If you think that the scientific evidence confirms that there is no God, this carefully argued book sets out in great detail the evidence and arguments around three key areas of scientific discovery and shows how they support a belief in a supreme transcendent being: God. On route he explores the Judaeo-

Christian roots of modern science. A truly impressive piece of work.

Mitchell, Colin (1994) *The Case for Creationism*, Autumn House Ltd 283 pages
 A broad discussion across many topics where the evidence points to a creator rather than evolution.

Mitchell, Elizabeth (2014) *Reverse Evolution Causes Darwin's Finches to go Missing?* Answers in Genesis March 20, 2014 https://answersingenesis.org/natural-selection/reverse-evolution-causes-darwins-finches-to-go-missing/

Pandit, Subodh (2015) *Come Search with Me, Book 1 Does God Really Exist? Is theism rational? Is evolution truly scientific?* 4th edition, www.searchseminars.org (Available from Amazon publishing)
A critical evaluation of evolution and attempts to explain life without God.

Pandit, Subodh (2015) *Come search with me, Book 2 The weight of evidence, Religions compared candidly, the basis for belief* 4th edition, www.searchseminars.org (Available from Amazon publishing)
An engaging review of the claims of the world's major religions, with a reasoned discussion of what led Subodh Pandit to becoming a Christian.

Nagel, Thomas (2012) *Mind and Cosmos, Why the Materialist Neo-Darwinian Conception of Nature is Almost Certainly False,* Oxford University Press
Nagel concludes that the inability of evolution to explain the mind undermines it as an explanation of origins, or indeed

anything else for that matter.

Sarfati, Jonathan (2014) *The Greatest Hoax on Earth? Refuting Dawkins on Evolution*, 2nd edition, Creation Book Publishers

Sarfati, Jonathan (2011) *Refuting Compromise: a Biblical and Scientific Refutation of "Progressive Creationism" (Billions of years)*, 2nd edition, Creation Book Publishers

Wallace, J. Warner (2015) *God's Crime Scene, A Cold-case Detective Examines the Evidence for a Divinely Created Universe*, David C. Crook 320 pages

J. Warner Wallace looks at the multiple lines of evidence that point inexorably to a creator God. Very thorough and very readable.

Walton, John C. (2021) *Compact Time, A Short History of Life on Earth*, Matador 167 pages

John Walton is a Professor of chemistry. He examines the process of radiocarbon decay and evidence that does not fit with the dominant long ages model of evolution, such as soft tissue in dinosaur bones, and concludes that conventional dating has significantly overestimated the age of fossils and rocks.

Christianity and the development of secular culture in western countries

Schaeffer, Francis *Escape from Reason*, IVP
Schaeffer, Francis *The God Who is There*, IVP
Schaeffer, Francis *He is There and He is Not Silent*, IVP

These three books by Francis Schaeffer are often published in one volume, (*The Schaeffer Trilogy*) and they belong together because they build on one another. I am immensely indebted to Francis Schaeffer's ideas in these and his other books.

Escape from Reason, traces the process of western culture moving away from a Christian world view to a secular one. He makes the case that truth (true truth as Schaeffer calls it) cannot exist outside the Christian framework and that within a secular world view everything must inevitably be seen as relative with no absolutes, with terrible consequences.

The God Who is There, makes the case that God exists and that that is an objective fact regardless of one's perspective.

He is There and He is Not Silent, addresses how we might know God, and how He has communicated with us.

Taken together these three books tell the story of a culture that has taken a wrong turn away from God and truth, but they also point the way back.

The life of Jesus, early Christianity and the Bible as history

Blomberg, Craig (2014) *Can we Still Believe the Bible? An Evangelical Engagement with Contemporary Questions*, Brazos Press 287 pages
A rigorous discussion on the nature of the text of the Bible and the criticisms levelled against it in the last century.

Blomberg, Craig (2016) *The Historical Reliability of the New Testament; Countering the Challenges to Evangelical Christian Beliefs*, B&H Academic 783 pages
Popular culture may sell the claims that the New Testament is unreliable, all made up later, not reliable history etc. Craig Blomberg works through a mountain of evidence in this substantial book to support a solid belief in the historical reliability of the New Testament manuscripts as we have them recorded.

Graves, David E. (2019) *The Archaeology of the Old Testament, 115 Discoveries That Support the Reliability of the Bible*, Electronic Christian Media, Canada (available via Amazon publishing) 305 pages
The popular view is that the Old Testament is all myth and not connected to history. This book presents solid evidence that the Old Testament books are anchored in a real historical context that testifies to their antiquity and integrity.

Gibson, Ty (2014) *The One*, Review and Herald Publishing Association (Hagerstown, MD)
Scripture predicted the Messiah's life in incredible detail.

Kitchen, K A (2003) *On the Reliability of the Old Testament*, Wm.

B. Eerdmans Publishing Co. 662 pages

This book argues for the solid historical basis of the Old Testament books and events. The scope of the book is immense, and the volume of evidence considered is incredible. The Old Testament is shown to be a collection of credible historical texts.

Makowski, Michael (2008) *The Book of Daniel, Prophecies for our Times, Simply and Clearly Explained*, Saatkorn 129 pages

A short commentary on and discussion of the book of Daniel highlighting its major themes and exploring the prophecies it contains.

Mangalwadi, Vishal (2011) *The Book That Made Your World, How the Bible Created the Soul of Western Civilisation,* Thomas Nelson 442 pages

A comprehensive and wonderful exploration of the influence of the Bible on western though as well as how that has spread to other countries with great positive effects.

McDowell, Josh (1999) *The New Evidence That Demands a Verdict*, Thomas Nelson Publishers 760 pages

An immense source book that collects evidence under many themes relevant to this book, *The Possibility of Belief*, including:

Is the New Testament Historically Reliable?

Is the Old Testament Historically Reliable?

Jesus, A Man of History

The Nature of Truth

There is a 2018 updated and revised edition also.

Page, Nick (2011) *The Wrong Messiah, the Real Story of Jesus of Nazareth*, Hodder and Stoughton ltd. 312 pages

This is an incredibly readable book. If you think you know who

Jesus was and what his life and teaching meant, you might be quite surprised. Nick Page does a wonderful job of peeling away what people think they know to get to something much more fascinating. It is worth a lengthy quote from the introduction. He says of Jesus,

> "He died a revolutionary leader. He was a peasant, not a king, and when people tried to make him a king, he ran away. Far from smashing Israel's enemies to pieces, he said we should love them and not even call them rude names. After his death not much changed, except that the fishermen who followed him started a cult. There was no new age. Looked at dispassionately, Jesus was a complete failure by any measure. (Except for being human. And according to the Christians he only scored 50 per cent at that.)
>
> To his opponents, Jesus had none of the qualifications that a Messiah should have. To them, he was a wino who kept bad company, had no respect for tradition and who ended up dying the most shameful death possible. Just how wrong can a Messiah be?
>
> And yet, despite that, those who followed him, those who, some fifteen years after his death got nicknamed Christians, came to see Jesus as the Messiah. They believed that the person who just didn't fit – the cornerstone which the builders rejected – turned out to be the Christ, the Messiah, the anointed of God. They were convinced that he was right all along.
>
> And this book is an attempt to find out why."

Page, Nick (2012) *Kingdom of Fools, the Unlikely Rise of The Early Church*, Hodder and Stoughton 389 pages
How on earth did Christianity survive and grow in the First Century and go on to turn the world upside down? Surely that

deserves investigation. On route Nick Page covers the historicity of Luke's accounts in Acts of the Apostles and reveals his work as a convincing first-hand witness account.

Wallace, J. Warner (2013) *Cold-case Christianity,* David C. Cook 288 pages

A forensic examination for the evidence for Jesus, his life and resurrection and the accounts of them that we have in the Christian gospels, by a cold-case detective. J. Warner Wallace uses the same techniques he uses to investigate cold-case murders where he patiently and forensically examines all the evidence available. He concludes that beyond any reasonable doubt, Jesus existed, died and was resurrected.

Becoming a Christian and the basis of Christian belief

Craig, William Lane (2008) *Reasonable Faith, Christian Truth and Apologetics*, Third Edition, Crossway 415 pages
A systematic and thorough defence of Christian belief.

Eldredge, J (2004) *Epic, The Story God is Telling*, Thomas Nelson 104 pages
An overview of the large story, the Christian view of history and where we fit in it

McDowell, J and McDowell, S (2011) *More Than a Carpenter*, Authentic media Ltd. 179 pages
An examination of who Jesus is and what that means for our lives.

McDowell, Josh (1989) *Skeptics Who Demanded a Verdict*, Tyndale House Publishers
Josh McDowell was once a sceptic who simply did not think there was a credible basis for belief. He looks at the different routes of several well-known people from unbelief to belief. For example, he tells the story of C.S. Lewis who went from atheist Professor to one of the best known and effective defenders of Christianity in the Twentieth Century.
Accessed at: http://www.josh.org/wp-content/uploads/Skeptics-Who-Demanded-a-Verdict-1.pdf

Pandit, Subodh (2015) *Come Search with Me, Book 2 The Weight of Evidence* 4th edition, www.searchseminars.org
A search for true religion. A thorough and systematic book evaluating the basis of Christian belief.

Strobel, Lee (1998) *The Case for Christ*, Zondervan 317 pages

Lee Strobel was a cynical journalist and atheist. When his wife became a Christian, he was really unhappy. He thought she must have been duped somehow and set out to prove she was wrong. The problem for him was that the more he looked for evidence to convince her that Christian belief was nonsense and based on nothing better than fairy stories, the more he encountered evidence that convinced him of the opposite. In the end he became a Christian.

Strobel, Lee (2015) *The Case for Grace*, Zondervan 230 pages

Life stories of how God's transforming grace has reached some unlikely people and how they describe it as transforming them.

White, Ellen (1892) *Steps to Christ'* 2003 Edition, Stanborough Press Ltd. 128 pages

Also available at https://m.egwwritings.org/en/book/108/toc Accessed December 2019

This little book first published in 1892 has been in print ever since. If you have got beyond the dead ends of atheism and agnosticism, and believe there is a God, then *Steps to Christ* sets out many steps of the experience of believing and living the Christian life. Millions of copies have been printed and it has been translated into numerous languages, a true Christian classic.

Other supporting references

These references are not part of the suggested reading but are referred to in this book.

Alberts, B, Johnson, A, Lewis, J Morgan, D, Raff, M, Roberts, K and Water, P (2015) *Molecular Biology of the Cell* 6th Edition, Garland Science.

For further detail have a look at Roche Metabolic Pathways; www.biochemical-pathways.roche.com

BBC (2018) *More or less, Are there more stars than grains of beach sand?* 7 July 2018

Bianconi, E, Piovesan, A, Facchin, F, Beraudi, A, Casadei, R, Frabetti, F, Vitale, L, Pelleri, M C, Tassani, S, Piva, F. and Perez-Amodio, S. (2013) *An Estimation of the Number of Cells in the Human Body*. Annals of human biology *40*(6), pp 463-471.

Camus, Albert (1947) *The Plague*, English translation published by Penguin Classics (2002)

Courtois, Stephane et al (1999) *The Black Book of Communism*, Editions, Robert Laffont, S.A. Paris 859 pages

Dawkins, Richard (1986) *The Blind Watchmaker*, Norton and company, Inc.

De Botton, Alain (2014) *The Art of Travel*, Penguin 272 pages

HuBMAP Consortium, 2019. *The Human Body at Cellular Resolution: the NIH Human Biomolecular Atlas Program.* Nature, *574* (7777), p 187

Kemp, Thomas (1985) *A Fresh Look at the Fossil Record,* New Scientist, Vol 188 5 December 1985 page 66

Kuhn, Thomas (1962) *The Structure of Scientific Revolutions,* University of Chicago Press

Martin, Roy C (1999) *Astronomy on Trial: a Devastating and Complete Repudiation of the Big Bang Fiasco,* University Press of America, New York

Newkirk, Pamela (2015) *The Astonishing Life of Ota Benga,* Amistad, Harper Collins

Page, Nick (2007) *What happened to the Ark of the Covenant: And other Bible Mysteries,* Authentic Media Word

Rayner, Steve (2012) *Uncomfortable Knowledge: The Social Construction of Ignorance in Science and Environmental Policy Discourses,* Economy and Society Volume 41, Issue 1 pp 107-125

Sender, R, Fuchs, S and Milo, R, 2016. *Revised Estimates for the Number of Human and Bacteria Cells in the Body. PLoS biology,* *14*(8), p.e1002533.

Zimmer, Carl (2013) *How Many Cells are in Your Body* National Geographic 23 Oct. 2013
https://www.nationalgeographic.com/science/
phenomena/2013/10/23/how-many-cells-are-in-your-body/

FOOTNOTES

---

[1] https://www.nytimes.com/2017/05/12/magazine/can-prairie-dogs-talk.html).

[2] https://spectrum.ieee.org/apes-with-apps

[3] This discussion was inspired by Francis Schaeffer's discussion of Albert Camus' book, The Plague', see *The Schaeffer Trilogy*.

[4] I first became aware of the Antikythera Mechanism and how it illustrates to us how we recognise design in an archaeology lecture by Kendal Down.

[5] I heard this argument first made by John McKay in a talk on evolution and origins

[6] This estimate is from a talk by Isabel Moraes, (National Physical Laboratory London)

[7] Quoted in a talk by Stephen Meyer to C4IDUK, 2020

[8] Stephen Meyer in a talk to C4IDUK, 2020

[9] I first came across this description of the state of affairs in a talk by John McKay.

[10] An estimate given in a talk by Isabel Moraes, (National Physical Laboratory London)

[11] This analogy of the Tube train and Mind the Gap was made by Alastair Noble in a talk about Intelligent Design based on an article by Anthony Latham called *Mind the gap – an outline of the philosophical positions held about the mind*. See Centre for Intelligent Design UK, c4id.org.uk/

[12] Written by Phillips speechwriter (Denis Healey) at the Socialist International Conference, Copenhagen, 1953. As reported in: Time and Chance (1987), James Callaghan

[13] Francis Schaeffer formulates some of these direct propositional statements in his books contained in *The Schaeffer Trilogy*. They inspired me to make a longer compilation of such statements.

[14] I heard this put so plainly by a Rabbi who had survived Auschwitz concentration camp. It made a great impression on me.

[15] https://en.wikipedia.org/wiki/39_Melachot

[16] York Minster is a cathedral in England famous for its impressive stained-glass windows

ABOUT THE AUTHOR

Duncan Bayliss

Duncan Bayliss has lectured Geography at University level for 30 years with a particular interest in environmental management. His other interests include cycling, travel and travel writing.